GARDENS IN TIME

GARDEN

S IN TIME

JOHN (AND RAY) OLDHAM

LANSDOWNE PRESS
Sydney • Auckland • London • New York

Edited by Peita Royle
Designed by Bruno Grasswill

Published by Lansdowne Press Sydney
176 South Creek Road, Dee Why West, NSW, Australia 2099
First published 1980

Produced in Australia by the Publisher
Typeset in New Zealand by Jacobson Typesetters Ltd
Printed in Hong Kong

National Library of Australia Cataloguing-in-Publication Data

Oldham, John.
Gardens in time.

Index.
Bibliography.
ISBN 0 7018 1350 4

1. Landscape gardening. I. Oldham, Ray, joint author. II. Title.

712

Theodore Osmundson, F.A.S.L.A.

FOREWORD

In the fall of 1963, I had the great good luck to be assigned a room at the East-West Center in Hawaii with the Australian landscape architect John Oldham. We, along with seven other landscape architects from the United States and South-East Asia, had been selected to study Hawaiian and Japanese gardens at first hand with a month in each locality. 'Cultural interchange between East and West' is East-West Center's mission and it works. At least with the Oldhams of Western Australia, who have become our great good friends, colleagues, travelling companions and reciprocal visitors in each others' homes. They are stimulating people, with broad intellectual and artistic interests and an abiding fascination and love for the world's landscapes.

I have known that they have been collaborating on this, their magnum opus, since we met. As Australians, they are compulsive and inveterate travellers and have visited and photographed almost every region which they discuss. The Oldhams perceptive intelligence and tenacity has resulted in a major history of what we call today, landscape architecture, and I am now more than ever proud to have nominated John for Corresponding Member of the American Society of Landscape Architects, a well deserved honour which he now holds.

John and Ray Oldham have written a book which presupposes that we have always been a creature of the landscape environment which we find and make for ourselves. In this they have taken the global view that wherever the interaction of people takes place, there too goes a deliberate modification in the landscape, first to survive, then to enjoy, and finally as history has demonstrated, to dominate. The Oldhams' story, therefore, eschews the course of the traditional writer of landscape history who leaps nimbly from Egypt, to Rome, Spain, the Renaissance and thence into the eighteenth and nineteenth centuries.

Their story begins with the Aborigines, as exemplified by the first natives of their own Australia, but quickly expands into all of the known dominant cultures of the world. The art of the landscape, unlike architecture, is a fragile one and, consequently, its presence in the ancient and vanished civilizations can, at best, be speculated upon from writings and drawings in stone and clay. Indeed, many of the finest gardens and parks of every epoch have succumbed before human destruction, neglect or the inexorable advances of their surrounding countrysides. The appearance of these are by far the most difficult to convey, but the Oldhams have not been deterred. In the absence of reality, they have gone to the written descriptions of the gardens' owners, designers, or contemporaries. However, landscape design is a visual art and the story is shared in full measure by text and photography.

They have done a particular service in demonstrating that the origins of our own Western landscape traditions go beyond Rome, Greece and Egypt as we so conveniently and erroneously believe. The philosophy and completed work in landscape design throughout China, Japan, the Mongol and Islamic Empires, including the Mughul, all of whose history we in the West know so little, is woven into the major events and forces dominating these countries and their cultures.

The Oldhams have made a very convincing argument for the origins of the Italian Renaissance garden. They refuse to repeat existing thinking with Europe as the focus of the world. They prove that history is much too complex for such a view. The presence of Islam, first flowing westward with irresistible force on the southern edge of the Mediterranean to Spain in the seventh century, and ultimately occupying the perimeter of the Mediterranean from what is now Yugoslavia, clockwise around to the border of present-day France in the fifteenth century, is an historical fact too great to ignore. The forces of Islam, which, ironically, have emerged as a threat that may be far more pervasive and destructive in the future than were their swords in the five hundred years of their dominance, are shown to be the predominent influence. One can certainly argue with this view from the standpoint of architectural detail but their case in overall design is difficult to refute.

This fresh and comprehensive examination of the social, economic and cultural evolution of history through its greatest epochs, in relationship to the landscape which man has experienced and made to satisfy his needs, makes *Gardens in Time* unique and of great importance to us at the present time.

It is especially gratifying to me to have such a comprehensive history of the art and science of landscape architecture appear a mere decade after the mindless branding of history as 'irrelevant' in the 1960s. Few landscape architects today are capable or willing to do the extensive time-consuming research necessary to produce a work of this kind. The excellent and comprehensive work *Design on the Land*, by Norman T. Newton, published in 1971, is the only American book of comparable scope, but does not deal with the historical context prior to the American experience in such depth.

This book should be read by both landscape architects and those aspiring to enter this humanly rewarding field. But of equal importance, it should be read by the decision makers and their advisors. It will demonstrate that the will to bring order and beauty to our environment is not a recent frill but a basic impulse in people since we first learned to live in groups. From this may come the fourth state beyond the domination of nature, that of a sympathetic accommodation for the survival and well-being of both people and their natural surroundings. It will also demonstrate the need for a sensitive and highly skilled landscape architectural profession throughout the world to bring about this harmonious state.

Theodore Osmundson

Theodore Osmundson, F.A.S.L.A.
Berkeley, California 1979

CONTENTS

INTRODUCTION

Men have made gardens since they first ceased to be nomads and settled along the shores of the great rivers of the world. Even before they formed settlements, they appropriated many splendid natural landscapes as meeting-places for conference, festival and dance.

Commencing with the earliest dramatic sites used by the nomadic Aborigines of Australia for their corroborees, we have traced, up to the present day, man's search for an earthly paradise.

We show how, through the ages, the great garden movements begun in Egypt, Asia Minor, Central Asia and the Far East have ebbed and flowed, met and inter-acted; to produce finally the wonderful garden heritage and landscape tradition that we enjoy today.

Our researches have taken us many times around the world, wandering through the gardens of many lands; and delving into museums, libraries and art galleries to discover the story of gardens that have long gone. Athens, Florence, Venice and Rome; Peking, Kyoto, Agra and Kashmir; Isfahan, Shiraz, Istanbul, Cairo and the Nile Valley; Granada, Lisbon, Paris, London and the English countryside; Stockholm, Boston, New York and San Francisco are some of the places we have researched on our travels.

These voyages of discovery were exciting and illuminating. Eventually they revealed the origins of contemporary garden art and landscape design.

This is a 'picture book' showing the beauty and character of the finest gardens in the world. But it also links them together in a continuous story . . . a story that at first seemed only a tentative theory, but, as more and more evidence was uncovered, became a firm conviction. We believe our study and observation establish beyond doubt that, though enormous contributions have been made to garden art and landscape design by the Western world – Europe and the Mediterranean – the basic theory of the natural garden was formulated in the Far East.

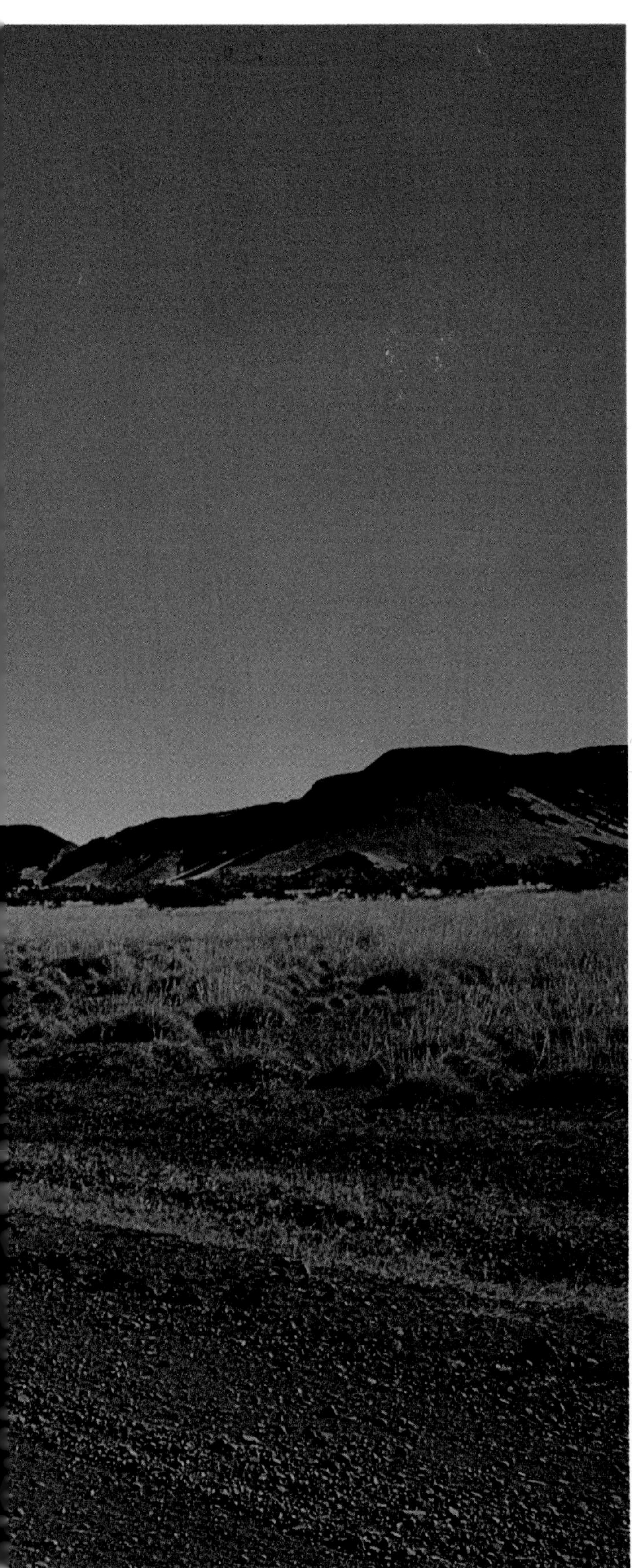

CHAPTER I

THE ANCIENT 'SENSE OF LANDSCAPE'

A 'sense of landscape' is older than civilised man. Tens of thousands of years ago, when mankind had no architecture and no landscape architecture, through his 'sense of landscape' he claimed the architecture of nature as his own.

Primitive hunters chose dramatic natural landscapes as the meeting-places for religious and social ceremonies. Even though such prehistoric men disappeared from the earth many thousands of years ago, archaeology and anthropology provide us with evidence for their way of life. Equally illuminating are those people who have survived in a primitive social organisation right up to the present day.

1

The Genius Loci, an appreciation of the spirit of a special place and of enhancing it for human use and enjoyment, existed in prehistoric times. Primitive hunters and food-gatherers had no architecture but they appropriated that of Nature. Pyramid Hill in the North-West of Australia was one of the many impressive natural sites used by the early Aborigines as a place of assembly. It is crowned by murals depicting their way of life.

PREHISTORIC LANDSCAPES

The Australian Aborigines are representative of these survivors of an ancient way of life. As a consequence, today we are fortunate in being able to examine in Australia some of these meeting-places of prehistoric man much as they were when he was using them.

Western Australia was isolated from the civilised world until early in the nineteenth century. It contained no plants or ruminant animals suitable for domestication, so its inhabitants were still hunters and food-gatherers. In the twentieth century, the authors were able to investigate the ancient sacred sites and meeting-places of the Aborigines while these were still almost untouched by civilisation.

The Australian Aborigine already had his pyramids. They were not built by him, but appropriated from nature. On the vast plains of the Pilbara, the sites of Aboriginal meeting-places were invariably chosen where the landscape assumes an unusual form: near mountains or in deep gorges, in caves or by river pools. On the huge boulders which constitute basic elements in the natural 'pyramids' of the Pilbara in north-western Australia, and in many other areas of the continent, he inscribed murals depicting his social life, his religious ceremonies and his philosophy.

Though the Aborigine had no written language, he was able to record his activities, his history, even his philosophy, in various art forms: in music and the dance, in legendary tales handed down by word of mouth from one generation to the next; and in graphic art forms. Music, dance and the spoken word were ephemeral; but the art is preserved for all time.

Russell Drysdale, a notable writer and painter of the Australian landscape, has described one of their sacred sites, Gallery Hill:

> The granite, weathered ... by nature, maintains a curious order and delicacy, and rises like architecture out of the plain. Rock on rock is incised with totemic

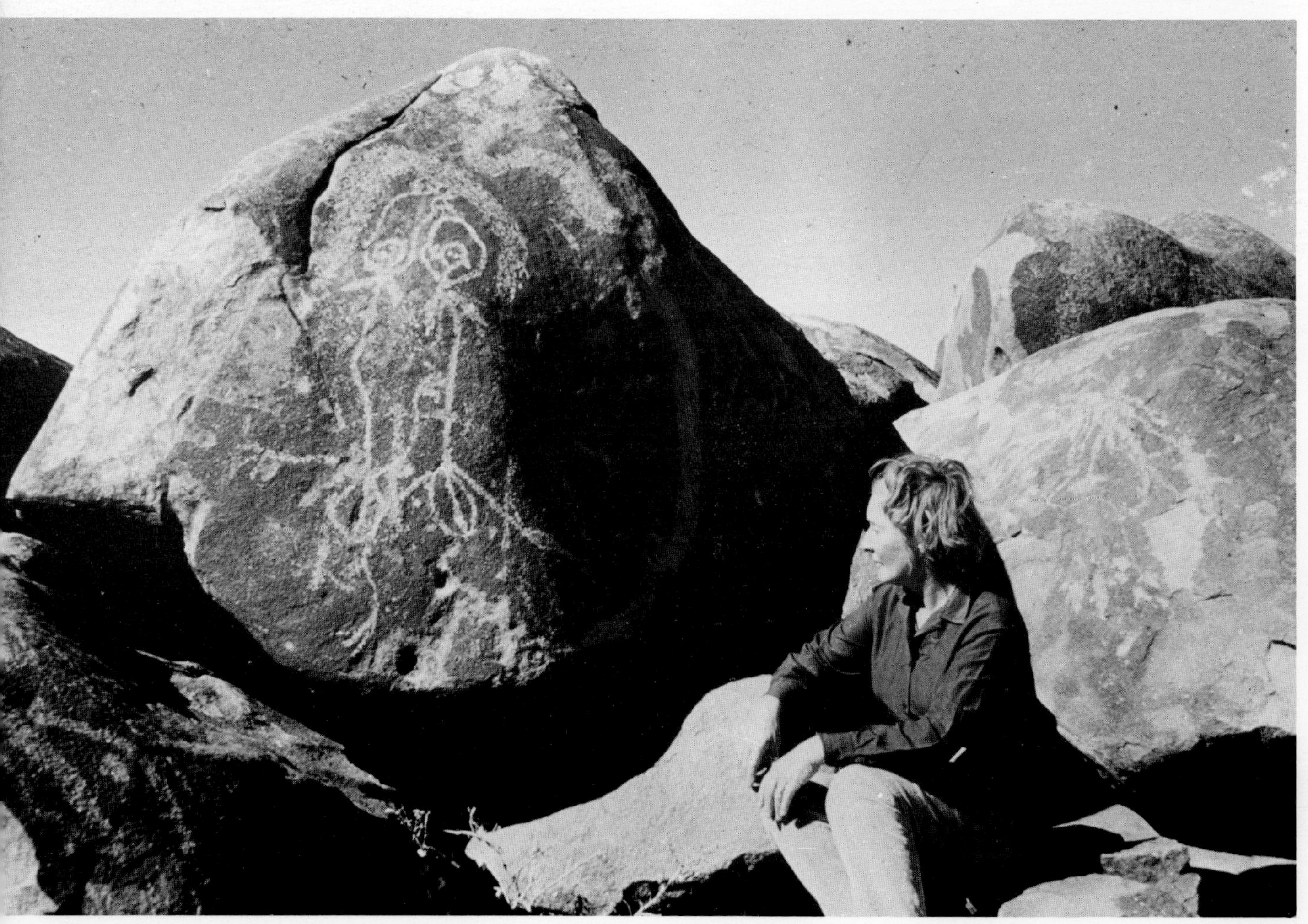

2

Corroborree. 'Dream-time' Aborigines of the Snake Totem dance on the great boulders at Saddle Rocks, in the north of Western Australia.

> figures of goannas, euros, tortoise, and particularly realistic interpretations of the coming into being of life. . . . The place had something of the quality of Chartres, but there was no music, only silence as the galleries stood ageless and immobile in the wind and desert air.[1]

When Russell Drysdale wonderingly passed this way in the 1960s, there was no music, it is true; but centuries before, when it had been the gathering-place for tribes from hundreds of miles around, there had been music. Music of men's and women's voices singing the age-old songs of the corroborees; rhythm of feet stamping the dry earth; of hands slapping and thumping thighs and arms and chests; thin chatter of the women's gonnae sticks; and the mysterious wail and roaring of the didgeridoo. These adjuncts to the sacred corroboree grounds have long since passed. Present-day local Aborigines attribute the exquisite rock engravings to the 'White Owl' people who were 'extinguished' before the present Aboriginal inhabitants arrived in Australia. However, the art is undoubtedly that of some earlier members of the same Aboriginal race.

Many of these sacred sites remain today much as the long-vanished Aborigines left them, although it is not easy to view many of these repositories of a long-lost culture. A local guide, a reliable four-wheel-drive vehicle, and an ability to 'rough it' in sometimes hazardous and isolated situations, are necessary to travel through the arid and unpeopled regions, as we found when we visited the Pilbara in 1967. We were able to penetrate the few roads into mountains, gorges, cliffs, caves, rivers and permanent pools in search of the magnificent art left in rock engravings and paintings . . . After several weeks thus engaged, we found that we had acquired an intuitive sense for the sites which had been selected by the long-ago Aboriginal people as suitable for their most moving and significant ceremonies. They were invariably dramatic and beautiful parts of the natural landscape.

Just as a 'sense of landscape' pre-dated civilisation, so also did a theory and practice of environmental planning. Quite early in his development, mankind learned that fire was a valuable tool and weapon which could help him to control and change his environment. The primitive nomads of Europe and Asia employed fire to clear forest country, to drive game animals as they hunted, to facilitate their own movement through heavily timbered terrain, and to encourage the growth of food plants. Alexander Marshak's recent researches have revealed that, more than twenty thousand years ago, man had a much clearer understanding of his environment and a greater appreciation of landscape quality, than has been previously supposed.[2] This is corroborated by our own study of the ancient ceremonial grounds of the first Australians. And from the comments of pioneer white settlers in Western Australia, the park-like appearance of much of the country when they first saw it, was probably the result of planned burning by the Aborigines.[3]

3

Windjana Gorge, Western Australia. Dramatic sites like this were converted by Aborigines into sacred meeting places.

4

Union of the Gods. An early pictograph showing the Aborigines' attitude to the creation of life. Gallery Hill, Western Australia.

A sense of landscape and of the environment, possessed intuitively by primitive man, prepared him for the further progress which revolutionised his whole pattern of life. The domestication of plants and animals laid the basis for permanent settlement, for greater control of his environment, and ultimately, for civilisation.[4]

THE NILE VALLEY

The first civilisations developed in widely separated regions and with considerable time variations. Civilisations appeared earlier in the West than in the East. As far back as 3000 B.C. the people in the Nile Valley and also those settled between the Tigris-Euphrates River had already established large towns.

Egyptian history is better documented because the stone temples and tombs of Egypt, decorated with murals, have been able to withstand the ravages of time better than the mud-brick with its cunieform writing, the main repository of the history of the civilisations of the Tigris-Euphrates.

Egypt consisted of a long, narrow valley containing large areas of flood plain. In some places it was fringed by cliffs; in others, separated from the neighbouring peoples by inhospitable desert. The arable land was irrigated and fertilised by the regular flooding of the Nile. Egyptian civilisation grew up over a period of four thousand years in this favourable environment, bringing changes and development to all aspects of life. However, we are concerned only with the environmental changes of man — to his arrangement, for decorative as well as functional purposes, of such elements as trees and plants, soil, rock and water, buildings, and some animals.

Gardens were designed in Egypt from very early times. Meten, an official and high priest under the last king of the Third Dynasty and the first king of the Fourth Dynasty, in 2720 B.C. built himself a garden around his house, which is described on his tomb. The house and garden were surrounded by a square enclosure of over ten thousand metres. '. . . It was planted with palms, figs and acacias for both ornament and use. Several ponds with green surroundings made a home for water-fowl. Before the house stood arbors and two fields of vine plantations yielded him an abundant supply of their fine wines.'[5]

In 1500 B.C. when the Pyramids were over a thousand years old, a magnificent temple complex was built at Thebes, surrounded by fine formal plantings. It is called the Temple of Deir-el-Bakhari and was built by Queen Hatshepsut who reigned from 1502 B.C. to 1479 B.C. Deir-el-Bakhari, which she built to honour the god Amon, was dramatically sited below over-hanging cliffs. A broad avenue of tree-flanked sphinxes formed an awe-inspiring approach, leading up to three large enclosed courts on rising levels, connected by ramps, the Temple being symbolically on the highest level. The whole complex was completely symmetrical. Temples such as this were later to inspire the architecture of the Greeks and Romans.

5

The Pyramids. These dramatic man-made mountains in the Nile Valley express the domination of man over nature.

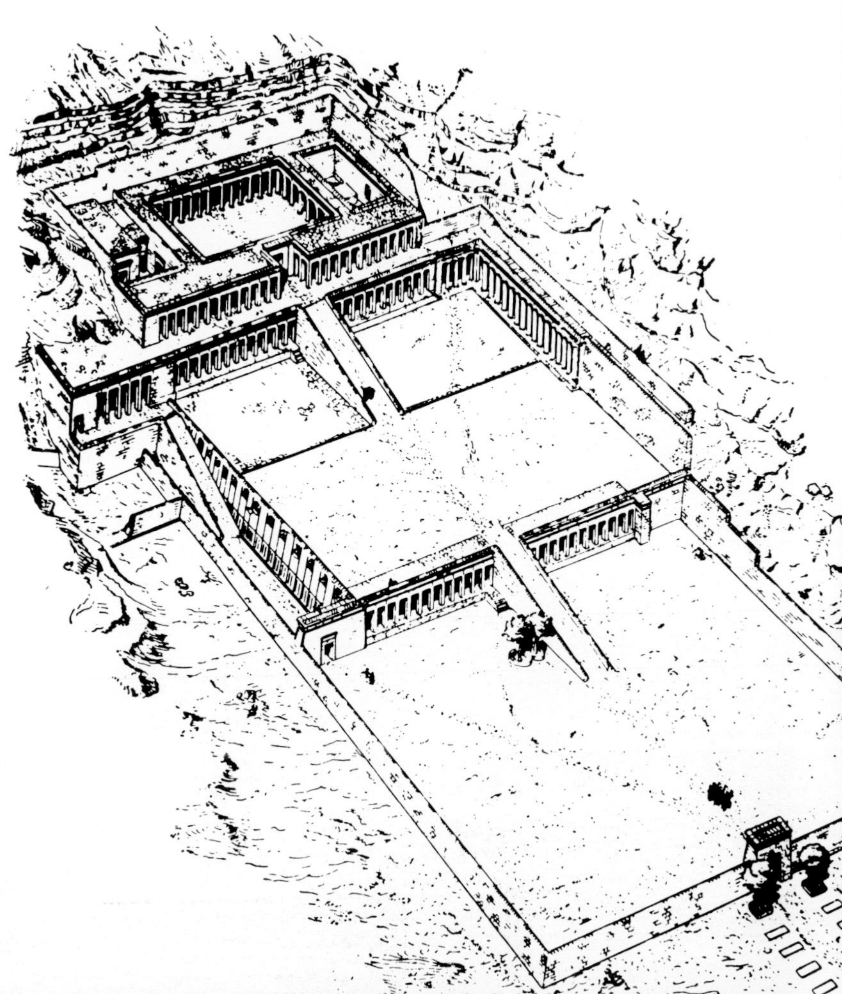

7

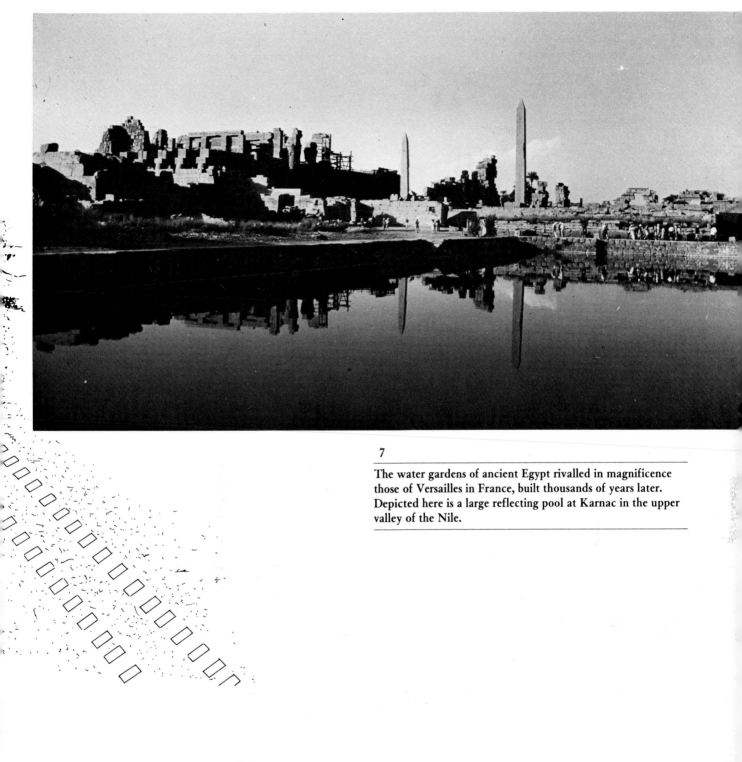

The water gardens of ancient Egypt rivalled in magnificence those of Versailles in France, built thousands of years later. Depicted here is a large reflecting pool at Karnac in the upper valley of the Nile.

6

The Temple of Deir-el-Bakhari, built by Queen Hatshepsut in the Nile Valley, is in ruins today. Long approach ramps were used between the various levels. The use of steps as a deliberate landscape experience came several centuries later.

The God-Kings of Egypt were very like the rulers that came later in history: far from being gods they were extremely human in most of their behaviour.

Hatshepsut was the daughter of Thutmose I, Pharaoh of Egypt; and she helped him govern while she was still a girl. She had an aptitude for government, and to secure her continued influence, married the heir-apparent, Thutmose, who was also her half-brother. They had two daughters, Neferure and Merytre. Hatchepsut's husband became Thutmose II but they didn't relate well. He died in 1501 B.C. Research has shown that his shoulders, hips, pelvis and breastbone were broken and there were symptoms of poisoning. These facts baffle Egyptologists! They can't imagine who could have been responsible.

Hatshepsut had arranged a marriage between her daughter Nefehure and her stepson Thutmose, who now became Thutmose III. Hatshepsut was his mother-in-law as well as his stepmother: but she didn't relate well with him either. She declared herself Pharaoh in 1495 B.C. and to avoid an unbreakable tradition that only a King could rule in Egypt, she appointed herself King as well. She then set up statues representing herself with a beard. She died in 1479 B.C. (For her, there had been perhaps a surfeit of Thutmoses!) Despite her somewhat complicated home life, Hatshepsut's reign was a productive one in both architecture and garden art.

The most detailed surviving illustration of the garden art of the Egyptians is the garden of a high official of Amenhotep III who reigned around 1390 B.C. at Thebes. It corresponds quite closely to Meten's garden, built over a thousand years earlier. To describe it, we shall quote Marie Louise Gothein, the first to bring it to the attention of Western garden enthusiasts:

> If we look at the beautiful regular plan, the fine alternation of trees planted with prudent forethought, the elegant shape of the sunk ponds, the judiciously disposed buildings in the garden – we recognise with astonishment that we have a formal garden in an advanced state of development on the very threshold of our history! Rhythm, symmetry and a happy combination of elegance and utility (fruit from the date palms, fig trees, pomegranates and grape vines – fish and water-fowl from the ponds), these have been fully attained, and with them a delight in quiet com-

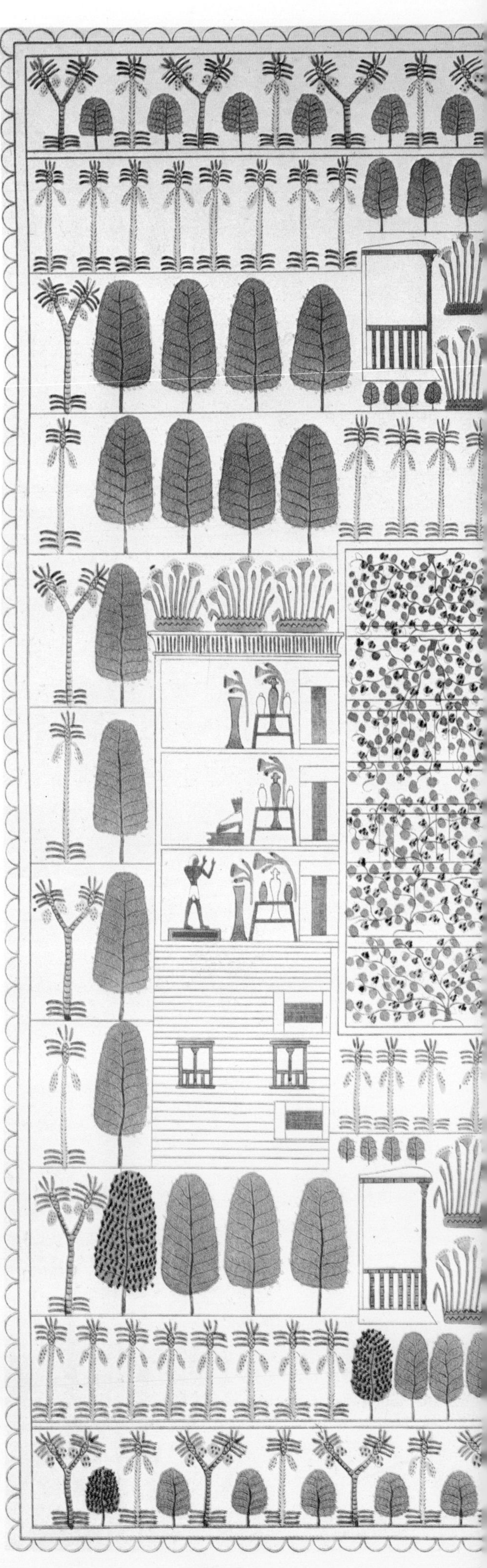

8

Garden plan for a noble of Amenhotep III (*c.* 1400 B.C.). 'If we look at the beautiful regular plan, the fine alternation of trees . . . the elegant shape of the sunk ponds – we recognise with astonishment that we have a formal garden in an advanced state of development on the very threshold of our [Western] history.'[6] As in most formal gardens, the planting is subordinate to the rectilineal architectural form of the buildings.

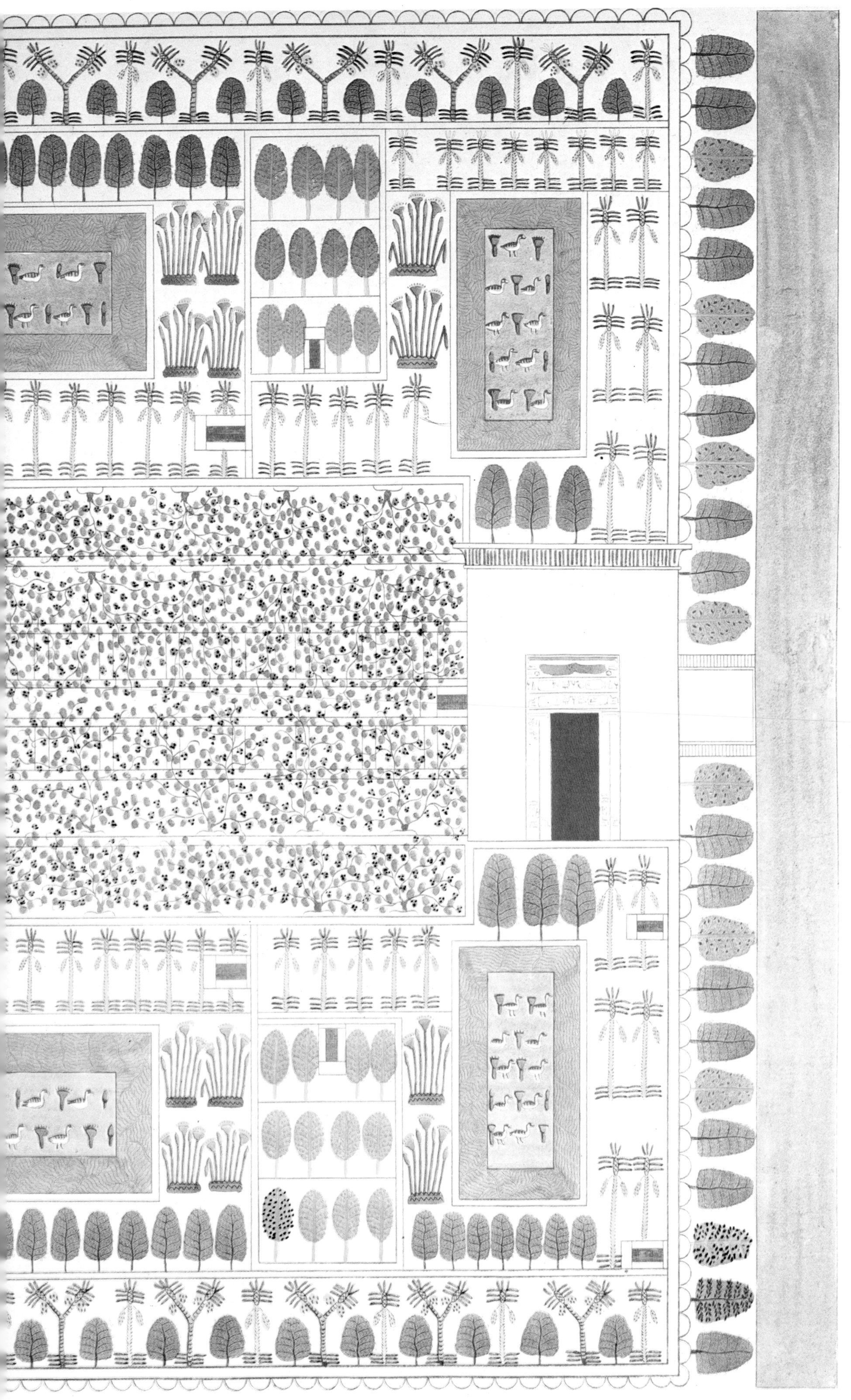

> munion with Nature, expressing as she does a sense of beauty in orderliness. . . . The next pleasing feature is the complete supremacy of the garden, to which buildings and the dwelling house included, are subordinate.[6]

Gothein's is a fine tribute to this early garden. But, being an enthusiastic protagonist of the formal garden, she failed to detect that the natural elements were completely subordinated to the architectural form of the whole. Trees are planted in straight lines, following and emphasising the lines of buildings and enclosures; water is used in straight canals or rectangular pools. Pergolas to support grape vines were used from earliest times and gradually became decorative in form. These were delightful central features providing grateful shade to important garden precincts.

Man-made structures dominated the Egyptian landscape. Earliest and most prominent were the Pyramids; then came the temples and lesser buildings; and later, the monumental images of the Pharaoh were sculptured, vieing with the cliffs in their scale.

Man's proud domination of his environment was everywhere made evident. The scale of the gardens of the Pharaohs was immense. We are accustomed to think of Versailles as the largest garden created by man, but the gardens of ancient Egypt rivalled Versailles in scale. Amenhotep III (1409–1379 B.C.) surrounded his palace with park-like gardens which included a pond 1½ kilometres in length and more than 300 metres wide. This was built to honour his wife and to celebrate the twelfth anniversary of his coronation. When the opening day arrived, the pond was filled with water and he took the Queen on the canal in the royal boat as part of the festivities.

The large quantities of water needed for these royal gardens were raised from the River Nile by means of a well sweep or shaduf. A beam was supported centrally with a heavy weight at one end and a bucket at the other. The weight as a counterbalance permitted the use of relatively large water containers. The system is still in use today both in Egypt and Asia. We saw it in Kashmir in Northern India just a few years ago.

By 1500 B.C. horticulture had reached a high level in Egypt. Queen Hatchepsut transplanted fully-grown incense trees, shipping them hundreds of miles to her temple at Deir-el-Bakhari. Rameses III (1198–1166 B.C.) boasted of creating wide places to walk in, with all kinds of trees that bear sweet fruits – a sacred way glowing with the flowers of every country, with lotus and papyrus numberless as the sands. Rameses also bequeathed gardens to others. He gave the religious houses of Egypt 514 gardens and tree sites.

9

Transporting incense trees to Egypt from the Land of Punt, over one thousand miles away, for the gardens of Deir-el-Bakhari. Queen Hatchepsut was justly proud of this achievement, and recorded it in bas-relief.

Listed in his same catalogue are gifts of over nineteen million nosegays.

This inclusion of nosegays and gardens together, illustrates another Egyptian characteristic, their love of flowers.

> Few Oriental nations can think of a festival without flowers, but nowhere were flowers so completely part of human life, so essential, as in ancient Egypt. If a feast were held, or a house made ready for the gods, everything was clothed in flowers. Garlands were worn on head and neck; the guests were presented with a nosegay, or at least with a single flower, as they entered; the servants were busy, not only with dishes for the feast, but always weaving new wreaths; and as each new kind of refreshment was served, fresh flowers were handed round. The guests carried nosegays in their hands all the time, enjoying the perfume.[7]

In this early civilisation of North Africa, flowers also inspired the forms for columns and their capitals in architecture, lotus and papyrus being the most used forms.

Despite Rameses' boasting, the range of plants available to the Egyptians would have been relatively limited. Trees would have included the sycamore (fig) – the most important shade tree – date palms, incense trees (probably Boswellia), tamarisk, willows, figs, pomegranates, acacia and elderberry. Among the flowering plants, the most loved was the water lily with its beautiful blue, red and white flowers (often referred to as lotus), papyrus, poppies, jasmine, delphiniums, oleander, convolvulus, gentian and cornflower. Mint would have probably been used as a garden plant as well as a culinary herb.

The gardens we have outlined were those of the ruling classes of Egypt. The life of the peasants would have been a harsh one. Both men and women worked from daylight to dusk and there were a number of peasant uprisings during Egypt's long history.

There would have been a middle class of priests, traders and artisans and the homes of some of these would have contained garden courts with pools of water for both use and ornament. They would have been enclosed for the same reason as the palace gardens. The larger ones would have had a tree or trees for both shade and fruit. The favourite tree would probably have been the sycamore fig. It was much admired by the Egyptians and its sign stood for trees in general in the early records. The delight of ordinary people in gardens and trees is well expressed in a poem from early Egypt depicting the sycamore tree as the friend of lovers . . .

When the tree is in all the glory of its flowering
it sends a message to the maiden:
'The little sycamore,
Which she planted with her own hand,
she moves her lips to speak
How fair are her lovely branches!
She is laden with fruits
That are redder than the jasper.
Her shade is cool,
She lays a little letter in a girl's hand,
The head gardener's daughter
She bids her hasten to the well-beloved:
"Come and stay among thy maidens,
We are drunken if we would go to thee,
Ay, before we have tasted aught,
The servants that obey thee
Are coming with their vessels;
Beer of every kind they bring
And every kind of bread,
Many flowers of today and yesterday,
And all refreshing fruits.
Come, and make it fine today,
Tomorrow, and next day, three days long . . .
Sit in my shade."
Her friend sits on her right hand
She makes him drunken
And yields to what he says . . .
But I am dumb
And say not what I see
I will say no word.'[8]

The contribution of Egypt to all of the arts is seldom fully understood, the reason probably being that, for the West, it has been over-shadowed by that of the Greeks, which became the standard for Western culture. The Egyptians produced an extensive literature; books on religions, morals, law, rhetoric, arithmetic, mensuration, geometry, medicine, travel and even novels. This became the basis of Greek culture.

Also to North Africa must go the credit for pioneering in architecture, and in formal landscape design. The development of sculpture Egypt shares with India.

However, it is apparent that, despite their joy in flowers and trees, the Egyptians had, to a large extent, lost touch with their origins in wild nature. In all their vast and splendid undertakings, the Pharaohs never forgot their role as God-King. Trees were no longer seen as majestic themes in a great pastoral symphony . . . they had become domesticated, well-mannered and subservient elements of Egyptian architecture.

MESOPOTAMIA

Parallel in time to Egypt, a separate civilisation had emerged a thousand miles away, beyond the Arabian desert, around the Euphrates River. In 1500 B.C. the land was occupied by the Assyrians. Though the climate was warm and dry like that on the Nile, the environment was very different. Large forests grew close to the settlements, high mountains arose to the North and East, giving a special character to the parks and gardens made in Mesopotamia. The Assyrians revered trees; but at first, the trees they worshipped were growing in the forest.

The Gilgamesh epic, probably the earliest surviving in history, tells the story of King Gilgamesh, king of Uruk between Babylon and Ur on the Euphrates River. With his friend Engidu, Gilgamesh ventured forth to destroy Humbaba, guardian of the cedar woods. Humbaba was a wicked Elamite tyrant who terrorised the people of the surrounding country. They sought him in his mountain stronghold, which was to the east of the Tigris River, surrounded by cedar woods. This extract from the epic illustrates the different approach to Nature of the Assyrians from the Egyptians. It describes a hunting ride which penetrates the virgin forest:

. . . (they) stand and look upon the wood,
They behold the high tops of the cedar,
The entrance to the wood
Where Humbaba goes in lofty tread.
The ways are straight, and the path is wrought fair.
They see the cedar mount, the dwelling of gods, the sanctuary of the Irnim.
Before the hill stands the cedar, abundant and tall,
Her good shadow is full of rejoicing.
It covers the thorn bush, covers the dark-hued sloe,
And beneath the cedar, the sweet smelling plants.[9]

This epic foreshadows the distinctive contribution which Assyria, Persia and perhaps India, were to make to the early 'Western' landscape movement.

10

A temple and 'hanging garden' at Quyundjig (Nineveh). Notice the water channel flowing down from the elevated garden terrace. The pointed arches are characteristic of the Middle East and were adopted by Islam and later by the Gothic cathedral-builders in Europe.

11.

An impression of 'The Hanging Gardens of Babylon', modified from a nineteenth-century artist's conception.

12

Reconstruction of part of the city of Assur on the Middle Tigris River about 1500 B.C. Note the way houses surrounding the city centre turn blind elevations to the street. They all have central courts for lighting and ventilation. Those of the more well-to-do would have developed gardens and pot plants.

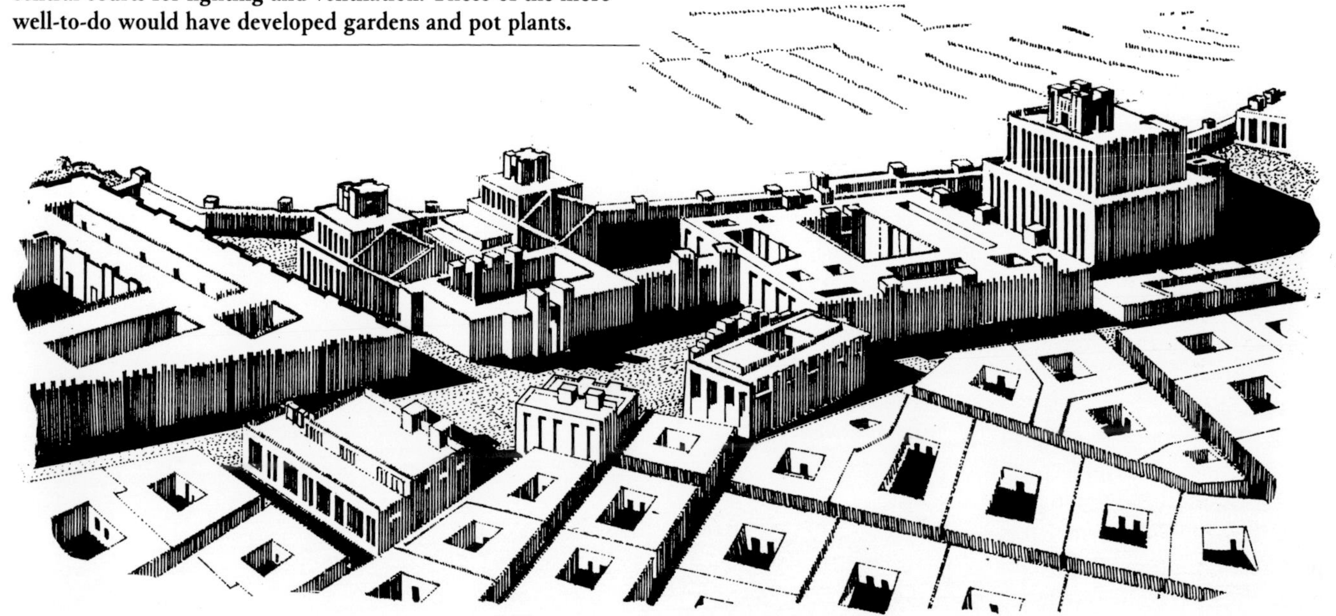

The 'fair wrought' avenues of planted trees which penetrated the virgin forest, forged a strong landscape link between the works of man and those of Nature. The original purpose of the avenues could have been functional, that is, simply to make hunting easier. The game animals were at first indigenous, no doubt; but exotic animals were soon introduced, and then enclosure became essential to prevent their escape. Eventually large enclosed hunting parks became associated with every important city. Once enclosure had taken place in Assyria, and exotic trees were introduced, the hunting parks would inevitably have taken on a regular appearance.

Tiglath-Pileser I (1116–1078 B.C.) was the first to put on record this pride in the royal parks: 'I carried off from the countries I had conquered trees that none of the kings, my forefathers had possessed, these trees I have taken and planted them in mine own country, in the parks of Assyria have I planted them.'[10] Tiglath-Pileser also brought to his capital, Assur young wild oxen, and stags and wild goats, even young elephants, and let them grow up like flocks of sheep in his park. He also imported dromedaries, and foreign kings sent him as presents 'beasts from the great sea' for which he had large fish-ponds made.

What was the appearance of these parks and plantings of the Assyrians? Apparently they soon became formal in their planting. Assyrian bas-reliefs dating from early times show trees and palms arranged in rows similar to those of the Egyptians. It is even probable that Egyptian design had

influenced such plantings because Assyrian princes had, in previous centuries, been taken as hostages to that country. Egyptian influence would have become much stronger when the Assyrians invaded Egypt around 700 B.C. and they would have become familiar with Egyptian gardens in detail. The imported trees mentioned by Tiglath-Pileser would almost certainly have been row-planted in order to make irrigation easier.

Describing how the parks were made in his time, Sennacherib (705–681 B.C.) son of Sargon II, writes:

> I have cut down and levelled mountain and field from the land about the town of Kisiri unto the country near Nineveh, so that the plants may thrive there, and I have made a canal; one and a half hours' journey from the Chusur river have I brought water to flow in my canal, and between my plantations for their watering.[11]

The method of irrigation practised by the Assyrians involved a central canal with branches leading off each side at right angles. The form is an ancient one: it appears on prehistoric pottery. At the present day, farms in Iran and other West Asian countries are irrigated in the same way.

From the earliest times in Mesopotamia private dwellings in the cities turned a blind face to the street. The rooms of the house faced inwards to a central court yard which provided light, air and access between them. In the more well-to-do houses these courtyards would have been adorned with pot plants and even trees and gardens. Similar Roman houses were preserved by the volcanic eruption of Vesuvius at Pompeii.

Probably due to their mountain environment, the Assyrians were more interested in contours than were the Egyptians. The Assyrians introduced a symbolic mount into their parks, and the Hanging Gardens of Babylon became one of the seven wonders of the ancient world. Legend has it that they were built for one of the King's consorts who, coming from a mountainous land, wearied of the flat plain and longed for a garden which would remind her of her own country.

In part of the Hanging Gardens were probably some rather gruesome decorations; the head of a conquered warrior, suspended from a tree is shown in a bas-relief of King Ashurbanipal enjoying a victory feast in 660 B.C.

13

Alabaster bas-relief of Assurbanipal relaxing in his garden at Nineveh, seventh century B.C. The head of a defeated enemy is hanging in one of the trees.

THE PERSIANS

The Persians now enter our story. Their influence has been a continuous one almost up to the present day. They have come to be regarded as the mainspring for garden design in Central Asia, in much the same way as their ancient rivals, the Greeks, came to be regarded as the main origin of all European culture. Though the Persians did make a most important continuous contribution in the sphere of landscape garden design, we shall show in later chapters of this book, that the Western preoccupation with Persia sometimes obscures decisive contributions from other cultures.

Persians succeeded the Assyrians to the hegemony of Western Asia in 559 B.C. Xenophon the Greek, who saw their parks on his travels, described the way they were laid out through the medium of Socrates:

> Everywhere the Persian king is zealously cared for, so that he may find gardens wherever he goes; their name is Paradise and they are full of all things fair and good that the earth can bring forth. It is here that he spends the greatest part of his time, except when the season forbids. . . .[12]

He continues

> When Lysander brought gifts from the allies, Cyrus himself showed him the Paradise of his palace at Sardis. Lysander marvelled at the beauty of the trees, at the evenness of their plantation, at the regular rows, at the neat way the corners were made, at the prettiness of it all, and moreover at the many sweet odours which followed their footsteps. 'All these things,' he said, 'do I admire; I admire the beauty of the whole, but far more, O Cyrus, do I praise the mind that has designed and ordered it.' Cyrus was much flattered by his praise, and informed Lysander that he himself had been the artist, and had even planted some of the trees.[13]

Persian palaces were built upon a series of raised platforms. This led to an important development in planning – the introduction of wide steps between levels – which replaced

14

View of the ruins of Persepolis today, showing the great stairway – an important step forward from the long ramps used in Egypt.

15

Another view of Persepolis, on the high plateau. Though it is in ruins, the fine scale of the open and enclosed spaces, still fills one with awe.

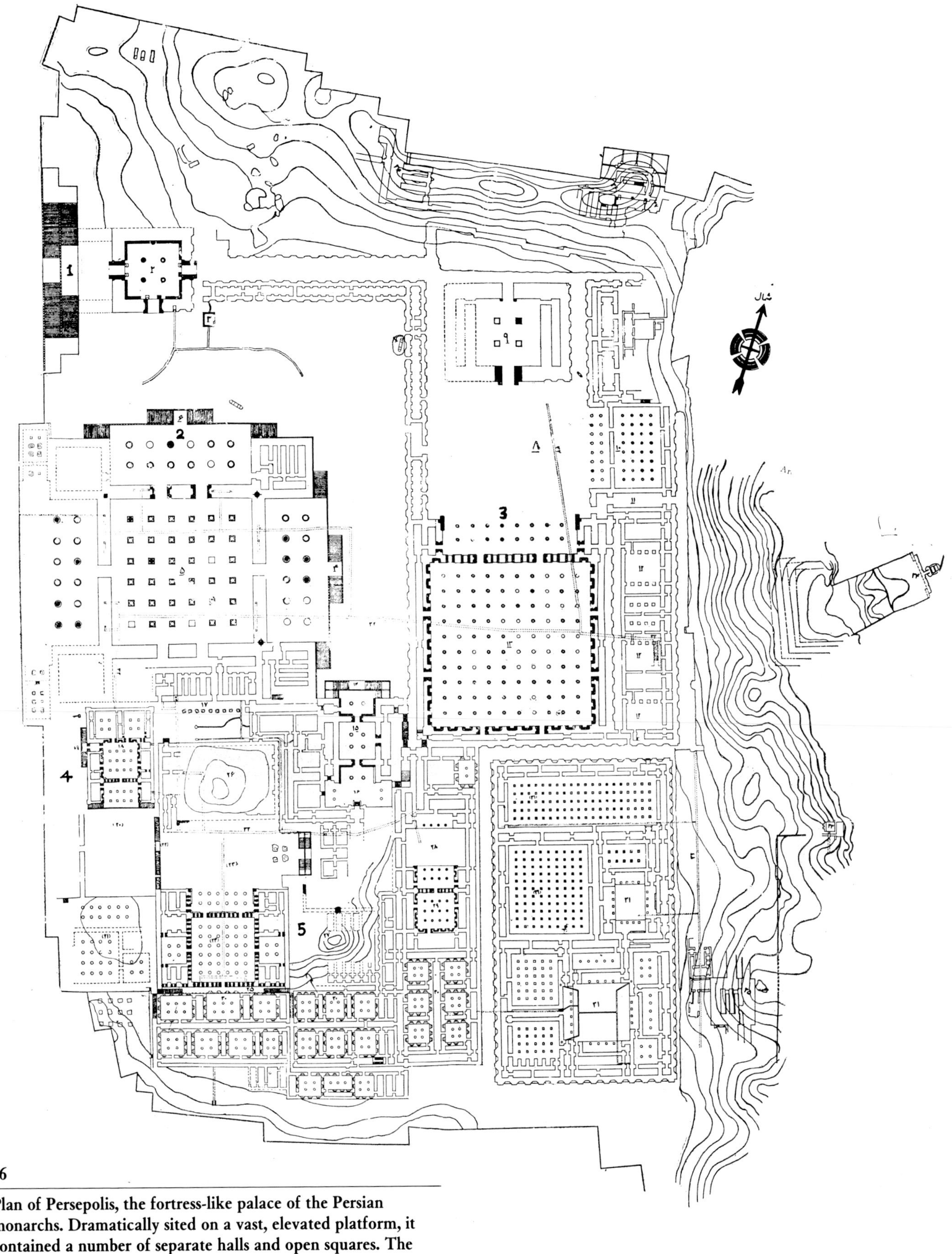

16

Plan of Persepolis, the fortress-like palace of the Persian monarchs. Dramatically sited on a vast, elevated platform, it contained a number of separate halls and open squares. The royal town spread out below it. Alexander the Great admired the royal gardens, but sacked Persepolis.
Key: 1. Entrance stairway. 2. Hall of Xerxes. 3. Darius Hall of 100 Columns. 4. Palace of Darius. 5. Palace of Xerxes.

the long, cumbersome ramps used by the Egyptians, as illustrated at Deir-el-Bakhari. The main approach stairway at Persepolis is a fine example. At Persepolis are also secondary stairways between the various upper levels. Bas-reliefs decorating their spandrils show delightfully formalised rows of cypress trees alternating with palms.

We do not know for certain the trees and flowering plants used by the Persians but they probably included plane trees, cypresses and date palms, poplars, elms, willows, pines, ash, cedars, oaks, maples and sweet myrtles. Fruit trees would have included oranges, apples, pears, pomegranate, almonds, figs and grapes.

The most popular flower was probably the rose and it is likely that narcissi, iris, daffodils, tulips, hyacinth and lilies-of-the-valley would have been added to the Egyptian vocabulary of flowers because all of these occur naturally in Persia.

When the Persians conquered Egypt in 525 B.C., the vocabulary of Persian landscape design would have been broadened and changed by knowledge of the Egyptian details of walled gardens.

ANCIENT GREECE

The Greeks, rising to dominance in the fifth century B.C., eventually became the heirs to the whole of the culture of both Western Asia and Egypt, as well as the Mediterranean. The Greeks, like the Phoenicians (from whom they obtained their written language) were essentially traders, largely divorced from the land. They showed little interest in garden design. They were much more pre-occupied with man himself.

But their new form of government changed the shape of the royal park, giving it a more democratic content. First it became a sacred grove, planted with trees and dedicated to the gods. Then gradually it changed into an arena for sporting activities and was called a Hippodrome. The more active sports, which included chariot racing, required large open areas. A long central open track was surrounded by formal plantings of trees similar to those of the sacred groves, but now giving shade to the spectators, for whom seats were also provided.

Sculpture was introduced; first as an image of the god of the grove, later as a recurring theme to honour successful competitors at the games.

Democracy also brought a new meaning to the city square, which became a place of public assembly. Each new Greek city was planned around an agora, as this city square was called; and the arrangement of buildings around the agora became as important as the design of the individual buildings.

The Acropolis and theatres at Athens are the most famous surviving examples of Greek space design but another delightful illustration of Greek town planning also exists in Priene in Turkey, on the coast of the Mediterranean. The town is now completely ruinous, but the form of the Agora remains, and the theatre could be used today.

17

The Odeon, behind the Acropolis in Athens. Though the Greeks built no gardens, they developed superb urban open spaces for public use.

THE MACEDONIANS

It has been customary to regard the Macedonian Empire as part of the Greek cultural heritage of the Western world, but in fact, the Macedonians played quite a different role from that of the Greeks. Although there had been a considerable interchange of ideas between the cultures of the Aegean, Egypt and Western Asia, Alexander brought these cultures together in a way that had not happened in previous times.

When Phillip of Macedon began to gain supremacy in the Aegean, the Greeks regarded the Macedonians as barbarians, not cultured like themselves. But Phillip had developed a better strategy of warfare and subdued the Greek States. They refused to accept him and hated him, calling him the Tyrant of Hellas. Phillip however greatly admired Athenian culture and appointed Aristotle, a Macedonian who had been Greek-trained, as tutor to his son. (Aristotle's father had been the family doctor of the Macedonian Royal house.) Phillip's son, Alexander was therefore imbued with Greek ideas and philosophy. He learnt the art of warfare from his father and soon extended Macedonia's hegemony far beyond Phillip's conquests. He went eastwards through Asia as far as India; westward through the Aegean to Egypt.

Like most people of his period, Alexander was quite a superstitious person. His mother, Olympias, was the high priestess of an ancient cult and kept sacred snakes in her bedroom. Her husband, King Phillip, detested them. He was renowned for his drinking habits and perhaps at times he frequently couldn't tell which snakes were the real ones . . . Queen Olympias brought Alexander up to believe that his real father was Zeus-Ammon, a Graeco-Egyptian snake god. Alexander used to boast about it; and once executed thirteen Macedonians because they had said he was *not* the son of a serpent.

Alexander's conquests took him through all the areas of the ancient civilisations we have been discussing. He penetrated Persia. Assyria and Babylonia, into Asia as far as the Indus Valley, and finally occupied Egypt. There his general, Ptolemy, who became its Governor, founded a famous dynasty of Graeco-Egyptian rulers. After his conquest of Asia, Alexander adopted many of the customs of the conquered countries and he deliberately pursued his objective of integrating European and Asian cultures. He did not achieve this integration in his lifetime, but it was carried out by his successors.

Alexander was deeply interested in the parks and gardens of the countries he conquered and instructed that the parks of already-subdued palaces were to be preserved and well tended. On his return to Parsargadae, when he found the tomb of Cyrus in the royal Paradise had been neglected and robbed, he severely punished the Magi who were the hereditary guardians.[14] During another military engagement, he made a detour on his march from Celonae to see the garden of Semiramis at the foot of the Mountains of Baghistan, where willows along the stream were renowned for their beauty.

Alexander adopted from the Oriental lands he conquered, the custom of doing affairs of State in the Paradise. He received his generals there . . . and 'when he came sick to Babylon, he had himself carried to the great park on the far side of the Euphrates, that he might die there.'[14]

One of the creative effects of his conquests was to unify the garden cultures of Asia, Egypt and the Eastern Mediterranean. Many new parks were built. Gothein points out that over a quarter of the city of Alexandria in Egypt was occupied by public parks and royal gardens.

Another famous garden city in the Alexandrian tradition was Antioch. Its main street was a long, continuous portico with houses on one side; on the other, gardens extended right to the foot of the mountain: they contained all manner of summer-houses, baths and fountains, which however did not appear on the hillside, so as not to destroy the impression of regularity. Seven and a half kilometres beyond the town was a famous park called 'Daphne'. Later generations could not praise it enough for its baths, porticos and places of amusement. For public use were excellent hostels where vines grew even inside the rooms, while in the gardens were wafted the aromatic scents of flower beds. 'Daphne' was often praised as being the fairest spot on earth.[15]

Unfortunately no illustrations of consequence survive. Alexander's raids into India and the consequent exposure of the Mediterranean culture to that of Buddhist India, possibly had a significant effect. But as far as landscape design is concerned, these influences are conjectural. We know that the ancient Hindu culture upon which Buddhism was built, regarded the tree as sacred. The Hindus also paid more respect to other living things than did their neighbours. Buddhism itself was strongly nature-oriented. Chinese sources reveal that at this period, the princes of India vied with each other in building parks and gardens in honour of Buddha. Much additional study is required to reveal the form taken by these parks and gardens.

Gothein believed that these Indian parks and gardens were formal in character, and did not vary substantially from those of Western Asia. She writes: 'Neither to the foreign invader like Alexander and his successors nor to the travellers arriving from the West does there appear to be anything different here (in India) from their own parks.'[16] It is important to realise that, when all these visitors came to the Indus Valley, that part of India had been a satrap of Persia for several centuries and therefore had long been under strong Persian influence.

THE ROMAN EMPIRE

From the beginning of the second century B.C. the Romans gradually succeeded to leadership in the Western world. It is commonly said that the Romans were not a creative people; that they were not innovators; that they appropriated the cultures of those nations who had preceded them – particularly that of the Greeks. We consider this attitude misleading. Do not all new and vital civilisations absorb as much as they can of the contributions others have already made towards human progress? Surely their success usually depends almost precisely on the extent to which they can do so. Did not the Greeks absorb a great deal of the architectural and sculptural advances of Asia and Egypt, and learn all they could from every country and culture with which they came in contact?

The Phoenicians, Greeks, Macedonians and the Carthaginians laid the economic base which permitted the Romans to establish political domination over the Mediterranean, Europe and Asia Minor. Though Roman art, science and literature were inspired by that of the Greeks, the Romans themselves made considerable contributions in all these fields.

Wherever the Roman legions went in the countries around the Mediterranean they found inspiration for garden art and landscape design. Roman gardens were architectural in character, and within closed colannaded courts, trees were arranged in rows, and garden beds formed regular patterns. Ivy was a favourite plant and we obtain an idea about its use in a letter from Cicero to his friend Quintus after a visit to Quintus' pleasure grounds: 'I praised your gardener; he has clothed everything with ivy, both the foundation-wall of the villa and the interspaces between the columns of the walk, so that, in short, those Greek statues of yours seem to be landscape gardeners crying up [selling] their ivy'.[17]

In the larger gardens and open spaces, avenues of trees repeated the regular rhythm of the columns of the palaces or porticos. Garden beds and flower boxes were carefully related to spaces between columns, statuary and trees. Water was used formally in straight canals, rectangular ponds or circular basins. These were often fed by fountains and falling water.

During the Golden Age of Roman literature, in the century before the Christian era, Catullus, Virgil and Horace found great pleasure in the freedom and beauty of the rural landscape and made it the background for many of their poems. Though their concept was that of man in a landscape much of which was of his own making, Horace, particularly in some of his private writing, expressed a deep love of nature. Here is an epistle to his friend Quinctius, describing his little estate among the Sabine Hills outside the city of Rome.

A chain of hills that stretches far and wide,
Unbroken save where runs a shady vale
Which catches on the right the morning sun,
And on the left his last warm evening glow.
The temperate air would gain your ready praise.
What if you saw my brakes of generous thorns
Laden with ruddy cornels and with plums;
My woods of oak and ilex that delight
My herds with fodder and their Lord with shade?
You would declare that to these Sabine Hills

18

Nilus and colonnade at Hadrian's Villa near Tivoli, Italy. The name Nilus (Nile) given to water bodies, indicates the Egyptian origin of this design idiom.

The verdure of Tarentum has been brought.
A sparkling fount that well might give a name
To some broad-breasted stream – Hebrus itself
That winds through Thrace is not more cool or pure –
Pours forth its limpid waters that bring health
To weary head and jaded appetite.
This hiding place so dear unto myself,
And, pray and believe so full itself of charm,
Will keep me here for you in safe retreat
Through all September's unsalubrious hours.[18]

There was a renewed interest in Egyptian monuments and gardens – evidenced by the graffiti scratched on the walls by the Roman centurions. Even the garden names were taken over from the Egyptians: narrow canals and pools of water received the name of 'Nilus' after the River Nile; and the colonnade around the Nilus at Hadrian's Villa outside Rome was called 'Canopus' after a town of that name near Alexandria. This was perfectly natural as the Roman Emperors, such as Julius Caesar, greatly admired Alexander the Great and all his works, both in Asia and Egypt. Caesar even believed in the divinity of his person as Alexander had done before him.

During his sojourn with Cleopatra in Alexandria, Caesar planned to conquer the world and bequeath it to their son, Caesarion. But alack! Caesar proved to be completely mortal; and after entertaining Cleopatra in his Imperial Garden when she visited Rome, he was killed in the Senate House by some of his best friends.

Caesar bequeathed his Imperial Garden to the people of Rome. Cleopatra quickly returned to Alexandria, to engage in her much-publicised love affair with Marc Anthony. It was not a material success. Octavian, the nephew-once-removed and adopted son of Julius Caesar, defeated Anthony at Actium; and after Anthony and Cleopatra had committed suicide, he executed Caesarion – just in case – and became the Emperor Augustus, ruling the Roman Empire for forty years.

Augustus was also a garden builder and, like Alexander and the Persian monarchs, conducted affairs of state in his gardens when he was resident in Rome. Roman aristocrats followed the example of the Emperor by building villas and gardens outside the city walls to escape the congestion of the city. The most famous of the Imperial gardens was The Golden House, built by Nero after the great fire of 64 A.D. The Imperial residence with its garden courts, was over a mile long. The three-storeyed, colonnaded entrance faced the Forum and had a colossal 120 feet high statue of Nero in the centre. Avenues and gardens extended far down the hillside to the valley now occupied by the Colosseum, where an immense oval pond was surrounded by secondary palaces and pavilions.

In addition to lakes, waterfalls and gardens, Nero's architects created secluded areas surrounded by thickets, open lawns, vineyards, pasture lands and hunting grounds. In the congested conditions of the surrounding city, Nero's expanse appeared much more luxurious than gold or precious stones. Nero's Golden House was the final straw that led to his downfall. It made him unpopular with everyone; a barrier across Rome, it disrupted the trade and communication of the city. After his death, there was a campaign to obliterate all memory of Nero; and Vespasian built the Colosseum down in the valley where Nero's oval pond and palaces had been.

The Romans took over the large vocabulary of plants that had been developed during the integration by Alexander of the Aegean, West Asia and North Africa. To these plants, were added others from the Romans' North-Eastern conquests in Europe. They included a wide variety of trees of which the most popular was the plane tree, still in widespread use in Rome to this day. Other popular species were cypress, elms, poplars, umbrella pine, laurel, lime, cinnamon, aspen, alders, oaks, myrtle, firs and spruce. Roses were the most widely used shrub, as they are today, and there were a number of varieties. Oleanders were planted extensively because of their persistence in difficult positions. Box was favoured for topiary. Fruiting trees included oranges, apples, pears, pomegranate, olives, almonds and figs. Grape vines were used both for fruit, wine and decoration, periwinkle (*Vinca minor*) and ivy were other popular climbers. Violets, hyacinths, Sweet Rocket, acanthus, narcissi, iris, anemones, poppies, verbenas, and crocus were among the smaller plants.

The Romans had stronger links with the land than did the trading Greeks. For this reason their contribution to landscape design was a more significant one. The republican form of government initially adopted by the Romans, though ogligarchic, permitted individual landowners to develop private estates in a way that would have been difficult, if not impossible, under the dictatorial kingdoms of Assyria, Persia and Egypt. The country estates of aristocratic Romans gave a new form and content to landscape design. They became one of the fore-runners of those of the landed gentry of Europe of a much later date.

From the letters of Pliny the Younger, we obtain a vivid impression of the new landscape thinking which accompanied this change. For the first time we can recognise very close parallels to the thoughts and feelings of Renaissance man. Pliny and his contemporaries had a passionate attachment to the natural landscape of Italy. They sited their villas on the coast or in the foothills, to obtain the most benefit from the surrounding terrain. Here is Pliny writing to his friend Caninius Rufus:

> How stands Como, that favourite scene of yours and mine? What becomes of the pleasant villa? The eververnal portico, the shady plane tree grove, the crystal canal so agreeable winding along its flowery banks, together with the charming lake below that serves at once the purposes of use and beauty? What have you to tell me of the firm yet springy avenue, the bath exposed on all sides to full sunshine, the public salon, the private dining room, and all the elegant apartments for repose both at noon and night? ... Leave, my friend (for it is high time) the low and sordid pursuits to others, and in this safe and snug retreat emancipate yourself for your studies.[19]

What a bewitching picture Pliny paints! His language and thoughts have a modern ring. It would be easy to imagine him living in Jane Austen's early nineteenth-century England. But this would be an illusion. One should always be on guard against clothing vague descriptions in images which are familiar to us . . . Pliny's villa was very different from *Mansfield Park*. To begin with, Rome was then a slave state and Pliny was a scion of one of the few ruling families. Crucified slaves would have been a commonplace along the Roman roads: the unsuccessful slave revolt led by Spartacus had been repressed with cruelty and bloodshed in the previous century. And the villa garden which he describes would almost certainly not have been similar to the one in your mind's eye. . . .

Fortunately, Pliny gives us more detail in his account of his own 'villa rustica' in Tuscany, a country estate on a much larger scale than Como. The central feature was a large open hippodrome enclosed by a formal planting of plane trees linked together on their trunks and lower branches by ivy, which was festooned from tree to tree. Water was piped to every part of the garden and used decoratively in the form of fountains and other more complex devices. Describing the hippodrome, Pliny writes:

At the upper end is a semi-circular bench of white marble, shaded with a vine which is trained upon four small pillars of Carystian marble. Water, gushing through several little pipes from under this bench, as if it were pressed out by the weight of the persons who repose themselves on it, falls into a stone cistern underneath, from whence it is received into a fine polished marble basin, so artfully contrived that it is always full without ever overflowing. When I sup here, the tray of whets and the larger dishes are placed around the margin, while the smaller ones swim about in the form of little ships and waterfowl . . . [20]

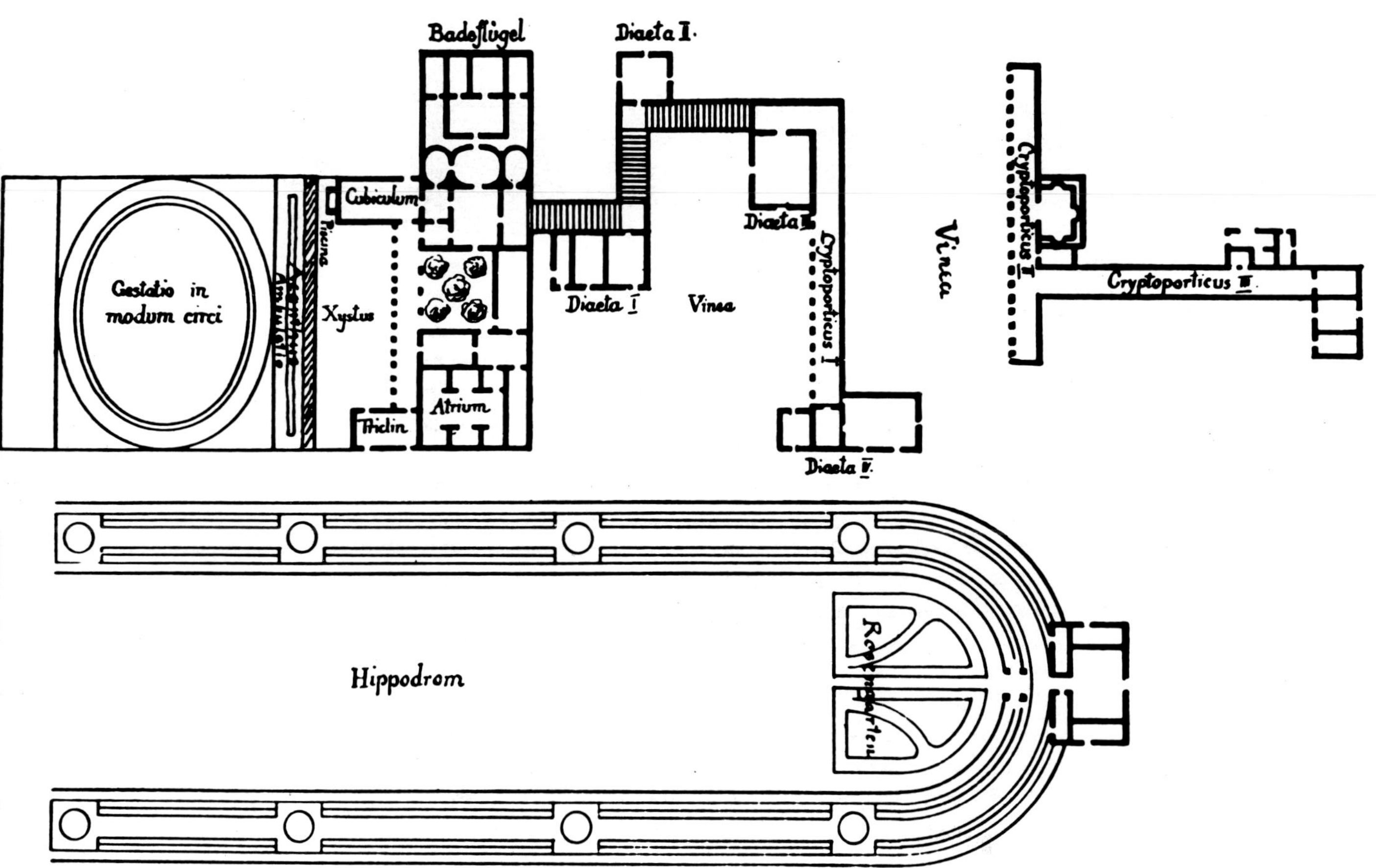

19

Plan of the Tuscan villa of Pliny the Younger, reconstructed by Gothein from his descriptions. The Roman gardens were developed from those of the Macedonians in Asia Minor and Egypt and were basically formal in character.

TOPIARY

But the garden innovation of which Pliny speaks with most pride and enthusiasm is that of topiary — that is, the cutting and shaping of plants into geometric and animal forms:

> The box is interposed in groups and cut into a thousand different forms, sometimes into letters expressing the name of the master or again that of the artificer; whilst here and there little obelisks rise intermixed alternatively with apple trees, when on a sudden, in the midst of this elegant regularity, you are surprised with an imitation of the negligent beauties of nature; in the centre of which lies a spot surrounded with a knot of dwarf plane trees. Beyond this are interspersed clumps of the smooth and twining acanthus; then come a variety of figures and names cut out in box.[20]

Gothein's reconstruction of the Pliny garden which we illustrate is based upon a thorough study of the whole remaining evidence of the period. But like all reconstructions relying upon literary description, it must be regarded as speculative.

A prominent characteristic of Roman gardens is the tendency towards ornate display. Is there not something repellent — verging on the decadent — in the clever artifices by which materials are made to appear what they are not? The enthusiasm for topiary is the final expression of man's domination over natural forms.

We can however, obtain a more accurate idea of the detail of such a garden from murals on the walls of villas at Pompeii. This city was entombed in 79 A.D. Pliny's letters were written in 62 A.D. The ruins of Pompeii illustrate an important element in garden design for the first time, the fully enclosed court open to the sky. This was called a peristylium by the Romans. The House of the Vettii in Pompeii is the best known example. It has been carefully restored and if this is completely authentic it was rather crowded and lacked the simplicity of the later Islamic courtyard gardens. Another instance is the House of Meleagre also at Pompeii. The pool here with its central fountain jet, has been shaped in an unusual way evocative of the pools of Mughal India which were built many centuries later. It was probably based on a Persian prototype.

The Romans made contributions in other areas of landscape design, however. They developed the concept of the Greek agora as a central city meeting-place; the best known example being the Forum Romanum. Reconstruction of the Forum made by scholars indicates that considerable attention was devoted to the arrangement of buildings around the central space. Scale, vistas and viewpoints were given careful consideration; though at this distance of time, it is difficult to know how much was deliberate design and how much the result of happy chance. The finest examples of city squares in the West (which were inspired in part by Rome) were planned much later, during the Renaissance.

As with relics of the Greek civilisation, many interesting Roman ruins can be found outside Rome, in areas where modern civilisation has not overrun them and obliterated much of their spirit. One of these survives at Ephesis, in modern Turkey. To roam around this town is an exciting experience.

One wanders down a marble-paved street between delightful ruinous shrines, baths, shops, pavilions and even a brothel . . . clamber up a steep slope on one side of the street, and a superb agora is suddenly revealed. Then, as a climax, a magnificent theatre appears, perhaps more dramatic as a ruin today than it was in its heyday, with its form more clearly revealed. The sea has receded from this town which was once a busy port; but the spirit of the ancient Roman Empire still persists and it is easy to imagine the street, the agora and theatre, peopled with toga-clad Roman citizens.

20

Levels Hall, Westmoreland, in the Lakes District of England. A fine surviving example of the art of topiary, which was very popular among the ancient Romans.

THE BYZANTINE EMPIRE

The fall of the Roman Empire is still usually dated by the fall of Rome to Germanic invaders in 476 A.D., but this is far from correct. Constantine I had dedicated Constantinople as the new capital in 330 A.D. Though a treaty with the Persians in 363 A.D. resulted in the loss of much of the Roman Empire's West-Asian territory, it laid the basis for the re-conquest of the Mediterranean by the Eastern Emperors. Under Constantine, Christianity also gained strength and became the dominant religion.

In 527 A.D. Justian became Emperor and dedicated himself to the re-conquest of the West. Under his thirty-eight year reign Constantinople reached its economic and cultural peak. Byzantium regained control of the whole of Italy and the Adriatic, the northern coast of Africa and

21

The Agora at Ephesus in Turkey. The Roman ruins at Ephesus are still undisturbed by later developments in Anatolia. One can almost imagine toga-clad figures moving through them.

southern Spain. The superb Church of Hagia Sophia, Constantinople was commenced in 532 A.D. to become the symbol of triumphant Christianity.

The Byzantine Empire, as it was now called, carried on the culture and traditions of the Roman Empire. But it incorporated far greater influences from Asia, to which the Empire was directly exposed due to constant interchange with the Persians in trade and warfare and, through Persia, these influences infiltrated from many other Asian countries and cultures.

The Byzantine Empire was an urban one and had largely lost its links with the soil. As a result, there was a decline in garden art and landscape design. Garden forms became more and more artificial in both Byzantium and in its Persian neighbour.

The most famous garden features of the sixth century were shown in a huge Persian garden carpet, 60 yards square, woven in the reign of Chosroes I (531–579 A.D.), the most important of the monarchs of the Sassinid Dynasty then ruling Persia: 'The ground (of the carpet) represented a pleasure garden with streams and paths, trees and beautiful spring flowers. The wide border all around showed flower beds of various colouring, the "flowers" being blue, yellow or white stones.'[21]

Another artificial feature developed by the Persians and adopted by the Byzantines, was to make artificial trees of precious metals and jewels. A famous plane tree in the Persian Throne Room was constructed of gold with golden leaves, precious stones for fruit, and sitting in the branches were artificial birds which sang when the wind blew through them. When Bishop Livdprand visited the court of Constantinople as ambassador for Berengarius and Otho I (962 A.D.) he gave an account of the Emperor's throne room of the Magnaura in the Palace grounds, he saw 'a brass tree, gold-plated, that stood before the throne, and on its branches gilt birds of different sizes, which sang each with its proper notes.'[22]

Parks and gardens continued to be built inside the Palace grounds in garden courts and outside the walls of the towns, but very little detailed information is available about them. Almost certainly they corresponded to those built in Asia and Rome during the earlier period we have discussed.

The Christian ethic was not sympathetic to Nature; and it perpetuated the concept of man dominating the natural environment, and imposing his will upon it.

EARLY EAST-WEST LINKS

Half a century before the Christian era, an interesting trade link was established between the Roman Empire and the Empire of China – 'the Land of the Ceres' as it was known by the Greeks. China was situated far beyond the geographic world known to the Romans. The basis of the trade was silk, a commodity new to the Western world. Silk had been produced in China from the very earliest times, probably from around the third millenium B.C. But techniques of its production were a closely-guarded secret, to reveal which to foreigners was punishable by death. The Western world had various explanations of the source of silk: Romans at the time of Virgil believed it was a vegetable fibre combed from a tree.

The finished product came from China along the Silk Road, handed from one trader to the next, over a distance exceeding five thousand miles. Passing through many territories controlled by China, it finally reached the Parthians of Central Asia. The Parthians, acting as middle-men, sold it to the Romans, whose Empire bordered them in Asia Minor. Trade with the Romans is supposed to have commenced in the following manner:

> At the Battle of Carrhae (53 B.C.) where the Parthians routed the Romans, towards the middle of the day the Parthians suddenly unfurled their gleaming banners; the effect was such that ... the famous valour of the Roman legions came abruptly to an end ... the brilliantly coloured and gold-embroidered banners ... were, if the historian Florius is to be believed, the first articles of silk that the Romans had ever seen.[23]

The startling effect of the silken banners is explicable if one remembers that other woven fabrics of this period were coarse, heavy and unyielding: the supple rippling of silk in the breeze gives an appearance of a living thing with muscles in play, vibrant with a hidden strength and apparent life and purpose. From this initial encounter, the silk trade with Rome began. As the years went by, the Romans' taste for silk grew to such an extent that in the year 14 A.D. the Senate had to issue a decree banning silk to men and limiting its use to women.

These silks were products of the Han dynasty (206 B.C.–220 A.D.). Some would have been embroidered with a wide range of design motifs taken from the life of the time, and so the distant civilisation in the East became known to the Western world, although it would not be seen directly for centuries. We can obtain some idea of the appearance of these Han embroideries from some surprisingly well-preserved archaeological discoveries made by Sir Aurel Stein at Lou han in 1914. Lou han was a garrison point on the old Silk Road to Parthia. The Stein embroideries have been described thus: 'The finds at Lou han and Tun Huang are polychrome-figured fabrics showing refined and intricate patterns in which many motifs familiar from other branches of Han art appear. There are the dragon and phoenix, animal-style ornamentation, with confronted beasts and birds, equestrian figures, strongly reminiscent of those shown on bas-relief.[24]

Additional Han embroideries have been unearthed in China in recent years. It is interesting to speculate as to whether landscape forms may have been included on the embroideries of this period; and if so, whether they influenced the art of the Romans?

Other Chinese artifacts had also reached Rome at this time. A Shang bronze dating from about 1200 B.C. has been discovered by archaeologists while excavating Roman ruins. Western scholars have written at length on the possible influences exerted on Eastern art by classic Greek and Roman trade contacts; but reverse influences have not, to our knowledge, ever been seriously investigated. Yet is it possible that the artist who depicted the 'Battle of Issus' at the House of the Faun, Pompeii, may have been influenced by the extraordinary vitality of Han art which had already reached Italy and the Mediterranean?

22

The extraordinary vitality and movement of the art of Han China (206 B.C.–220 A.D.) is well expressed by these flying figures performing a Monkey Play. Han figures like these were also embroidered on silks for export, and may have reached ancient Rome.

未央宮

CHAPTER 2
CHINESE GARDENS

IMPERIAL GARDENS AND PARKS

Two hundred years before Pliny was writing about his garden estate in Tuscany, a very different kind of garden-park was being described, five thousand miles away.

The poet Ssu-ma H'siang-ju writes of a Chinese* hunting park and pleasure ground built by the Emperor Ch'in Shih Huang Ti of the Ch'in dynasty (221–207 B.C.). This Emperor it was who completed The Great Wall, an extensive construction of fortified walls and towers which winds over the northern mountains of China for a distance of 1,400 miles. Its purpose was to keep out the barbarian hordes from the North, who constantly invaded the settled agricultural areas and attacked the great cities of a civilisation which was already over one thousand years old. In the poem, the Emperor's pleasure-ground was conceived on the same huge scale as The Great Wall itself.

This poem is the earliest expression which we have found, of the Chinese landscape concept based upon man as part of universal nature. It is an epic poem of great length. The extract we quote, though much abridged, is in itself considerable. We reproduce it here in order to illustrate the very different attitude of man towards Nature which was already accepted in China at this remote period.

As you read it, remember the gardens we have been discussing from the earliest civilisations of the West. Remember the gardens of Egypt – the row-planted trees which continue geometrical lines of palaces and the temples: water lying quiescent in rectangular ponds; man-made mountains standing up dramatically out of the flat plain, in the form of straight-sided Pyramids, each stone smoothed and cut at precise angles. Remember the hunting parks of the Assyrians, where broad avenues of exotic trees, evenly planted in rows, cut through the indigenous forest; where water is harnessed in straight canals; where mountains are levelled and palaces rise on a series of horizontal platforms. Remember too the Romans, who extended the use of water by aqueducts, and developed decorative play of water by movement in fountains. They employed the beautiful marble of their country, fashioning it into these fountains, into ponds and pools and baths, the stone everywhere cut and polished so that it acquired a texture quite different from its original character. They utilised trees and shrubs, flowering plants and creepers. And the Romans initiated the craft of topiary, clipping and cutting and training plants into the shapes of animals and birds, of men and geometric figures, so that these finished creations have little relationship to the original plant, and bear mute testimony to man's proud domination of nature.

It seems 'natural' for us today to admire the beauty of untamed nature. But remember that this is a comparatively recent attitude in the Western world. Until the seventeenth century, bold mountains, deep ravines, rushing torrents and other manifestations of untamed nature were regarded with horror and disgust.

Now, remembering these things, let us read the poem written in 179 B.C., twelve hundred years before William the Conqueror came to England.

23

Unlike those of Europe, the early Imperial Gardens of China were informal. They embraced the natural environment and deliberately incorporated it within their bounds. The scale was immense; as seen in this painting showing a Han Emperor on a bridge in his garden, watching the approach of a Dragon boat.

*As the history of China (the subject of this chapter) is less well known to most readers than that of Europe and the Middle East, we have prepared a brief summary, Appendix 11.

Have you not heard of the Shang-Lin Park of the Son of Heaven? Within the park spring the Pa and Ch'an rivers, the Feng, the Hao, the Lao and the Chueh, twisting and turning their way through the reaches of the park ... they race and tumble, pouring through the chasms of Pepper Hill, skirting the banks of the river islets, winding through the cinnamon forests, and across the broad meadows ... Behind them rise the tall mountains, lofty crests lifted to the sky; clothed in dense forests of giant trees, jagged with peaks and crags ... About their base, hills and islands raise their tall heads; ragged knolls and hillocks rise and fall ... while from their folds the mountain streams leap and tumble, spilling out upon the level plains.

There they flow a thousand miles along smooth beds, their banks lined with dikes blanketed with green orchids and hidden beneath selinea, mingled with snakes-mouth and magnolias; planted with yucca, sedge of purple dye, bittersweet, gentians and orchids, blue flag and crow-fans, ginger and tumeric, monkshood, wolfsbane, nightshade, basil, mint, ramie and blue artemisia, spreading across the wide swamps, rambling over the broad plains, a vast and unbroken mass of flowers, nodding before the wind, breathing forth their fragrance, pungent and sweet ...

Here the country palaces and imperial retreats cover the hills and span the valleys, verandahs surrounding their four sides with storied chambers and winding porticoes, painted rafters and jade-studded corbels, interlacing paths for the royal palanquin, and arcaded walks stretching such distances that their length cannot be traversed in a single day ...

Here sweet fountains bubble from clear chambers, racing in rivulets through the gardens, great stones lining their courses; plunging through caves and grottoes, past steep and ragged pinnacles, horned and pitted as though carved by hand ...

Here grow citrons with their ripe fruit in summer, tangerine, bitter oranges and limes, loquats, persimmons, wild pears, tamarind, jujubes, arbutus, peaches and grapes, almonds, damsons, mountain plums and litchis, shading the quarters of the palace ladies, ranged in the northern gardens, stretching over the slopes and hillocks and down into the flat plains ...

Here crab apple, chestnut and willows, birch,

maple, sycamore and boxwood, pomegranate, date palm, betel-nut and palmetto, sandalwood, magnolia, cedar and cypress rise a thousand feet, their trunks several arm-lengths around, stretching forth flowers and branches, clustered in dense copses, their limbs entwined, their foliage a thick curtain over stiff bending trunks, their branches sweeping to the ground amidst a shower of falling petals. They tremble and sigh as they sway in the wind . . . screening the quarters of the palace ladies; a mass of sylvan darkness, blanketing the mountains and edging the valleys, ascending the slopes and dipping into the hollows, overspreading the horizon, outdistancing the eye . . . [1]

24

The Great Audience Hall. **Scene One of The Forty Scenes depicting the famous Yuan Ming Yuan (The Garden of Perfect Brightness) built in the first half of the eighteenth century during the Ch'ing Dynasty. It was the Summer Palace of the Emperor Ch'ien Lung. In constructing these gardens, old legends were followed; famous pictures and well-known Chinese beauty-spots copied; and history was delved into to provide additional inspiration, the architects using as their models, many palaces and gardens in other parts of China. The Emperor brought back to Peking many scrolls of the gardens he most admired, to guide the architects, who copied them faithfully. The garden was destroyed as a reprisal by the English and French in the nineteenth century. The only remaining visual records are The Forty Scenes.**

25

The Beautiful Scenery of Fang Hu. **Scene Twenty-nine of The Forty Scenes. In forming these Imperial gardens, the soil excavated to make the lakes was used to create a landscape of mountains in miniature. These were planted informally with trees to re-create idyllic scenes.**

26

The Fairy Isles of the Blest. **Thirty-second picture of The Forty Scenes. This is a recurring concept in the Imperial gardens. Its origin is lost in antiquity. The original Islands were believed to be inhabited by immortals who had discovered the secret of eternal youth.**

27

The Double Mirror and the Sound of the Lute. **Thirty-fifth picture of The Forty Scenes. This scene echoes one that was described much earlier in the following words by Hsi Ma Kuang, in the Sung dynasty: 'At the border of the first stream that falls in cascades, stands a steep rock with overhanging top like an elephant's trunk. At the summit stands a pleasant open pavilion where people may rest and where they can enjoy, any morning, the red sunrise.'[13]**

28

Great stones horned and pitted 'as though carved by hand', described by the poet Ssu-ma H'siang-ju before the Christian era, were greatly prized by Chinese garden-makers. This detail of a palace garden, painted by Chiu Ying (1510–1551 A.D.) shows such a stone. Notice how the tree in front of it has been carefully shaped by removing its lower branches in such a way that they can heal easily.

29

Streams and Mountains without end. **Handscroll Northern Sung dynasty (960–1126 A.D.). By the time of the Sung, landscape garden design in China had reached a very high level of accomplishment. During the Sung we believe that garden design reached its zenith, as did landscape painting. This scroll illustrates the masterly way man's activities were integrated into the natural landscape in this period.**

For many centuries before this poem was written, great hunting and pleasure parks had been used by the feudal princes of China. The images used by Ssu-ma H'siang-ju would have been taken directly from these Imperial and princely establishments. The poet has made a composite of all the landscape concepts of his time. His obvious joy in the beauty and drama of high mountains, vast rivers, deep valleys, dense forests, reflects the early Chinese nature aesthetic, showing an acceptance of the natural forms of the landscape, very similar to our acceptance today.

What an extraordinary difference of approach between the civilisations of the East and West! While the gardens of the great Western civilisations expressed, in unmistakeable terms, man's dominance over nature, in the East nature is seen as the guiding force: man himself, not as something separate from and superior to nature, but as a part of the natural world. In China, man has striven to understand the principles on which Nature's beauty is created and has applied these principles to his own man-made landscapes, keeping them in harmony with the environment.

It is evident that much of the park is composed of natural landscapes (similar to our great National Parks of today) enclosed for man's enjoyment and utilised for his sport and recreation. But man has exerted considerable control; changing existing forms, creating new landscapes. The author's joy in the drama and beauty of natural scenery reflects not only his personal reactions, but the attitude of his contemporaries.

Another aspect of the poem is the pleasure taken in rock arrangements. Lining the rivulets which meandered through the park were rocks with steep and rugged pinnacles, horned and pitted as though carved by hand. Here already we find the sculptural use of rocks and their symbolic association with mountains, which was to become so characteristic of the later Chinese and Japanese gardens. The presence of these rocks and the poet's comment on them, show that they are one of the elements added by man to this Ch'in park.

The Chinese poet also expresses his delight in the form and movement of water . . . water pouring through chasms, twisting and turning, racing and tumbling; water in fountains bubbling out from clear chambers; chattering away in serpentine streams.

He makes a vivid impression on us by his joy in enumerating the large range of trees, shrubs and flowers contained in the park; his pleasure in their scale, form, texture, colour, taste and scent. He did not need to exaggerate nor use his imagination here. China is endowed with a remarkably rich flora; and at the time the poem was written, her horticulturalists and garden designers had been working with their native plants for over a thousand years. Here is a

factual description of the flora of China by E. W. Wilson of Arnold Arboretum:

> The flora of China is beyond question the richest temperate flora in the world, a greater number of different kinds of trees being found there than in the whole of the other north-temperate regions. Every important genus of broad-leaved trees known from temperate regions of the northern hemisphere is represented (except the Plane and False Acacia); all the coniferous genera of the same region except the Redwoods (Sequoia). In North America about 165 genera of broad-leaved trees occur; in China the number exceeds 260. Of the 300 genera of shrubs enumerated in the Kew Hand-List of Trees and Shrubs (1920 edition) fully half are represented in China.[2]

Our final comment on the poem concerns the man-made structures in the park. When describing the palaces, pavilions, terraces, verandahs and covered walks, Ssu-ma H'siang-ju sees them as part of the landscape. They and the people who occupy them are one with the landscape in which they are placed.

In very extravagant terms, the poet was describing a park such as had been created by the rulers of his country for the last thousand years. Freed from the confines of reality, he made his park a composite of all the landscape concepts of his time: in one landscape garden he combined both hunting park and pleasure ground. But actually at the time Ssu-ma H'siang-ju wrote, hunting park and pleasure garden were more often separate entities.

A hunting park which was actually called Shang-lin was built by the Emperor Shih Huang Ti, and some years later, when the Han Emperor Wu took it over, he extended it for one hundred miles up and down the Yellow River. Adjacent to his palace and the capital, across the river, Emperor Wu (140 B.C.–89 B.C.) built a separate pleasure garden. The pleasure park was seven miles in circumference. It was composed of lakes, waterways, hills and islands and contained many palaces and pavilions to house his consorts.

Nearly one thousand years later, in the seventh century A.D., Sui Yang Ti built an imperial park near his capital city of Lo-Yang. It was 120 kilometres (75 miles) in circumference, and over one million workers made it. Residential palaces were scattered through the park, and its 'water garden' was in scale with its enormous size, containing nine lakes, four of which were large enough to be called 'seas'. Soil and rock which had been excavated to form the lakes, were used to make miniature mountains; and hilly islands were constructed in the lakes. The Northern Sea, the largest of the lakes, was 22 kilometres (13 miles) around. The lakes were joined by waterways so that pleasure boats could travel over the whole water system: these pleasure boats were given the form of dragons and phoenixes.

The vast extent of the park is of less importance than its design, similar to the poetic description of the Shang-lin park of ancient times, a real version of Ssu-ma H'siang-ju's

dream garden – for the first time, a composite of hunting park and pleasure ground.

Six centuries later, Marco Polo wrote his eye-witness account of a similar park which was built in the thirteenth century during the Southern Sung dynasty (960–1279 A.D.) It was in the 'celestial city' of Hangchow and was reserved exclusively for the Emperor. He combined hunting with other pleasures: his consorts accompanied him in the chase, and after the hunt, they 'rushed into the water in a state of nudity, sportively swimming about' to entertain their 'Sun of Heaven.'[3]

The clearest visual impression we can obtain of such imperial gardens is The Forty Scenes of 'The Garden of Perfect Brightness' or Yuan Ming Yuan. This famous place was built during the Ch'ing dynasty (1644–1912 A.D.). It was the summer palace of the Emperors Yung Cheng (1723–1735 A.D.) and Chien Lung (1735–1799) and was indubitably a superb garden, embodying the whole range of Chinese landscape idiom up to that time. Although 'The Garden of Perfect Brightness' was deliberately destroyed by the British and French as a reprisal during a punitive expedition in 1860, its loveliness still lives on, in The Forty Scenes, which were painted during its time.

The landscape principles embodied in the epic of Shang-lin formed the basis upon which the whole Chinese landscape design ethos was built, reaching a high point during the Sung period over one thousand years later, and continuing on into the twentieth century. Imperial parks such as the one described in the poem are a main theme running through the history of landscape design from the very earliest times in China. Conservative in character, they became repositories of traditional landscape forms. As in Egypt, the result is that one can find landscape concepts which originated in early periods, being re-created many centuries – even a thousand years – later.

Such a recurring concept in the imperial gardens is that of 'The Mystic Islands of the Blest'. On these imaginary floating islands lived the Immortals (the hsien) who were believed to be human beings who had discovered the secret of eternal youth. Their palaces were build of jade, even more precious to the Chinese than pearls and other gems. The birds and animals on the Islands were all of purest white; and the trees, as in the Muslim Paradise, bore precious gems as well as fruit.

The origin of the myth of the Mystic Isles is lost in antiquity, but the early Chinese firmly believed in them. The first Ch'in Emperor Shih Huang Ti even organised naval expeditions to try to discover them, in the hope of obtaining the secret of immortality. Later, the Han Emperor Wu created on Lake Tai-I near his capital Chang-an, 'mystic islands' in imitation of the 'real' ones. He did this in an endeavour to induce the Immortals to inhabit them, thus hoping to gain their secret. Wu and his court considered this was perfectly logical because they believed the Immortals could fly through the air with the greatest of ease from one end of the Flowery Kingdom to the other. Much later, in the seventh century A.D., Sui Yang Ti furnished his vast Northern Sea with 'Isles of the Blest' complete with pavilions and terraces. But these were built for real people – the Emperor and his consorts – who reached them by dragon boat.

Another detail which has been used extensively in gardens throughout the long history of China, is that of the Sacred Tortoises. This was also taken from the Myth of the Mystic Isles. It was believed that the floating islands were unanchored in earliest times, and the movement of the sea inconvenienced the Immortals. This discomfort was overcome by huge tortoises who kindly anchored and stabilised the Islands. Initially there were five Islands; but after a giant had stolen away the tortoise-supporters of two of them, these two Islands drifted away and were lost. The Isles and the tortoises became a favourite theme in Chinese garden art from the Han period onwards. They were adopted by the Buddhists, and with them travelled to Japan, and even to the West with Marco Polo.

The Chinese natural philosophy was expressed through a wide spectrum of the arts. Landscape design, literature and painting are most revealing; ceramics and embroidery are also important.

Landscape gardening preceded landscape painting in China by many centuries. It is not until the fifth to seventh centuries A.D. that landscape painting reaches any significant proportions, and we must rely for our knowledge of the more early gardens upon descriptions in prose and poetry.

From the earliest times we have seen how the Chinese Nature aesthetic was in complete contrast to that of the Western world. When discussing the landscape painting of the Sung dynasty, the noted historian, C. P. Fitzgerald, remarks on this difference:

> More clearly than any other pictures, or any other branch of art, these landscapes reveal the wide difference between Western and Chinese artistic traditions. Until the nineteenth century the West had no feeling for wild nature other than marked aversion. No one admired the English Lake scenery before Wordsworth. In the seventeenth century the West Highlands, the Alps and the Pyrenees were shunned by men of taste. Mountains were 'horrid rocks', moors 'blasted heaths'. This aversion to un-

30

***An Imperial Palace of the Han Period*, style of Chao-Po-chu, Sung Dynasty. This could be an illustration to the Shang-lin Park, 'screening the quarters of the Palace ladies, a mass of sylvan darkness blanketing the mountains and edging the valleys.' (See text.)**

tamed scenery has been explained by the insecurity of the time. Mountains and wastelands were associated with brigands and highwaymen. It has been suggested that an efficient police was the foundation of a delight in wild nature.

This explanation is refuted by the fact that in China, where mountains have always been the haunt of bandits, and the dangers of travel at least as great as in Renaissance Europe, poets, painters and scholars of the highest intellectual status have for centuries delighted in the wild beauty of the high hills, and frequently retired from the comforts of civilisation to some remote mountain solitude.

> *Perhaps an appreciation of natural scenery uncontrolled by the work of man is a product of long and continuous civilisation, of sophistication in fact, which is only achieved after many generations of culture.*[4]
> (Our italics.)

Fitzgerald's comments, which he applied to painting, apply with equal force to garden design. He mentions the poet Wordsworth, but makes no reference to the renowned English landscape designers who flourished in England in the eighteenth century – Kent, Capability Brown, Repton and Paxton – whose works in this field of art cause us, the authors, to date by a century earlier the revolution in the English approach to nature. This variation in our timing does not alter the value of Fitzgerald's comment.

BUDDHISM COMES TO CHINA

We have seen how the Chinese nature aesthetic was developing many centuries before the Han period; during the Han, it was still in a formative state, not maturing until many centuries later. Late in the Han dynasty, a new cultural stimulus came from the north. Unlike most things which then came from the north, this was a peaceful influence. Over The Silk Road – usable once more by the expansion of the Han empire – came some Buddhist monks from India.

Penetration of Buddhist thought into China was at first slow; but when the Han empire collapsed in 221 A.D. under the impact of the Northern Tartars, in their insecurity both the common people and the dispossessed scholar-administrators, turned their thoughts to salvation in another and a better world. Buddhism flourished after the fall of the Han, and by the fourth century A.D. its influence was widespread throughout the whole country.

The preaching of the Amida sect was partly responsible. Amida had forsaken Nirvana until all living things could be saved, and Amida only required a simple affirmation of faith. This had a tremendous appeal to the common people, who could not afford the long penances demanded by other denominations. Hui-Yuan (334–417 A.D.) was the monk who is reputed to have established the Amida teachings in China. He received considerable support from wealthy southern landholders through whom he was able to establish a monastery in the Lu Shan range, an isolated mountain complex rising abruptly out of the plain within view of the river Yangtse in central China.

The monastery was built close by the main peak of Lu Shan, which towered above it, and was sited above a deep ravine down which fell many waterfalls. The White Lotus Society had its headquarters in the monastery, to which came seekers after knowledge from all denominations, including Taoist and Confucian. Hui-Yuan was famous throughout China for his ability to plan within the landscape. His monastery became a centre for the discussion and dissemination of landscape ideas and a vivid description of it follows:

> The retreat which Yuan (Hui-Yuan) had founded made the most of the beauty of the mountains. It stood back from the foot of Incense Burner Peak and was girdled by Waterfall Gorge. Around it were heaps of boulders, amongst which pines grew thickly. Clear springs encircled its steps, and white cloud filled its rooms. Within the Monastery Hui-Yuan had planted another grove for meditation. Among its trees the mist hung like rime, while the stone courtyard was covered with moss. Everywhere the eye could see, or foot could tread, all was of such spiritual purity it struck one with awe.[5]

Many of the most brilliant men of the period visited Hui Yuan at his Eastern Forest Monastery; and lay members of the White Lotus Society were free to come and go as they pleased. Some of these men, working in a different artistic medium, can enlarge our understanding of the way in which the Chinese landscape aesthetic was developing. The nature poet Hsiah Ling-yun (335–433 A.D.) describes in charming detail in one of his poems, how the contemporary Chinese intellectual appreciated and enjoyed the natural environent around Lu Shan:

. . . I know that dawn has broken,
Though yet no sun has touched this shadowed valley;
Around the peaks the clouds begin to gather,
While dew still glistens brightly on the flowers,
My path winds round beside a curving river,
Then climbs far up among the rock-bound crags.
With cloak held high I wade the mountain torrent,
Then toil up wooden bridges ever higher.
Below, the river islets wind around,
But I enjoy following the sinuous stream.
Duckweek floats upon its turbid deeps,
Reeds and cat-tails cover its clear shallows.
I stand on a rock to fill my cup from a cataract.
I pull down branches and pluck their leafy scrolls . . .
With a handful of orchids I grieve for my lost friendship.
I pluck the reeds, yet can tell no one how I feel.
The sensitive heart will find beauty everywhere –
But with whom can I discuss such subtleties now?
When I look at all this, the world of man disappears
And in a flash of enlightenment everything falls from me.[6]

Ling-yun loved to clamber through steep mountainous country, and he designed a special pair of sandals with sprigs to assist him in steep places. Within sight of Lu Shan, he owned a property which he describes thus:

I placed my house against a northern slope
And opened its doors towards the stream.
The rushing torrent I used instead of a well.
I planted hibiscus instead of a surrounding wall.
Above them, from my window I can see masses of mountains.

Another friend of Hui Yuan was Tsung Ping (375–443 A.D.) who was an accomplished musician and is famous as a painter and calligrapher. Writing about the art of landscape painting, Ping illuminates another aspect of Chinese landscape design: the deliberately evocative qualities introduced by the garden-maker, which are intended by suggestion to induce the beholder to let his imagination flow far beyond his present confines. Tsung Ping expresses it in this way:

> Take a giant mountain like the Kun-lun and consider the small size of the pupil of our eyes. Place something an inch before the eyes and they cannot see it, but place it a few miles away and it can be encompassed by the small pupil no longer than an inch. This is because the further away an object is, the smaller it appears. Take a distant view over a piece of silk and the forms of the Kun-lun and Lang-chung mountains can be perceived within a square inch. A vertical height of three inches can represent a thousand fathoms, while a horizontal stretch of several feet can

31

Part of the horizontal scroll after the style of Wang Wei (699–759 A.D.), the first known Chinese pure landscape painter. Landscape garden design preceded landscape painting in China by many centuries. The building group up in the mountains among the pines, is almost certainly a monastery. Buddhist monks played an important part in developing the art of landscape design in China.

stand for the distance of several hundred miles. In this way all the delicacies of the Sung and the Hua mountains and the beauties of this universe can be recaptured in painting. For what which meets the eye and calls forth the response from the heart as the true form of things, will also meet the eye and call forth the response from the onlooker if the representation is skilful. When this spiritual contact is established the true forms are realised and the spirit is captured. Is it not as good as to see the mountains themselves? . . . If these things are skilfully represented, they are truth itself. Therefore, in my leisured life, having put my mind in order, I wipe a wine cup or strum the ch'in (lute) and sit alone looking at a painting. Without leaving the crowded human habitations, I roam and wander in the solitary wilds of nature. There the mountains peaks soar aloft and the clouds and forest spread deep and far away.[7]

Notice how Tsung Ping uses the flat graphic forms of his painting to take him in imagination to the actual distant landscapes which he knows. This same deliberate purpose guides Chinese garden designers. For them, much of the pleasure in quite small landscaped places, is the power the garden possesses to evoke the beauties and pleasures of far distant natural themes.

Some technical details of garden-making of the fifth century, we obtain from Ju Hao 'who was by nature a subtle craftsman, chose fine rocks from the quarries of Pei-mang and Nan-sham, transplanted bamboos from Ju and Ying, directed the construction of two-storied pavilions, laid out trees, all to give the impression of rustic wilderness.'[8]

In the sixth century, Chang-Lun, Minister for Agriculture under the Emperor Hsiao Ming (516–527 A.D.) was renowned as a garden maker. One of his creations is described thus:

With its hills and ponds this garden excelled in beauty many princely pleasure grounds. Here had been built

32

Partridge and Sparrows. A painting by Huang Chutsai (_c._ 940 A.D.) shows a corner of a garden with an informal arrangement of rocks and plants. It belongs to the Five Dynasties Period which preceded the Sung.

33

Buddhist Monastery in stream and mountain landscape, attributed to Chu Jan, Northern Sung. This might almost be a picture of the monastery built by Hui-Yuan, referred to in the text. 'It stood back from the foot of Incense Burner Peak and was girdled by Water Fall Gorge. Around it were heaps of boulders where pines grew thickly. Clear springs encircled its steps and white cloud filled its rooms.'

up a number of hills that were called the Chin Yang Mountains. They looked as though they had been formed by nature. Within these heights were double peaks and curving ridges by the side of deep streams and valleys, and there were plenty of tall leafy trees which afforded protection against the rays of the sun and the moon, and hanging creepers which did not prevent the mist from stealing in. The paths ran zig-zag up the hills and down the valleys. It looked as though they had been suddenly broken off at certain points, although actually they continued in another direction. The stony and curious water courses flowed in some places in winding bends and in others straight on. Nature lovers were so captivated by this spot that they forgot to go home.[9]

From the earliest times the Chinese were remarkably successful at creating an harmonious relationship between the rectilineal character of man-made buildings and the informal quality of natural rocks and plants. One of their methods was to organise groups of buildings asymmetrically in relation to each other and the spaces they occupied, while maintaining an harmonious total effect. The open spaces between the buildings were carefully related in scale and shape, both to the buildings and to each other. Tree and rock forms were introduced to contrast with the formal building shapes and to link them in a relationship with the natural landscape beyond.

The best surviving example of this from this period is not in China, but Japan – the Horyuji Temple in Nara. Its style

34

Garden stones in China frequently became renowned. The one illustrated was admired so much by Mi Fei, a celebrated painter and art critic of the early twelfth century, that whenever he approached it, he would bow to it and greet it reverently as his elder brother.

35

Birds and other animals added animation to Chinese gardens. A garden built by Hsi Ma Kuang in the Sung period is described in some detail in the text. Swans, rabbits, song-birds and fish, all gave vitality to the scenes.

36

San Tan Yin Yueh (Three Pools Mirroring the Moon). The largest of the three islands in Outer West Lake, Hangchow, as it is today. Hangchow was the capital of the Southern Sung dynasty and was described by Marco Polo at the end of the thirteenth century. It was very beautiful and famous throughout China at that time, as The Celestial City. The West Lake was used extensively for recreation by the Sung people, and still is today.

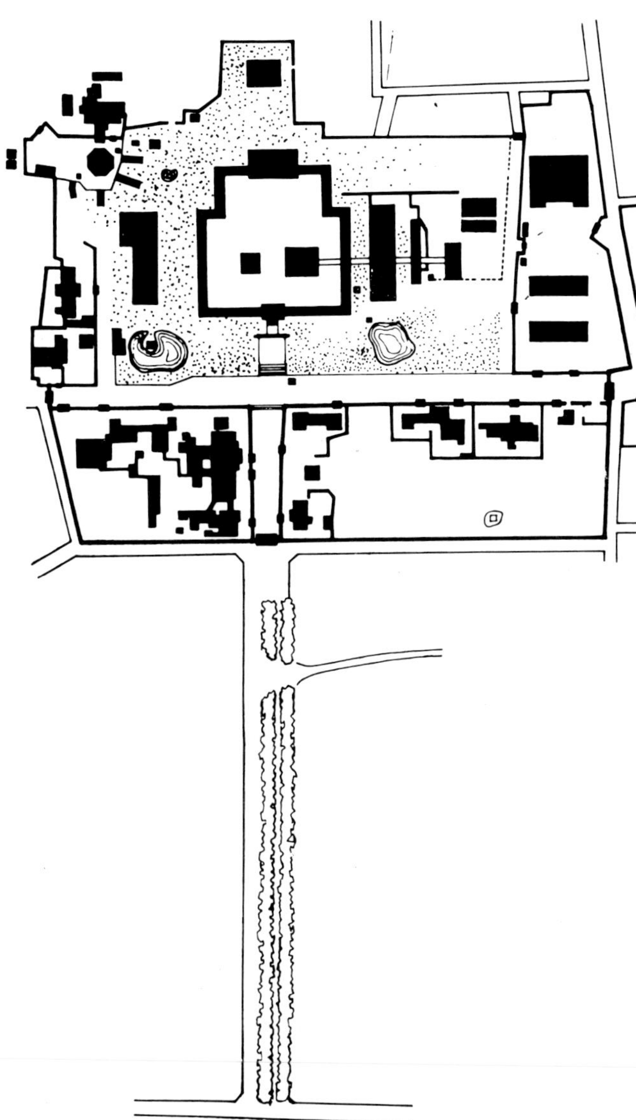

37

An aerial view of Horyuji. Temples, courts, cloisters, ponds and trees are combined harmoniously in a superb composition. The temple is in Nara, the old capital of Japan. Its style is T'ang Chinese (618-906 A.D.).

38

Horyuji Temple is sited so that its high pagoda is the most prominent feature in the townscape of Nara.

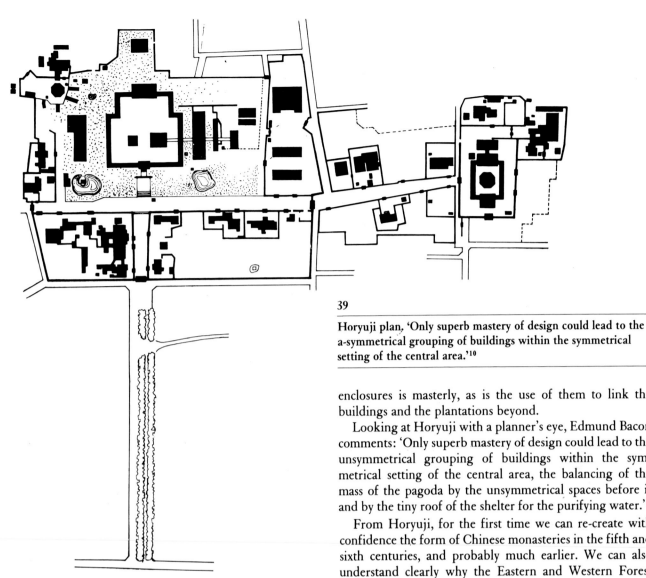

39

Horyuji plan, 'Only superb mastery of design could lead to the a-symmetrical grouping of buildings within the symmetrical setting of the central area.'[10]

is pure T'ang Chinese and it is in an excellent state of preservation. Commenced in the seventh century and completed in the eighth, Horyuji is a most satisfying arrangement of open and closed spaces. Temples, courts, cloisters, ponds and trees are combined harmoniously in a superb composition, the tall, many-tiered pagoda forming an inspiring focal point. The placing of the trees within the enclosures is masterly, as is the use of them to link the buildings and the plantations beyond.

Looking at Horyuji with a planner's eye, Edmund Bacon comments: 'Only superb mastery of design could lead to the unsymmetrical grouping of buildings within the symmetrical setting of the central area, the balancing of the mass of the pagoda by the unsymmetrical spaces before it and by the tiny roof of the shelter for the purifying water.'[10]

From Horyuji, for the first time we can re-create with confidence the form of Chinese monasteries in the fifth and sixth centuries, and probably much earlier. We can also understand clearly why the Eastern and Western Forest Monasteries, built by Hui-Yuan in the fourth and fifth centuries, became the Mecca for scholars and artists who wanted to learn about landscape design.

From earliest times, as can be seen from the Shang-lin epic at the beginning of this chapter, the Chinese saw buildings and their environment as a unity. Designers deliberately studied the relationship of palaces, pavilions, terraces and covered ways, to the garden areas or to the natural landscape in which they were placed. It is clear from Horyuji that, by the seventh century, this aspect of landscape design had reached a high degree of refinement.

One of the most important contributions to landscape design by the Chinese and Japanese masters, is in handling the relationship between exposed and covered areas; between open and closed spaces; between formal shapes and outlines and informal ones. These designers were constantly aware of the need to overcome the tensions resulting from the impact of geometric structures upon natural forms. For centuries, Eastern designers have excelled in these skills: we in the West are only beginning to learn them today.

These same design principles were also applied in city buildings, streets and squares. Peking today is a magnificent example. Edmund Bacon has described it as 'possibly the greatest single work of art on the face of the earth.'[11]

THE GARDENS AND PAINTINGS OF THE SUNG

The practice of landscape garden and park design based on capturing the spirit of nature for the use and enjoyment of man, continued to be practised during the T'ang period (618–906 A.D.); and parallel to it, landscape painting was developed as a fine art. Both reached their zenith during the Sung dynasty (960–1280 A.D.).

Assessing the landscape paintings of the Sung, C. P. Fitzgerald writes,

> When peace and unity were restored under the Sung dynasty, the artists who assembled at the new capital, Kai Fing Fu, had a living tradition to work on. The Sung inherited a great tradition, but they did not merely imitate earlier work. In the absence of sufficient T'ang pictures to form a judgment, it is perhaps untrue to say that the Sung landscapes had never been equalled by the T'ang painters. Nevertheless, it is certain that Sung work is of unsurpassed excellence and reflects the changed spirit of the new age. Sung landscapes are in a class apart, unrivalled in their own Far Eastern art and unequalled in the paintings of any other land.[12]

The gardens of the Sung, as well as their landscape paintings, also achieved this excellence. Here is a description of a famous Sung garden, by Hsi Ma-Kuang, a high official who built it in 1026 A.D.:

> I have built a garden where at my leisure I may find repose and hold converse with my friends. Twenty acres is all the space I need. In the middle is a large summer house, where I have brought together my five thousand books, so as to consult the wisdom therein and to commune with antiquity. On the south side there is a pavilion in the middle of the water, by whose side runs a stream which flows down from the hills. On the east the waters make a deep pond, whence they part in five branches like a leopard's claws. Numbers of swans swim there and are always playing about. At the border of the first stream which falls in cascades, there stands a steep rock with overhanging top like an elephant's trunk. At the summit stands a pleasant open pavilion where people may rest, and where they can enjoy, any morning, the red sunrise . . .
>
> Several pavilions are on the north of the large summer house, scattered about here and there; some of them are on hills, one above the other, standing like a mother amongst her children, while others are on the slopes. Several of them are in little gaps made by the hills, and only half of them can be seen at one time.
>
> This whole region is overshadowed by a forest of bamboos, intersected by sandy footpaths where the sun never penetrates. Towards the East is some level ground of irregular shape, protected from the cold north winds by a cedar wood.
>
> All the valleys are full of sweet-smelling plants, medicinal herbs, bushes and flowers. In this lovely place there is always spring.
>
> At the edge of the horizon there is a copse of pomegranates, citrons and oranges, always in flower and in fruit . . .
>
> On the West, a walk through weeping willows leads to the bank of the river. All around are rocks piled casually with an effect like that of an amphitheatre. At the base is the entrance to a grotto, which as one goes in, gets wider, making an irregularly-shaped room with an arched ceiling. Light comes from above through an opening hung around with wild vines and honeysuckle. Rocks serve as seats and here on the blazing dog days one can sit in the cool shadowy cave, refreshed by the sight and sound of water, for a small stream comes out on one side and fills the hollow of a great stone, and then trickles to the floor, winding about in cracks and fissures till it falls into an open basin. The basin becomes deeper, turns, and flows into a pond at the bottom of the grotto, leaving space for a little path which wanders between the water and the great natural-shaped rocks which are heaped around. A whole family of rabbits plays around the rocks and fishes dart to and fro in the pond . . .
>
> Another pond has little islands on it, bordered by sedges and the larger island contains birds and bird houses. The way to the islands is by large stepping stones which project out of the water, or by small wooden bridges, some of which are arched, some straight or zigzag. When the water lilies near the bank are in full flower, the pond seems to be wreathed in purple and scarlet, like the edge of the Southern Sea when the sun rises.[13]

Many such gardens would have been built in China during the Sung period, and though we believe none survive there, we are fortunate in being able to enjoy similar ones which were constructed on the Sung model in nearby Japan, and which have been preserved to the present day. In these we see rock arrangements, just as described by Hsi Ma-kuang; streamlets and lakes, bridges and stepping stones; garden pavilions set near the water and even over water; pebble paths and rocky amphitheatres. The forty scenes of the Garden of Perfect Brightness also help us to visualise Sung gardens. Based as they often are on earlier famous landscape gardens, 'The Double Mirror and Sound of Lute' is an

40

Garden entrance and arch of the Pei Ling, Shanyang burial place for the imperial family of the Ch'ing Dynasty. Built in 1651 A.D. in north China.

example, with its 'steep rock and overhanging top like an elephant's trunk'.

The superb landscape gardens and paintings of the Sung period are regarded as the finest expression of the Chinese nature-oriented creative art. But it is important to remember that this high point was reached as a result of over two thousand years of continuous development. Sophisticated and beautiful art forms do not spring suddenly into being. They are the products of a long and complicated process of social development, with associated aesthetic and intellectual growth.

Sudden and rapid creative surges do take place: but these are the result of the impact of ideas and inventions of an old and mature civilisation upon a new and vigorous one, in which the objective situation is exactly suitable to absorb these ideas, and to transform and develop them.

The Natural Landscape School in Europe seemed to spring suddenly into being, almost fully-fledged, to replace the out-moded formality of the Renaissance. This is an illusion . . . the English School of Landscape Gardening was the product of thousands of years of landscape-design experience which had accumulated in China and Japan, five thousand miles away. This will be discussed in later chapters of the book.

THE MONGOL INTRUSION

While these developments were taking place under the Sung dynasty, forces had emerged in North-East Asia which were to shake the foundations of the civilised world. Tartar tribes of nomadic horsemen had been unified by Genghis Khan. Adopting the name of Mongols, they set out under his leadership to conquer the world. In common with Alexander the Great and the Romans, constant and unremitting warfare was the weapon Genghis Khan used to achieve his imperial aims. In less than one hundred years he and his descendants held sway over the whole of Central Asia, China, Persia, parts of Northern India, Russia, Hungary and Austria. The Mongols established the largest empire the world has seen. They made cultural contributions of immense significance. Some of these will be dealt with in a later chapter.

After finally over-running the Southern Sung China, the Mongols controlled the whole country until 1366, when they were expelled by the Chinese and a new dynasty established, the Ming (1366–1644 A.D.)

The Ming dynasty consolidated and diversified the cultural achievements of the Sung. However, Ming artists lacked the spontaneity and brilliance of the Sung masters, and much of their work contained signs of cultural decay similar to the baroque during the European Renaissance. Most of the surviving historic memorials and landscape parks and gardens in present-day China belong to the Ming period. These include the Forbidden City and Sea Palaces, The Temple of Heaven and much of the central city area in Peking, The Ming Tombs and the Ming reconstruction of the Great Wall in the environs of the capital, and many of the surviving landscape precincts in and around Hangchow and Soochow. It is still understandably difficult for a foreigner to make any kind of a comprehensive survey beyond the main cities of China, and the monumental work of Siren is the most complete reference material available.

41

A 'moon gate' in a park at Tsinan, Shantung Province. This was a favourite device used by Chinese designers to frame a view or to lead from one garden precinct to another.

European penetration commenced during the Ming period; first by Portuguese traders, followed by the Dutch, British and French. But it was during the succeeding Manchu dynasty of the Ch'ing (1644–1912 A.D.) that a real invasion of China took place. Like all the previous invaders by land, the Manchu emperors themselves adopted the Chinese culture. Most renowned of the Manchus, Ch'ien Lung (1736–1795) completed the famous Yuang Ming Yuan (Garden of Perfect Brightness), begun by his father Yung Cheng. This comprised a superb collection of man-made precincts, palaces and pavilions, and landscaped lakes, mountains and streams, covering approximately six square miles. French and Italian Jesuits lived and worked in the Yuang Ming Yuan, and constructed some European-type buildings and gardens in one of its precincts.

Evocative impressions of many famous Chinese landscapes were created in the Yuan Ming Yuan together with reproductions of man-made landscapes of former periods. This process was continued in the Summer Palace by succeeding Ch'ing Emperors. The Yuan Ming Yuan also became a repository for a magnificent collection of historic and contemporary works of art, including literature. Paintings commissioned by Ch'ien Lung and his father to record visual impressions of the whole of the gardens, became known as the Forty Scenes. A set sent to France by the Jesuits is now in the Bibliothèque Nationale in Paris.

Ch'ien Lung maintained effective control of his empire; but under his successors, foreign trade penetration was followed by military intervention by the British, supported by the French. In 1860 the Yuan Ming Yuan was pillaged

42

Black Tiger Spring, Tsinan. The recently created bridge, and treatment of the river banks, show how present-day China still continues the tradition of their early landscape designers.

43

Stone ships were a favourite idiom in Chinese gardens. This one in Nanking was built for Hung Hsiao-chuen, founder of the Taiping Kingdom (1853). He loved to sit in it while he worked.

44

The Liu Garden of Soochow. A famous garden in a city of gardens. It runs a zig-zag course throughout 2,000 feet and dates from the Ch'ing Dynasty (1644–1910 A.D.). To our eye, it is somewhat overcrowded, lacking the refinement of the gardens of the Sung period.

45

Bamboo was a favourite plant in China, both in garden-making and painting. It became a symbol of Chinese art and was a popular idiom in post-Mongol painting in Central Asia. From there it was carried to pre-Renaissance Italy.

and destroyed by a force under Lord Elgin, and gradually China became a vassal state to Britain who, under pressure, granted trade concessions to many other countries including U.S.A. The penetration and exploitation of China, primarily by Great Britain, with other countries of Europe, and the U.S.A. as junior partners, continued into the twentieth century' though the Chinese made many attempts to throw off the yoke. During the period following the First World War, Japanese trade penetration followed by invasion reduced the whole country to a state of disorder and impoverishment.

The power of the Chinese people to recover from such desperate conditions has been demonstrated by the progress that has taken place since the liberation of the country by the Communists led by Mao Tse Tung in 1949. When the authors visited China in 1972, it was already clear that a powerful cultural renewal was taking place. Everywhere we saw signs of love and respect for the natural environment and for the masterpieces of garden art of former ages. Tree planting is taking place on a breath-taking scale. Everywhere, ancient parks and monuments are being restored and new ones being built. These are no longer 'forbidden' but are for the use and enjoyment of the people. They are extensively used, appreciated and loved.

Perhaps to us of the Western world, the most reassuring evidence was that the present rulers are widely cultured men with a deep understanding and love of their country and its magnificent cultural background and traditions. This was most clearly expressed by a poem by Mao Tse Tung which we first saw, prominently displayed at the Canton Airport, with an English translation. Later we noticed the poem in many places – in historic monuments, newly-built pavilions, hotels and workers' homes. Its title is 'Snow'. Ray learned the English translation by heart, and at our farewell banquet, recited it: our Chinese hosts were delighted and immediately two of our personal guides sang it back to us in Chinese. Here is the poem:

Snow

This is the scene in that Northern land:
A thousand leagues of swirling snow;
A hundred leagues are sealed with ice.
On either side of The Great Wall
One vastness is all you can see.
From end to end of the Great River
The rushing torrent is frozen and lost.
The mountains dance like silver snakes.
The uplands roll like waxen elephants
As though they sought to vie with heaven in their height.
And on a sunny day, a red dress is thrown over the white –
Enchantingly lovely.

Scenes such as these in all our landscape
Have caused unnumbered heroes to bow in homage.
But alas! these heroes – the Emperors Shi Huang Ti and Han Chang Ti were rather lacking in culture.
Rather lacking in literary talent were the Emperors T'ang Ti Sung and Sung Ti Cho
And Genghis Khan.
Beloved Son-of-Heaven-for-a-Day only knew how to bend his bow at the Golden Eagle.
Now they are all past and gone.
To find men truly great and noble-hearted
We must look here in the present.

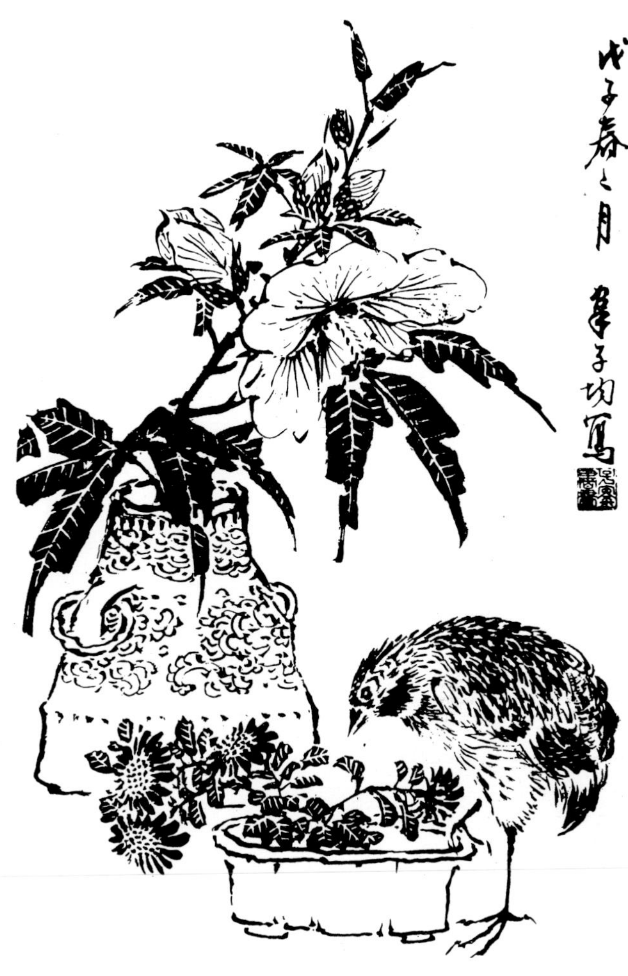

46

Flower arrangement has always been considered as a fine art in China and was adopted enthusiastically by Japan where it flourishes as an art today: this in turn has influenced the whole world.

But we are moving too far ahead in our story. From the time of Marco Polo onwards Chinese aesthetic ideas came to Europe and profoundly affected Western culture but before we examine the effect of Chinese culture on that of Europe, we must first discuss two flows of ideas from China, of a much earlier period.

Long before the arrival of the Mongols, important cultural exchanges had taken place, between China and Islam in the West, and China and Japan in the East. Both exchanges were important to garden and landscape development. Let us look first at the easterly flow. Not only because this occurred earlier in time; but also because we can then examine beautiful Chinese-inspired landscape gardens which are often in a state of excellent preservation, whereas many of their prototypes in mainland China have disappeared.

CHAPTER 3
THE GARDENS OF JAPAN

Should you be rambling among the forested foothills west of Kyoto, the old capital of Japan, and be prepared to scramble over a bamboo fence or two, you could come upon an enchanting moss-covered open sward. The ground-cover is shaded by a grove of graceful maple trees, whose slim, dark trunks give an illusion of mobility – they seem to dance over the undulating surface of the soft green moss.

The prospect is most inviting: as one moves forward, the mossy surface dips down to the edge of a small, irregular lake. An island and promontories formed by the curving banks, conceal the full extent of the lake, enticing one to stroll further. The only sign of man is a small rustic bridge which gives access to the island.

Green of the moss is echoed by a tracery of lichen on trunks and branches of the maples, giving them an appearance of considerable age. In summer the predominant colour is green: glowing green of the moss; delicate lighter green tracery of lichen; translucent fresh green of young maple leaves; deeper green reflections in the mirror-surface of the lake. In autumn the leafy canopy of the maple trees flushes into brilliant red, contrasting vividly with the moss.

47

Saihoji (Moss Garden) Kyoto. Commenced in the twelfth century A.D., this superb landscape garden has become even more beautiful than when first created, due to the intrusion of moss which now covers much of the ground and many of the original stones. The arrangement of trees with their lichen-covered trunks is very fine. The mossy ground dips gently down to a small irregularly shaped lake. Promontories formed by the curving banks conceal the full extent of the lake, enticing one to stroll further.

Moss is everywhere. It covers everything on the ground – undulations and rocks – both on the 'mainland' and on the island and extends to the water's edge. It even covers the surface of the bridge. The total effect of this is breath-takingly beautiful.

This is the famous 'Moss Garden', an ancient garden of the Saihoji Temple, and one of the many superb historic landscape gardens which surround Kyoto.

Commenced in the late twelfth century, it is one of the oldest surviving landscape gardens which, inspired by the landscape paintings and gardens of China, were built throughout Japan during the succeeding centuries.

Japan is a relatively young country and there is still some doubt concerning its origins. Early Chinese legends associated the Japanese archipelago with the Islands of the Blest. Within historic times, it has always had a close cultural affinity with China.

Intermittent contact between Japan and the Chinese mainland had existed from Han times. In the mid-sixth century Buddhism came to Japan from China, quickly triumphing over the original Shinto religion by a process of absorption. A new wave of cultural activity was the result, creating a hunger for things Chinese. The T'ang dynasty was in power in China, with its outward-looking policy; and contact between the two countries strengthened, permitting an easy flow of ideas.

At first the Japanese were overwhelmed by the power of Chinese culture. In the eighth century when a new capital was built at Nara, the layout and architecture were based on the T'ang capital at Chang-an. All Chinese forms, such as language, administration, costume, architecture, painting, sculpture and landscape gardening were deliberately copied by the Japanese aristocracy and priesthood. But underneath these imitations, the former Japanese structure continued to exist, including the Shinto religion. Unlike mainland China, where administrators were selected by examination, the Japanese aristocratic control continued, though cloaked by the new form.

After less than a century at Nara, the Imperial Court established a new capital some 48 kilometres (30 miles) away, today called Kyoto. In the hills around Kyoto are the best surving examples of early Japanese landscape gardens because Kyoto survived as the nominal capital of Japan for nearly a thousand years; and, though often experiencing civil disturbances, the city has never been subjected to devastating foreign invasion. During this period, China remained the mother country of Japanese culture. The flow of ideas from the mainland was constantly renewed; but as the Japanese artists and craftsmen gained confidence and skill, the gardens of Japan became imbued with their own pronounced national character.

Due to the long and relatively undisturbed history of Kyoto, some of these beautiful landscaped parks and gardens still exist there today, parts of them dating back to the twelfth century. This was the period when the mainland culture of the Sung had reached its peak; but there are few, if any, examples surviving in China itself. Thus the historic gardens of Japan have for us today a twofold significance: first, they are one of the finest expressions of the culture of Japan; secondly, they constitute some of the best surviving examples of the early Chinese school of landscape design.

Perhaps this dual significance of Japanese landscape architecture can be understood by comparable examples from the Western world ... The Gothic cathedrals of Europe reached maturity in France as an expression of the Christian spirit and the power of the Church during the medieval period. This architectural movement crossed the Channel to England where similar religious background and social structure existed. The glorious English Gothic cathedrals were the result. Imagine that, prior to development of the modern world, the whole of the French cathedrals had been destroyed ... and that we had only literary descriptions and graphic representations of them. Then the English cathedrals would acquire a dual significance – both as English masterpieces of Gothic architecture, and also as the only surviving example of a vanished architecture which was originally motivated by the culture and spirit of French Catholicism.

A similar, and perhaps closer, parallel, can be drawn from landscape design. The English, or Natural School of landscape gardening, reached its peak about the middle of the nineteenth century, after which it became temporarily overwhelmed by the emphasis on horticulture caused by an influx of thousands of plant species from abroad.

North America at that time had a European population with a culture and background almost identical to that of England, but set in an entirely new environment, with vast areas of virgin country to be tamed and controlled. An inherited love of nature was shared by many of these new Americans; and led by Andrew Jackson Downing and Frederick Law Olmsted, a movement developed in North America which applied the theory and practice of the English School to the new set of conditions. The famous U.S. urban park system, the National Parks movement, and a new profession of trained landscape architects, were some of the results.

Despite the genius of men like Olmsted, and the special national character that was given to the landscape movement in U.S.A., landscape architecture there was nevertheless developed deliberately and directly as a regional extension of the English School, and consisted of the application under new circumstances of the theory and practice of William Kent, Capability Brown, Humphrey Repton and Joseph Paxton.

If the whole of Europe had later been destroyed, Central Park, New York, and the park systems of New York and Boston would still illustrate clearly to landscape architects of the future, the spirit and motivation which led to the creation of the English Landscape School. These two imaginary situations, showing the French source of English cathedrals, and the English source of American landscape design, have been used to help us understand the importance of the Chinese content of Japanese landscape gardens.

48

Though the Imperial garden described by the Lady Murasaki (in our text) has long ago disappeared, surviving Imperial gardens in Kyoto can give us some idea of its appearance. This water-garden at Shugaku-in, used in his retirement by the Emperor Gomizunoo (1596–1680 A.D.) is a fine example. It is said to have been designed by Gomizunoo himself.

49

Another delightful traditional Japanese landscape garden is in the grounds of the Mitsui Club in Tokyo.

NARA

Japan's earliest historic gardens were in the grounds of the palaces of the nobility and in the monasteries which surrounded the Court established at Nara. Many of Nara's ancient buildings and precincts are in an excellent state of preservation. In addition, the ancient capital contains a magnificent collection of historical material, the personal possessions of the Emperor Shomu, who reigned there in the mid-eighth century. The Emperor lived in the Shoso-in, an eighth-century building in Nara's central park and the valuable historical evidence to be found there includes architecture, painting, pottery, sculpture and almost every other form of art or artefact used by the nobility.

Of special interest to us is a symbolic 'tray garden' made entirely of wood. The landscape depicted is obviously a Chinese one, with towering mountains and craggy cliffs of a type which do not occur in Japan but are common in parts of China. Such 'tray gardens' which were popular in China, would have been an additional source of inspiration for Japanese garden makers from the eighth century. Much of the garden construction in the early years was carried out by Korean gardeners who emigrated to Japan. There would also have been a considerable influx of artists and artisans from T'ang China.

Perhaps the most important surviving example of landscape design in Nara, is the Temple complex of Horyuji (see page 55). Commenced in the seventh century and completed in the eighth, it has been beautifully maintained, so that today it retains the appearance it had when Nara was the living capital of Japan. Built almost entirely of timber except for its tile roofs, Horyuji shows clearly why so little of the surviving architecture of China and Japan dates back more than a thousand years. Timber is, in historic terms, a short-lived material and even the Nara buildings have been constantly and lovingly restored to keep them in their fine state of preservation.

Fire is a constant hazard and few of the historic buildings of Japan have escaped its effects; but painstaking repair and reconstruction have overcome much of the loss by fire. Thanks to this, Nara is not only a Japanese historic town of great character and distinction but it gives us a most vivid surviving picture of the arts and artefacts of T'ang China.

THE HEIAN PERIOD

When Nara had been established less than a hundred years, the Japanese Court moved to a new capital in 781 A.D. The reason for the move was a conflict between Church and State. Powerful monastic orders had established themselves at Nara: the Emperor and his Court wished to remove themselves from their influence.

The site for the new capital was well chosen. It was in a spacious valley sheltered by surrounding hills, rising to Mt. Hiei, a high peak on the north-west . . . a green and pleasant countryside, the hills thickly forested, the valley watered by two rivers, fed by many streams. The new city lay between the rivers occupying an area three miles wide and three and a half miles long, with an Imperial enclosure about a mile square near its northern boundary.

Originally called Heian-Kyo, the Capital of Heavenly Peace and Tranquility, it later became known as Kyoto. Its plan, like that of Nara, was based on the layout of Chang-an, the T'ang capital of China. Heian-Kyo in those early centuries must have looked a gay and beautiful city. The nobility and gentry, freed from the restraints imposed by the monks, led a life of pleasure. They continued to build palaces and gardens on a lavish scale.

Chinese influence would have continued during the Heian period. In 814 the nobility of Japanese birth numbered about 800 families while nearly half as many were of Korean or Chinese origin.[1]

Emperor Kammu, who organised the move to Kyoto from Nara, constructed one of the largest of the early gardens, which occupied over thirty acres and contained the full Chinese vocabulary of lakes, islands, streams, groves of trees and tree-lined walks. The Emperor and his Court used the garden extensively for banquets, sporting activities and even military exercises.

Though only a few relics of these early gardens of Kyoto remain, contemporary literature elucidates them. *The Tale of Gengi* was written by a lady-in-waiting at the Fugiwara Court in the eleventh century. This was at the peak of the 'Heian' period (so-called after the first name of the city) when for three hundred years the Fugiwara clan dominated life in the capital. Gengi, the hero of the tale, was modelled on the Regent Fugiwara Michinaga; and the authoress, whose name is unknown, has become identified with the heroine of the tale, the Lady Murasaki, favourite of Gengi.

Gengi built gardens to suit the favourite season of his principal consorts, each of whom loved a different season. Murasaki's favourite season was Spring:

> Towards the end of the third month (April), when out in the country the orchards were no longer at their best and the song of the wild bird had lost its first freshness, Murasaki's Spring garden seemed only to become every day more enchanting. The little wood

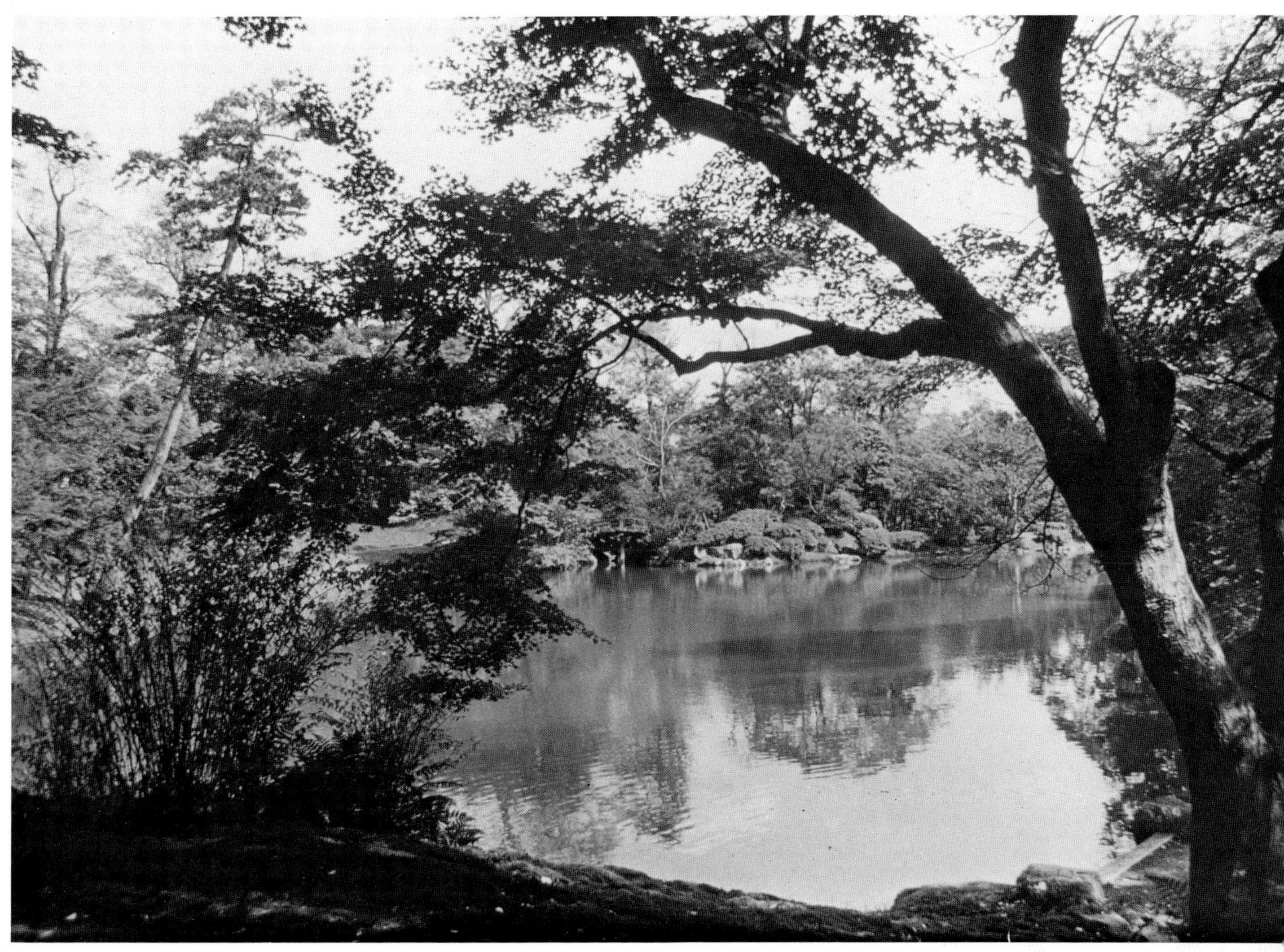

50

Prior to his retirement to Shugaku-in, the Emperor Gomizunoo built a garden, Sento Gosho, next to the Imperial Palace in the heart of Kyoto. It dates from the 1630s A.D. Koburi Enshu, a famous Japanese garden designer, was employed on the Sento Gosho. This is a view of one of the lakes.

on the hill beyond the lake, and the bridge that joined the two islands, the mossy banks that seemed to grow greener not every day but every hour – could anything have looked more tempting ... 'If only one could get there!' sighed the young people of the household; and at last Gengi decided there must be boats on the lake. They were built in the Chinese style. Everyone was in such a hurry to get on board that very little time was spent in decorating them, and they were put into use almost as soon as they could float ...

It was possible to go by water all the way to the Spring Garden, first rowing along the Southern Lake, then passing through a narrow channel straight towards a toy mountain which seemed to bar all further progress. But in reality there was a way round and eventually the party found itself on the Fishing Pavilion (on the main lake). Here they picked up Murasaki's ladies who were waiting at the pavilion by appointment ...

The lake as they now put out towards the middle of it, seemed immensely large, and those on board, to whom the experience was new and deliciously exciting, could hardly believe they were not heading for some undiscovered land. At last however the rowers brought them close in under the rocky bank of the channel between the two large islands, and on closer examination they discovered to their delight that the shape of every little ledge and crag of stone had been as carefully devised as if a painter had traced them with his brush. Here and there in the distance the topmost boughs of an orchard showed above the mist, so heavily laden with blossom that it looked as though a bright carpet was spread in mid-air. Far away they could just catch sight of Murasaki's apartments,

> marked by the deeper green of the willow boughs that swept their courtyards, and by the shimmer of her flowering orchards, which even at this distance seemed to shed their fragrance amid the isles and rocks. In the world outside, the cherry-blossom was almost over; but here it seemed to laugh at decay, and round the Palace even the wisteria that ran along the covered alleys and porticos was all in bloom, but not a flower past its best; while here, where the boats were tied, mountain-kerria poured its yellow blossom over the rocky cliffs in a torrent of colour that was mirrored in the waters of the lake below . . . [2]

The garden thus described was obviously based upon an actual Imperial garden; and though the prototype does not survive, some other gardens do which were modelled upon it. As in China, Imperial parks and gardens became repositories of well-known and beloved landscape forms from the past.

Lady Murasaki mentions a country estate of the Regent at Katsura; and we have historical evidence that the real Regent did in fact build a garden at Katsura. When the actual garden had disappeared, its description remained in *The Tale of Gengi* which became a classic of Japanese literature. Five hundred years later, Prince Toshihito was to build the now-famous Katsura villa and garden – perhaps even on the site of that of the original Fugiwara Regent. Many of its details were certainly based upon *The Tale of Gengi* which was greatly admired by the Prince.

Towards the end of the Heian period, garden designing had become a preoccupation of the court. Rulers and their courtiers participated directly in garden design and a gentleman of the court produced a book on gardening, *Sakuteiki*, based on the design theory prevailing in the eleventh century in Kyoto. The landscape gardens of China were still the main source of inspiration. However, their principles, not just details, were studied; and the Japanese masters learned to apply them in a way suited to the special qualities of their own environment.

THE SHOGUNATE

But the peaceful Heian development lasting three hundred years was drawing to a close. The ruling Fugiwara Emperors had come to depend on the support of two military clans, the Taira and the Minamoto. In the second half of the twelfth century, the Taira clan used its military power to seize control of Kyoto. The rival Minamoto warriers and their leaders were not prepared to accept the situation: they attacked the Taira, and after a few years, were victorious. Their leader, Yoritomo assumed power as Shogun or Supreme War-lord.

The new system of government, with a nominal Imperial Court but with the real power in the hands of the Shogun, was to persist with few interruptions, right up to the mid-nineteenth century. This change in government had important consequences for landscape design. Often the Shoguns, to avoid Court intrigue, established their military headquarters away from the capital. Kyoto and its environs became a cultural centre in which literature and other arts could flourish, where great works of architecture, landscape design and painting have survived intact into the present era.

The earliest of these historic landscape gardens built under the Shogunate is the 'Moss Garden', Saihoji, with which we introduced this chapter. Saihoji was built after the Japanese landscape designers had overcome the initial domination of Chinese form. The 'natural' principles are still applied, but the spirit of the garden is Japanese.

Saihoji is unique in another way – nature has added its own quality to the garden which was not originally intended, particularly in the lower part of the garden where moss tends to obliterate the original rock forms. The garden is in two parts, the upper section divided from the lower by a low wall. In the upper section, some stone arrangements are still intact: these include a shallow, stone-lined pool, a tortoise island in a sea of moss, and a dry cascade and 'pool'. In the lower garden through the centuries, moss has grown over everything, softening the outlines of stones and creating an effect which was never visualised by the original designers. It is significant, however, that the sensitivity of the Japanese has enabled them to accept nature's addition and to incorporate it into the design, to the benefit of the whole concept.

Saihoji was restored in the fourteenth century by the Zen Buddhist, Muso Kokushi. A series of well-preserved landscape gardens from this time onwards gives a continuous and comprehensive picture of landscape design in Japan.

51

During the Heian period the Japanese aristocracy developed delightful residential structures which established an indoor-outdoor link very like we use today in the finest of our contemporary houses. This seventeenth-century album leaf shows Gengi-sitting on an open terrace conversing with some of his friends.

THE ASHIKAGA PERIOD

Muso Kokushi was a friend and adviser to Ashikaga Takauji who in 1338 A.D. became Shogun of Japan. Under Ashikaga the Court and Shogunate became extremely wealthy due to expanding trade largely with mainland China; and with wealth and leisure the court devoted itself to the arts. An influx of new ideas had come from Sung China, including the Ch'an or Zen Buddhist movement with its emphasis on emotional communion with nature, derived in part from Taoism. Zen Buddhism with its simple tea ceremony and cult of asceticism, was adopted by the warrior class of Japan, and developed by them into the cult of the Samurai.

But parallel to the growth of Buddhism, Shinto, the ancient Japanese form of nature worship, had survived, and the followers of Shinto were also attracted by the simple, intuitive, direct inspiration from nature which was practised by the Zen. A new enthusiasm for the mainland culture followed: China and all things Chinese again became the ideal for intellectuals of the Ashikaga period – scholars, painters, potters and landscape designers. The landscape paintings of the Sung dynasty were the main influence on both painter and landscape designer (who were often the same person). Some of the Japanese landscape gardens of this period have been described as Sung

52

The Kinkaku-ji (Golden Pavilion) Ashikaga, Kyoto (*c.* 1394–1427 A.D.), was built by Shogun Yoshimitsu as a place of retirement. Essentially for leisure, it was intended for contemplation of the landscape of water, islands and mountains, for moon-watching and the enjoyment of the tea ceremony. Like the Sung paintings which inspired them, such gardens were essentially monochrome, but changed the black-and-white of painting to the greens of nature.

paintings in three dimensions.[3]

Sherman Lee, author of a most comprehensive study of Far Eastern Art, and Director and Curator of Oriental Art at the Cleveland Museum of Art, writes about paintings of this period:

> If one knows that this painting is Japanese, one can see elements different from the Chinese style, but the overwhelming impression of the painting is completely and utterly Chinese . . . These artists believe in the culture and style of China with such force and fervour that they were literally able to recreate the lyric style of Southern Sung to such an extent that their work equals, or in some cases surpasses that of the Chinese Masters of Southern Sung.[4]

Ashikaga Takauji, after his victory over the Kamakura Shogunate, established his headquarters in Kyoto. The vigour of the new Sung landscape influence and the simplicity of the Zen cult, combined happily with the sophistication of the Kyoto court; the result was a flowering of Japanese landscape garden art. Ashikaga's grandson Yoshimitsu, gave the lead to this movement, aided by Shubun, the Abbott of Shokoku-ji Temple in Kyoto. In the city Yoshimitsu built himself a magnificent palace in a large lake garden, which has since been destroyed. But still surviving is his most famous garden built on the outskirts of the city, now known as The Golden Pavilion (Kinkaku-ji).

Built after his retirement in 1394, on the site of an earlier garden, the Golden Pavilion is given an air of seclusion by the many large pine trees which fringe the lake. The form of the lake is skilfully contrived so as to give an illusion of much greater space than really exists. (The present garden is only 4½ acres.) The lake contains many islands, the largest of these creating an effect of foreground and middle distance. The foreground, as seen from the pavilion, is replete with intriguing islets, some in the shape of tortoises (a far-off echo of the Isles of the Blest) while a dwarf pine on the main islands repeats the theme of the large pines which frame the pavilion view, thus increasing the illusion of perspective.

53

A pine-framed view of the lake at Kinkaku-ji, beyond the Golden Pavilion.

54

Ginkaku-ji (Silver Pavilion) built towards the end of the fifteenth century. It is a 'stroll garden', as the scale of the lake is too small for boating.

The focal point of the garden is a two-tiered Pavilion which seems to float on the mirror surface of the lake. Originally the Pavilion blended happily and inconspicuously into the surrounding pine trees, but after it was burnt down in 1950 by a demented monk, it has been replaced by a replica in which the name 'Golden Pavilion' has been taken too literally. In the original building, the upper ceiling only was in gold leaf; but the new building's exterior is covered with gold leaf on the two upper storeys, giving rather too much prominence to the pavilion.

The garden, designed by Yoshimitsu himself, was intended to be viewed both from the Pavilion and then by boat. As the boat glides around the lakes, the beautiful landscape is revealed in a succession which could not be seen effectively from any other viewpoint.

The Golden Pavilion and its garden were built essentially for leisure and pleasure, to contemplate the landscape of water, islands and mountains; for moon-watching and the enjoyment of the tea ceremony; and, when afloat, for quiet contemplation of the changing panorama unfolding before one. Like the Sung paintings, these gardens are essentially monochrome, but change the black and white of the painting to the greens of nature. In Spring cherry blossom, azaleas and iris bring colour to the garden but in other seasons it is predominantly green. A favourite season is winter. Then the lake is frozen; snow covers the ground, the roofs of the Pavilion, caps the foliage of the pines, and lies on the rocky islets.

In the hands of Japanese masters of landscape design, the scale of the Sung paintings was subtly softened and modified to suit the more intimate quality of the flowing forms of the Japanese landscape. Rocks, which in the gardens of China were often active and tortuous, in Japan took their form from the gigantic mountains of the paintings, but became smoother and more restful in form. The huge, awesome rivers and vast seas of the paintings became intimate little lakes with tiny, rock-sized islands. The actual mountains of Kyoto were 'borrowed' as a visual extension of the gardens; but these are rounded forms clothed with

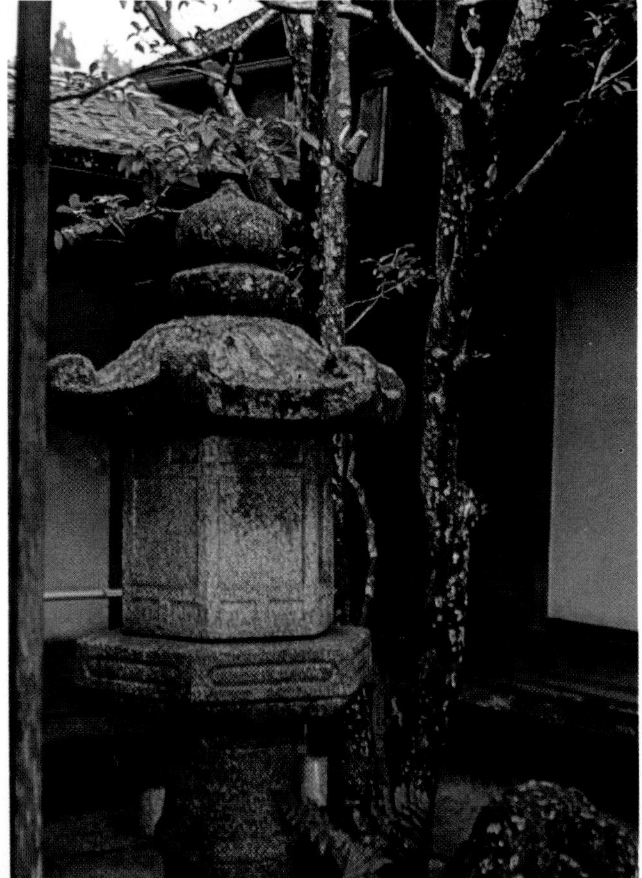

dense forests, and quite unlike those depicted by the Sung painters.

Thus a new landscape garden art came into being, evoking in miniature the changed and changing landscape of Japan. This is now an inspiration to the landscape architecture of the Western world. The Golden Pavilion, Ginkakuji (or Silver Pavilion), Daisen-in, Shugaku-in and Katsura in Kyoto; Rikugi-en and Karako-en in Tokyo, have become household words in the landscape design centres of the West.

Kyoto must have looked its most beautiful in the mid-fifteenth century when hundreds of gardens had been built in and around the capital. But this had been at the expense of a neglected peasantry, and civil war broke out in the capital and the city was devastated. Even the Golden Pavilion and Saihoji (the Moss Garden) were partially destroyed. When peace was restored the Ashikaga Shogunate remained in power but its position was far less secure.

Ginkaku-ji, popularly called The Silver Pavilion, was built by Yoshimasa, grandson of Yoshimitsu, after the Shogunate was in decline. He began its construction towards the end of the fifteenth century when conditions had become more settled. A cultured man, he had a great admiration for Saihoji which he had seen in its prime in all seasons. Because he decided to model Ginkaku-ji upon it, his garden was in two parts: one part in the foothills and the other on level ground. The upper garden formed a link between the lake and pavilions of the lower garden and a natural hillside and forest above. This hillside, which had an unusual silhouette, became part of the garden visually. The link with the natural landscape is one of Ginkaku-ji's most renowned qualities and one of the most successful instances of 'borrowed landscape' in all the Japanese gardens.

The lower garden is intimate in scale with a small irregular lake in the centre. It is a 'stroll garden' as the lake is too small for boating. The Silver Pavilion garden has suffered a number of vicissitudes through the years, including a long period of neglect. The present lower garden lacks unity. It is dominated by two sand features which were added at a later period and which conflict unhappily in scale with the rather intricate stonework of the little lake.

The surviving Pavilion, which has given the garden its popular name, is in natural timber, exquisitely detailed and presents an excellent idea of the original Golden Pavilion. The Silver Pavilion was modelled upon a pavilion built by Muso Kokushi in the Moss Garden: this had been destroyed in the civil war.

55

A stone lantern in a corner of the garden of the Ginkaku-ji. The original purpose of the lanterns was for lighting the garden walks at night, but they soon became an important design idiom in garden sculpture.

Yoshimasa promoted the ceremonial use of tea. Tea drinking became a transitional act when moving from the workaday world to a world of contemplation and communion with the beauties of nature. The elaborate and formalised 'tea ceremony' has since assumed great importance in Japanese life.

THE SAND GARDEN

Zen Buddhists played a leading part in the development and refinement of Japanese garden art. Their art developed parallel with that of the Ashikaga Shogunate. One most interesting facet of the garden design developed by Zen Buddhism in Japan is the Sand garden, culminating in a universe in microcosm called Ryoan-ji.

This small garden court is part of a much larger garden. It consists of fifteen stones set in coarse raked sand. Conceived purely as a subject for contemplation, the garden itself cannot be entered, except in spirit, yet the effect upon the sensitive observer can be quite overwhelming ... a masterpiece of abstract landscape design. Created in the fifteenth century, the spirit of this garden is completely Japanese, perhaps inspired by the water and islands of the Inland Sea.

Another excellent example of a Zen Buddhist garden is the Daisen-in, portion of the Daitoku-ji monastery.

Many of the sand gardens of Japan have a simplicity of form and an abstract quality that is reminiscent of contemporary painting. Sometimes sand was combined with moss in a quite delightful way. This was done in the garden of Sambo as illustrated in plate 66.

56

Ryoan-ji, Kyoto. Ashikaga period, probably 1488 A.D. A universe in microcosm, this small garden court consisting of fifteen stones set in coarse raked sand, was created purely as a subject for contemplation. Except in spirit, it may not be entered, and perhaps was inspired by the water and islands of the Inland Sea. In the hands of Japanese masters of landscape design, the scale of Sung paintings was subtly softened and modified to suit the more intimate scale and flowing forms of the Japanese landscape. Rocks which in the gardens of China were often active and tortuous, and used because of their intrinsic beauty, in Japan frequently were employed more symbolically to represent mountains and islands.

57

A garden court of Daisen in Temple. In what was called the Kare-Sansui style, impressionist landscape is created by an arrangement of many stones of varying shape and character.

THE EDO PERIOD

During the mid-sixteenth century Portuguese navigators had arrived in Southern Japan. They brought with them Christianity and firearms. Though Christianity flourished for a while in the early seventeenth century, Japan was soon closed to foreigners: Christians were persecuted and expelled and Japanese were forbidden to leave the country. This period, called Edo or Tokugawa, lasted 250 years. The administrative capital was moved to Edo (which is now called Tokyo).

But it was too late for Japan to isolate herself from the rest of the world. Commander Perry of the U.S. Navy arrived at Urago in 1853. This was followed by the opening of Japan to the benefits of foreign trade, and ushered in the modern period.

The landscape gardens of Japan which have had the most direct influence on contemporary landscape architecture of the West, are probably Katsura in Kyoto and Koraku-en and Rikugi-en in Tokyo. All belong to the Edo period. The two latter are quite large stroll gardens; Katsura is more intimate and perhaps more distinctly Japanese, with a happy combination of architecture and landscape.

58

Plan of the grounds of Katsura Imperial Villa.

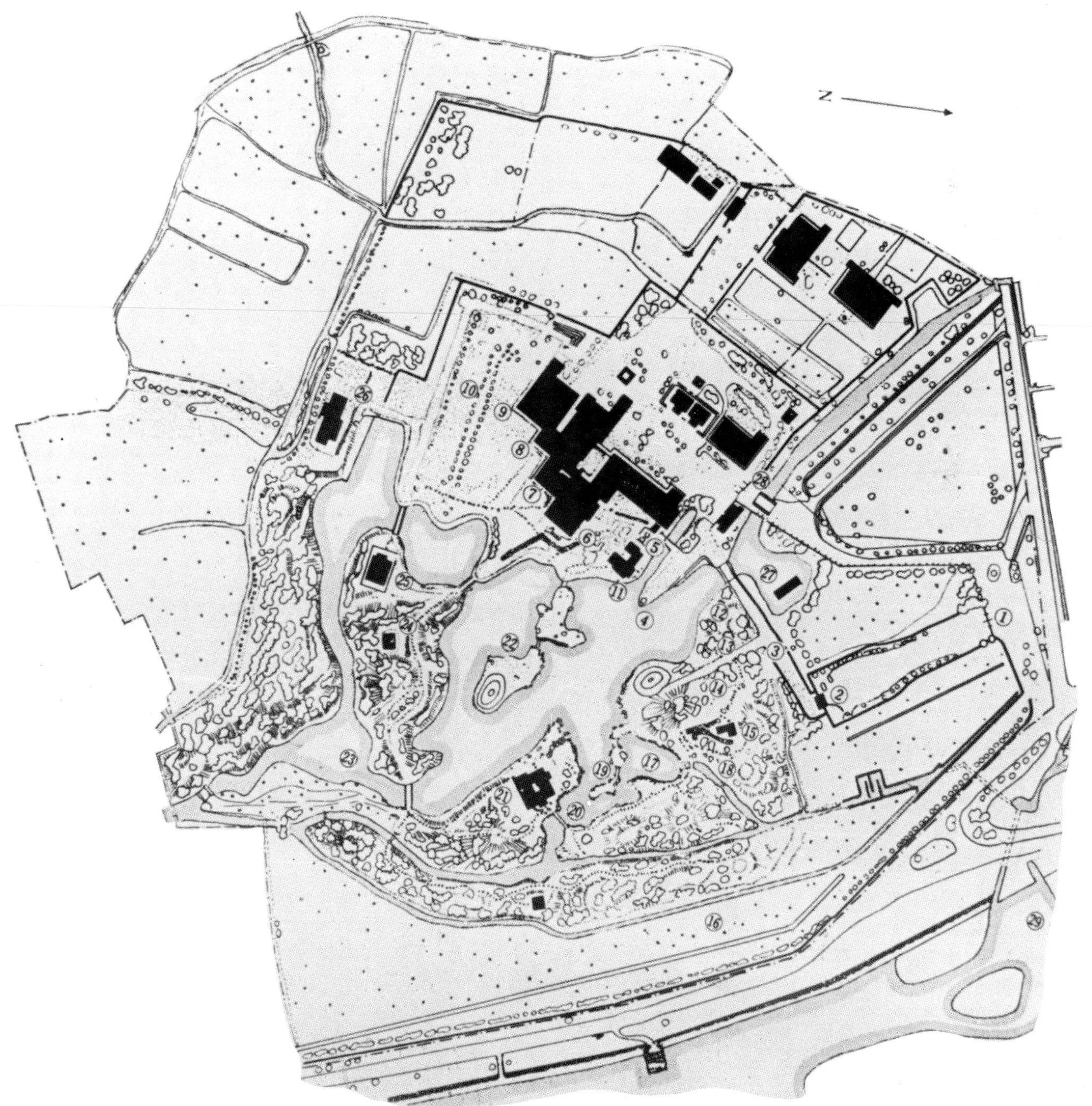

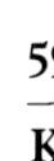

59

Katsura. View over the lake from the Shoken-rei tea-house. The garden and its villa have had considerable influence on the aesthetics of the Western world in the twentieth century. Katsura Detached Palace is not only a masterpiece of Japanese landscape garden art; it is also the finest surviving garden illustrating the spirit that created the Sung stroll gardens of China – of which otherwise we have only literary descriptions.

60

A group of cycads form a tropical corner in the stroll garden at Katsura Detached Palace.

61

Rikugi-en. Constructed originally in 1702 A.D. by Yanagisawa Yoshiyasu, it fell into disrepair but was skilfully restored by Baron Iwasaki in recent times. Like Koraku-en, it is a large stroll garden around a lake with islands, the excavated material being used to create miniature mountains. One of these hillocks gives this commanding view of the gardens.

62

Koraku-en. This earliest of the 'stroll garden' parks built at Edo (now Tokyo) during the Edo period, was created in the seventeenth century by Tokugawa Yorifusa (1603–1661 A.D.) and his son Mitsukuni (1628–1700 A.D.) and so was contemporary with Katsura. It still has great beauty; and of special interest is that a Chinese migrant, Chu Shun-shui, participated in the later stages of its design. Mitsukuni took a deep interest in things Chinese. Noted beauty spots in China and Japan were reproduced in this garden, in the same way as in the Yuan Ming Yuan. Both Koraku-en and Rikugi-en are now public parks.

63

Katsura Imperial Villa garden was partly inspired by *The Tales of Genji.* During the stroll through the garden, the scenes change, creating many different impressions. Here is a miniature alpine scene looking through pine trees back to a lake and islands.

Katsura was commenced by Prince Toshihito, a favourite of the Shogun Hideyoshi, during the Momoyama Period. The garden itself was begun in 1620 or a little earlier. You will recall that Prince Toshihito greatly admired *The Tale of Gengi*, thus in Katsura one can see in miniature many of the garden scenes so charmingly described by the Lady Murasaki. The garden was completed by Prince Toshihito's son, Prince Toshitada. A famous garden maker, Kobori Enshu, is also said to have participated in the design.

During the stroll around the garden at Katsura, the scene changes subtly from tropic to 'seascape' and even to a miniature Alpine landscape. The whole is successfully unified around a delightful indoor-outdoor pavilion, while resting places for quiet contemplation are provided in tea houses which are placed harmoniously into the landscape. The villa and tea houses of Katsura are superbly designed and the link between covered and open space is brilliantly contrived. Walter Gropius combined with Kenzo Tange, the notable Japanese architect to write a book devoted to the buildings alone. Katsura, now an Imperial villa, is one of the best-maintained of all the historic gardens in the foothills of Kyoto.

64

Stroll gardens such as Rikugi-en were designed to induce a mood of leisurely contemplation. Here a two-span stone bridge has (though it is not apparent in the picture) a central break and no handrail, so that the eye is directed to the beautiful form and placing of the stones. There were more than eighty view-points of literary significance on the stroll around the lake at Rikugi-en.

65

Stepping stones in a garden in The Silk House, Kyoto. They were frequently used by the Chinese and Japanese in lieu of a bridge, as described by Hsi Ma-Kuang in his eleventh-century garden. These are particularly fine.

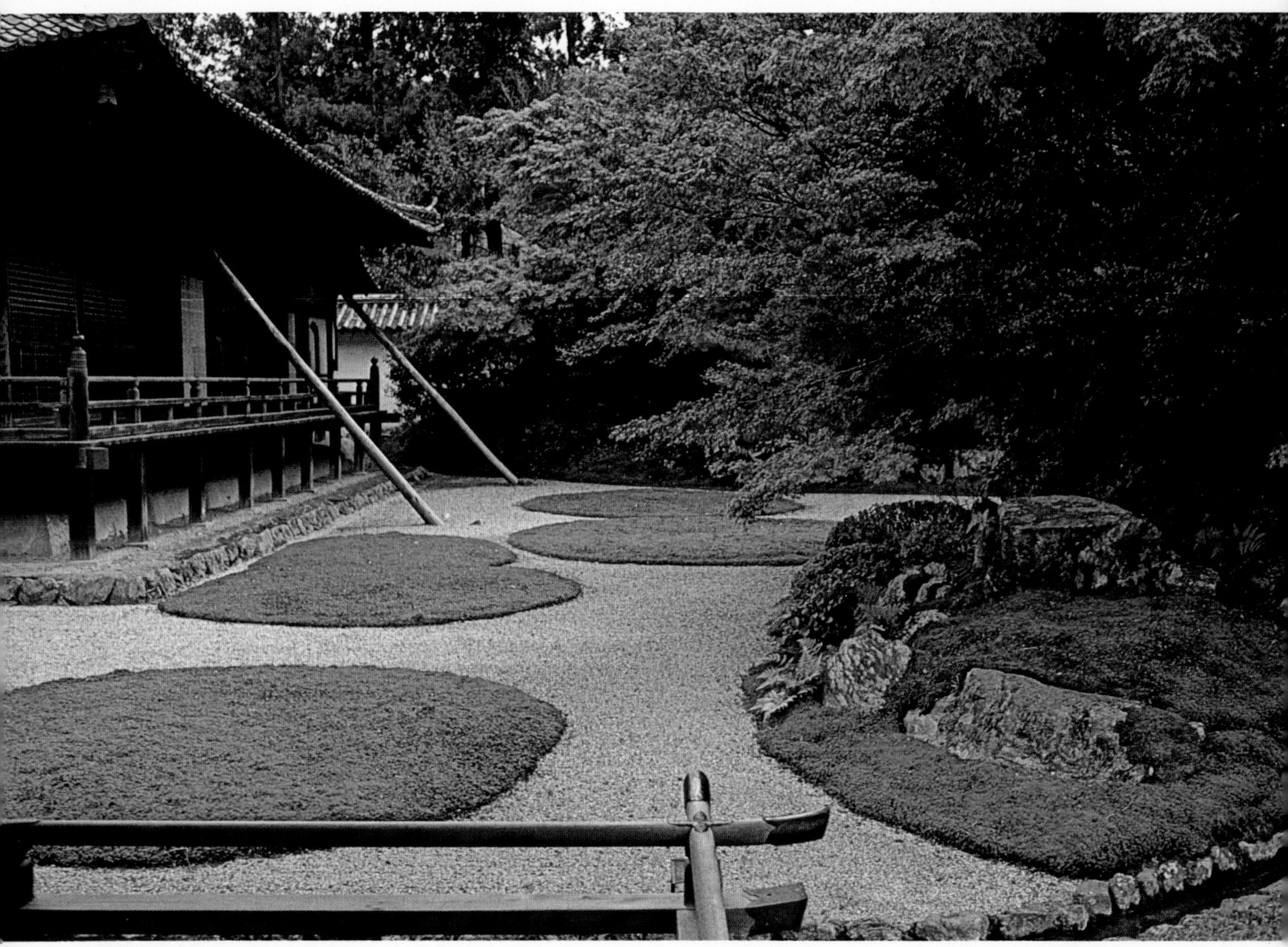

66

The abstract pattern of moss and white gravel at Sambo-in, Kyoto, has a considerable appeal to modern Western eyes. This is related to the earlier sand-gardens such as Ryoan-ji.

Koraku-en, now a public park, formerly belonged to the lords of Mito. It was commenced by Toguwara Yorifusu (1603 - 1661) and is a stroll garden with a strong Chinese influence. Contemporary with Katsura in Kyoto, there are inevitable similarities between the two gardens. The most notable is the arrangement of the main path around the lake. The original designer was Tokudaiji Sahyoe, a minor noble from Kyoto. The design was further developed under Mitsukuni, the second lord of Mito, assisted by a Chinese Confucian scholar Chu Shun-shui.

Rikugi-en, originally constructed in 1702, was later restored and renewed by Baron Iwasaki and is now a public park. It is a mature example of a large Japanese stroll garden. Now surrounded by busy streets, new high-rise buildings also overlook Rikugi-en and invade its privacy, despite excellently designed screen planting. There are several hills well-clothed with trees. From one of the hills a fine panoramic view of lake and island is obtained.

The Japanese landscape gardens we have been discussing are full of delightful and interesting details. We have endeavoured to demonstrate this where possible in our illustrations. There are many important Japanese gardens which we have not had space to mention; and for more comprehensive illustrations of these, we refer our readers to Loraine Kuck's *The World of Japanese Gardens.*

We have stressed the influence of China – especially of Sung China – on the landscape gardens of Japan. It was historically inevitable that the main source of inspiration should come from China: but the entirely original Japanese interpretation and the contribution of Japanese landscape designers was of the utmost importance to the development of the environmental arts.

Japanese landscape designers studied their own landscape, its special qualities and forms. In the masterpieces of landscape design which they created, they captured the spirit and the nature of the Japanese environment, re-interpreting it in superb man-made works of art. Though these ranged from quite complex and elaborate gardens such as Katsura and Rikugi-en to the austere simplicity of Ryoan-ji, they are all unmistakably Japanese and their contribution to the landscape design of the rest of the world has been of the greatest consequence.

To summarise the landscape design aesthetic developed in China and Japan in the first three-quarters of our present millennium: the basis of the landscape design concept is a love of, and respect for, nature and natural forms of water, land, rocks and plants. The forms deliberately set out to evoke much broader and comprehensive landscape themes than the space available could encompass, stimulating the mind of the beholder to create these grander scenes in his own imagination.

By using both a space and time dimension, the whole concept is gradually disclosed by a progression through changing spaces of varying contours. This is in complete contrast to the great gardens of the Western civilisations, where the whole garden is laid out before the beholder, and wide avenues, planted in geometrical lines, give an overpowering sense of man's domination over nature. The best-known example is the famous garden of Versailles, which represents the climax and culmination of this idiom.

In moving through the Eastern garden, a sense of enclosure is often followed by an illusion of illimitable space. This is achieved by 'borrowed scenery', which appears to be part of the design though it is physically far beyond its confines. In this way the scale can sometimes change quite suddenly, from intimate and elaborate to bold and awe-inspiring.

By such techniques, feelings of anticipation, suspense and surprise are engendered. All our senses are called into play with colour, form and line; texture underfoot of gravel, pebbles and stepping stones; the scent of flowers or pine needles . . . Contrast in form is used extensively to accent the qualities of important elements of the design, especially in the counterpoint between man-made and natural objects. But always the unity of the whole design is preserved, whether the scale and the detail is vast or miniscule; and man himself is made to feel at home in it and part of it.

In the fifteenth to eighteenth centuries, unique historic gardens of China and Japan became known in Europe, where they inspired the establishment of the English or Natural School of Landscape Garden Design. A second important flow of ideas went from Japan to America and Europe in the twentieth century, carried there by men such as Frank Lloyd Wright, Antonin Ramond and Thomas Church.

But we must now go back to Western Asia, to examine an interchange which occurred much earlier . . . in the eighth century, when the forces of T'ang China clashed, and finally came to terms, with the growing power of Islam.

67

A 'shin' style Hill garden, from an illustration in *Tukiyama Teizo-den* published in Tokyo in 1828 A.D. By this time Japanese gardens, though informal in character, had become highly stylized.

CHAPTER 4
ISLAM AND THE MONGOL EMPIRE

The contribution of Islam to the gardens of the world has been magnificent, but has often been obscured by religious intolerance. The first flowering of Islamic culture took place when Europe was experiencing the Dark Ages and the Byzantine Empire was fighting for its life against Persia, and then against the Muslims, who were expanding in the Middle East and along the Mediterranean to Spain. These conflicts put blinkers on European and other Western scholars for centuries.

A further confusion is caused by the tendency to describe all Central Asian gardens as Persian. And an additional complication is the strange paradox that the finest surviving gardens created by the early Muslims do not occur in the Middle East (the heart of early Islam) but in Spain.

Misunderstandings arose not as in the case of China, because of its remoteness from the Western world. The general failure to acknowledge the debt of Western garden art to Islam arises because the supremacy of Islam was achieved at the expense of Europe and in conflict with Christianity.

EARLY ISLAM

In the seventh century, while China and Japan were establishing significant cultural links, far-reaching changes were taking place in Western Asia and the Mediterranean. The powerful Byzantine Empire, which had grown out of that of the East Romans, was at war with Persia; when quite suddenly, taking them both by surprise, extremely mobile armies of Arab horsemen appeared on their borders, making lightning raids, then retreating into the desert wastes where they could not be followed. These armies fought under the banner of a new faith, Islam. In less than a hundred years they destroyed the power of the Persians, and the Byzantine Empire became confined to southern Italy, part of Greece and part of Anatolia. Islam created an Empire greater than that of the Romans.

The prophet Muhammed who founded Islam, was born in Mecca in 570 A.D. At that time, the Arabs were a group of nomadic tribes in constant conflict with each other. They did not appear to be a threat to their powerful neighbours. But the Arabs were traders as well as pastoralists and trade

68

This seventeenth-century Persian rug illustrates the formal garden layout that prevailed in Central Asia and India at that period. It is based on the methods of irrigation and garden-making used in Central Asia from the earliest times. Miniatures indicate clearly that, after the Mongol invasion and the introduction of Chinese cultural influences, informal gardens with meandering streams became the vogue in Central Asia. This style was reversed by Barbur, the first of the Mughal conquerors in India, and by Shah Abbas in Isfahan. This rug dates from their time.

was the secret of their growing power. The old trade routes from the West to the East – past the Tigris and Euphrates to the Persian gulf; and along the Nile to the Red Sea – had been disrupted by the war between Byzantium and Persia. Cautious traders were taking a new inland route, longer but safer through Arabia, which had brought immense wealth to the Arabs. Mecca, the largest town, had become a thriving centre of trade.

Arabs at that time worshipped many gods and Mecca contained their most popular shrines. To all of them Allah, the Creator of all things, was the most important. His black stone, a meteorite in the Kaaba Temple in Mecca, was sacred to all Arabs. Many thousands of pilgrims visited Mecca annually to kiss the stone. This influx of religious tourists increased Mecca's wealth, power and importance.

As Muhammed grew up, he saw and deplored the disunity among the Arabs. At the age of 40 he became religiously inspired. He established a new, broad, unifying faith in Allah as the one and only God with him, Muhammed as His prophet, through whom Allah spoke. He preached the idea, new to the Arabs, of an after-life for true believers, where they would be rewarded in the gardens of Paradise for their devotion to Allah. He taught that those who shared their wealth on earth with other believers, would receive far greater rewards in Paradise. Unbelievers would be doomed to damnation.

These ideas had a broad appeal and he quickly made thousands of converts. Unbelievers' wealth was regarded as fair game, so that fighting for Allah you either obtained wealth on earth by booty or if you died, you obtained everything you wished for in Paradise. Muhammed's teaching became embodied in the Koran, which has been the basic law of Islam ever since.

Once the Arabs had achieved unity as a nation under Muhammed and his followers, the progress of Islam was almost incredible. They defeated the Byzantines and Persians and occupied much of their territory. Then, under a series of Caliphs (successors to Muhammed) they conquered a number of less powerful peoples, most of whom were converted to Islam.

The Islamic Empire was extended to the borders of China and India in the east, and through North Africa to Spain in the west. Arabic was the official language throughout the Empire and Muslims (Believers) established their law over ninety million peoples – one-seventh of the world population at that time.

As with most Empires, there was internal strife and one dynasty of Caliphs succeeded another, often with considerable bloodshed. The Abbasid dynasty came to power in 750 A.D. replacing that of the Umayyads, and most surviving Umayyad leaders were annihilated. The Abbasids ruled for five hundred years. A new capital was established at Baghdad on the shores of the Tigris River. The celebrated Harun-al-Rashid (786 – 809 A.D.) was an Abbasid Caliph.

The inflow of booty, trade and taxes from the vast Empire made Baghdad a city of fabulous wealth and power. The splendour of the Court has been perpetuated in the *Tales of the Arabian Nights:*

> Vessels arriving at Baghdad docks brought with them the varied resources of the world. From China came silk, ink, peacocks, porcelain, saddles and spices; from India rubies, silver, sandalwood, coconuts, ebony and dyes; other cargoes included grain and linen from Egypt; glass and fruit from Syria; silk and other textiles from Persia, perfumes from Arabia; pearls from the Persian Gulf. Slaves and gold came from Africa; drugs, trinkets and slaves from Byzantium; leather from Spain; furs, amber, ivory and swords from as far away as Russia and Scandinavia.[1]

Though Persia was the strongest influence at the Baghdad Court, the administration there was international, chosen from all races which had embraced Islam. The Arabian Caliphs intermarried with the Persians and other conquered races, seldom selecting Arabs to mother their heirs.

The Muslims learned willingly from every people they subdued. Baghdad became the world centre of learning. When the Arabs overran Egypt, the great libraries there, originally collected by the Ptolemies fell into Muslim hands and the books became the treasured possessions of the Arab scholars. Philosophy, science, medicine, mathematics, astronomy and geography made enormous progress. The arts of poetry, literature, painting, architecture and landscape design received Court patronage and flourished. Scholars, artists, architects, scientists and garden designers flocked to Baghdad as the cultural centre of the known world.

Some examples of Islam's contribution to world culture are those by Ibn Sina (Avicenna in Latin), who wrote an encyclopaedia of medicine which formed the basis of European medical science; Khwarizion, who wrote a textbook on algebra – a science developed by the Arabs – which served as the principal mathematics text book in Europe until the sixteenth century. In addition, the whole of the heritage of classical Greece, both scientific and philosophical, which had been decaying in the West for centuries, was given new vitality by the translations made in Islamic lands.

69

The main vista alley of cypresses in the Bagh-i-Eram, Shiraz. It is delightfully shady and cool in the hot summer sun.

ISLAMIC GARDENS

The gardens of the early Caliphs and their officials would have been predominantly Persian in character. However, the Muslim rulers would also have been heirs to the whole of the Egyptian, Alexandrian and Roman garden culture.

In most of the countries controlled by Islam, rainfall was minimal and water had to be brought into the garden by irrigation. Through the centuries, the Persians had become masters in this sphere. By a system called the quanat, melting snow from distant mountains quite often provided a constantly renewed, year-round water supply. By tunnels and then by open channels, water was brought many miles to towns and villages. The system of irrigation used in farming – major water channels with minor channels leading off at right angles on each side – gave the form to Islamic gardens. This form was gradually developed and refined.

At its simplest it was known as Chahar Bagh or four gardens. But the divisions were often much more complex, and some gardens would have sixteen or more compartments divided by water channels. The simplest explanation of this garden form is given by the garden carpets of much later centuries, one of which is illustrated. These garden carpets acquire an additional importance, as none of the early central Asian gardens as originally planted, survive today.

As the Islamic Empire extended across Asia to India and China, the gardens of Islam were subjected to quite different influences. Professor Joseph Needham describes how, after the battle of Talas River (751 A.D.) where the armies of China were defeated by those of Islam, Chinese paper makers, artists and artisans were captured and induced to continue their crafts in Samarkand. A Chinese officer prisoner, Tu Huan, returned to China eleven years after the battle, and fortunately his brother, a great scholar Tu Yu, recorded what he had to tell of the influence of Chinese art on that of the Arabs: 'As for the weavers who make light silks, the goldsmiths and the painters, the arts which they practice were started by Chinese technicians. For example, for painting Fan Shu and Liu Tshu from the capital (Sian), and for silk throwing and weaving Yueh Huan and Lu Li from Shensi.'[2]

The victory at Talas River was not followed by an invasion of China, but trade links were established between Islam and China, both by land and sea. 'By the end of the eighth century in 798 A.D. Haroun-Al-Raschid sent a mission to Chang-an to arrange for co-ordinated strategy against the Tibetans who were annoying both parties ... and during the time of the Chin and Sung dynasties in the eleventh century, there are records of more than twenty semi-commercial, and semi-diplomatic Arab missions.'[3]

Through war and then trade the Arabs were exposed to the influence of the highly sophisticated Chinese painting and poetry, calligraphy and garden art, over a long period when these arts were reaching their peak. Early Arab painting, poetry and landscaping undoubtedly owe much to the influence of China; and it was inescapable that the Muslims, along with this artistic inspiration, should also absorb Chinese garden techniques. Some of their philosophy of man in the landscape would have penetrated too, countering the older concept of man as conqueror and subduer of recalcitrant natural things. The nature poetry of China appealed strongly to the Arabs, who during their early nomadic and illiterate period, had used verse as the traditional art form for communicating their history from one generation to another.

As a result of these new influences, topiary never played an important part in the gardens of Islam – plants were encouraged to grow naturally, though often arranged in a formal manner.

The new attitude to Nature is well-expressed by the poet Firdawsi who wrote towards the end of the tenth century:

Mazanderan is the bower of spring,
Tulips and hyacinths abound
On every lawn; and all around
Blooms like a garden in its prime,
Fostered by that delicious clime,
The nightingale sits on every spray
And pours his soft melodious lay;
Each rural spot its sweets discloses,
Each streamlet is the dew of roses.[4]

The new sense of harmony with nature was at first incorporated into the old form of water channels in Islamic garden-making. Water, the most prodigal element in the gardens of China, was the most precious element in the Central Asian gardens. Its decorative use was elaborated by the Muslims in a multiplicity of ways ... water channels were gradually widened into broad canals which were decorated with beautiful arrangements of fountain jets ... the informal waterfall of nature was often used as a broad cascade, and also as a 'water ladder' where the stone was carved with indentations to create a foaming, iridescent white panel.

The Muslims inherited a superb vocabulary of plants

70

The best-preserved of the early Islamic gardens are not in Central Asia but in Spain. This lovely arrangement of water jets is in the Generalife in Granada. The Moors had occupied the Spanish Peninsula from the eighth century, bringing with them the whole vocabulary of Central Asian garden art. Granada was the last Moorish Stronghold in Spain. It did not survive the Christian conquest of the fifteenth century.

from the civilisations that preceded them. Plane trees were the favourite large shade trees but poplars and cypresses gave vertical contrast; elms, ash, oak and willows gave shade in the summer and let through the sun in the winter, while pines were used where large scale dark contrasting foliage was required.

A whole range of prunus were used both for their flowers and their fruit including plums, apricots, peaches (from China) and almonds. Other flowering and fruiting trees were also popular such as apples, pears, quinces, cherries, pomegranate, mulberries and figs. Citrus fruit trees such as oranges, lemons and limes were treasured both for their fruit and perfumed flowers; and hazelnuts, pistachios and filberts for their nuts.

As with Rome the rose was the favourite flower but it was supplemented by daffodils, tulips, jonquils, hyacinth, lily-of-the-valley, marigolds, gilliflower, ranunculi, pinks, carnations, jasmine, violets, sweet marjoram and water lilies for pools.

Animals were used to give animation to the gardens including swans, pelicans, pheasants, pigeons, ducks on the water bodies; singing birds both in aviaries and in trees included nightingales, gold finches and linnets; deer wandered in the larger gardens.

MUSLIM GARDENS IN PERSIA

Shiraz in Southern Iran was famous for its gardens. This was the home of the poets Sa'di (1181–1291) and Hafiz, who died in 1189 A.D. Both poets loved their birthplace and extolled the beauty of its gardens. Hafiz, who died in Shiraz, wrote:

> *Joy be to Shiraz and its unrivalled borders*
> *O heaven preserve it from decay.*[5]

None of these gardens survive in Central Asia and Shiraz has lost its former beauty. When the authors visited Shiraz in 1969 eagerly anticipating the sight of the beauties so loved by the poets, we were bitterly disappointed, for the town's reputation has outlived its decline. When we went to view the Tombs of Sa'di and Hafiz, there were many young people, reading aloud from the works of these much-loved poets – but the Tombs, though on the sites of the original tombs, are of relatively recent construction and the surrounding gardens are undistinguished and show no trace of the once-beautiful form of the early Persian garden.

In the grounds of the Park Sa'di Hotel where we stayed at Shiraz, is a large pool which was formerly the centrepiece of the Bagh-i-Naw, built in the early nineteenth century. It is a lovely circular pool, and we enjoyed dining at night when tables are set out around it, and the central playing fountain is illuminated.

The best preserved garden we saw in Shiraz, the Bagh-i-Iram, is also dated from comparatively recent times, having been constructed in the nineteenth century in the traditional manner. It had recently been restored and was used as a 'guest-house' for distinguished State visitors.

Its central water channel and pavilion were both interesting in their form. Here it was that we experienced the delight of coming from a hot, arid countryside where no trees grew, into a dark shaded alley whose high walls are dark green cypress, in the shadows almost black. The 'walls' of the alley shut out the hot dry winds and the blazing sun. The cypress are not clipped, their natural habit providing its own formality. Here one enters a secluded world of coolness and beauty, a lovely microcosm of retreat from the harsh environment.

The air was deliciously cooled by a murmuring water channel, and scented by the sharp tang of the cypress and sweet perfume of roses – pale pink, deep crimson, white – growing in a 'border' along the water course, each plant set in the silver-grey gravel which paves the whole alleyway.

Only one alley is maintained in its original form, others in the garden have their simplicity and design marred by irrelevant and distracting additional planting. But we could find nothing remaining of the older, historic gardens – those famous Persian Gardens which we had hoped to see. Today if one wishes to see the gardens of Islam it is not to Central Asia that one must go. It is to the westernmost part of the former Islamic Empire, thousands of miles away, that one must travel. The Islamic Empire at its height extended around the Southern shores of the Mediterranean to the Iberian Peninsula; and when, in the thirteenth century, the whole of Central Asia was devastated by the armies of Genghis Khan, the South Mediterranean and the Iberian Peninsula remained unscathed.

So, paradoxically, it is to Spain that one must go to find the surviving gardens of the remarkable, influential early Islamic culture.

THE MUSLIM GARDENS OF SPAIN

The Arab conquerors brought with them as part of their cultural luggage, their traditional garden art; when they built fortresses in the hostile land, the buildings and the gardens were nostalgic replicas of those in their far-distant homeland. Many of the early Muslim gardens in Spain have disappeared or are in ruins. The Gibilfaro and Alcazaba complex at Malaga in Southern Spain are the earliest which the authors have examined in detail.

Because of their surviving evidence, these Spanish gardens are our main reference here, although there is in India a greater number of tombs, mosques and precincts illustrative of the architecture and garden design of Islam. These are to be found in the countryside around New Delhi and comprise the ruins of no less than five previous Delhis. The surviving Spanish gardens are in a much better state of preservation than those Indian ruins, which will be discussed in Chapter 5.

Commenced with the first conquest in 711 A.D., the Alcazaba-Gibilfaro complex was built on a site containing earlier Carthaginian, Greek and Roman ruins – for Malaga has long been a vital strategic port for invading armies. This treasure house of architecture and landscape design continued to be occupied by Islamic forces until the re-conquest of Malaga by Ferdinand of Aragon and Isabella of Castille who ousted the Muslims from Spain in 1487 A.D. Though occupied for a time by the Christian monarchs as a palace after its capture, it later declined and became ruinous. A partial restoration took place in 1933.

The significance of the Gibilfaro and Alcazaba is that it precedes by several centuries the much better preserved

71

The Alcazaba, Malaga, in southern Spain. Part of a castle fortress built by the Arabs to defend the town from pirate raids. It is older than the better-known Alhambra in Granada, and the water channels that irrigate the garden have not yet become decorative canals. Here we look down from a central tower to a restored garden court behind the defensive walls.

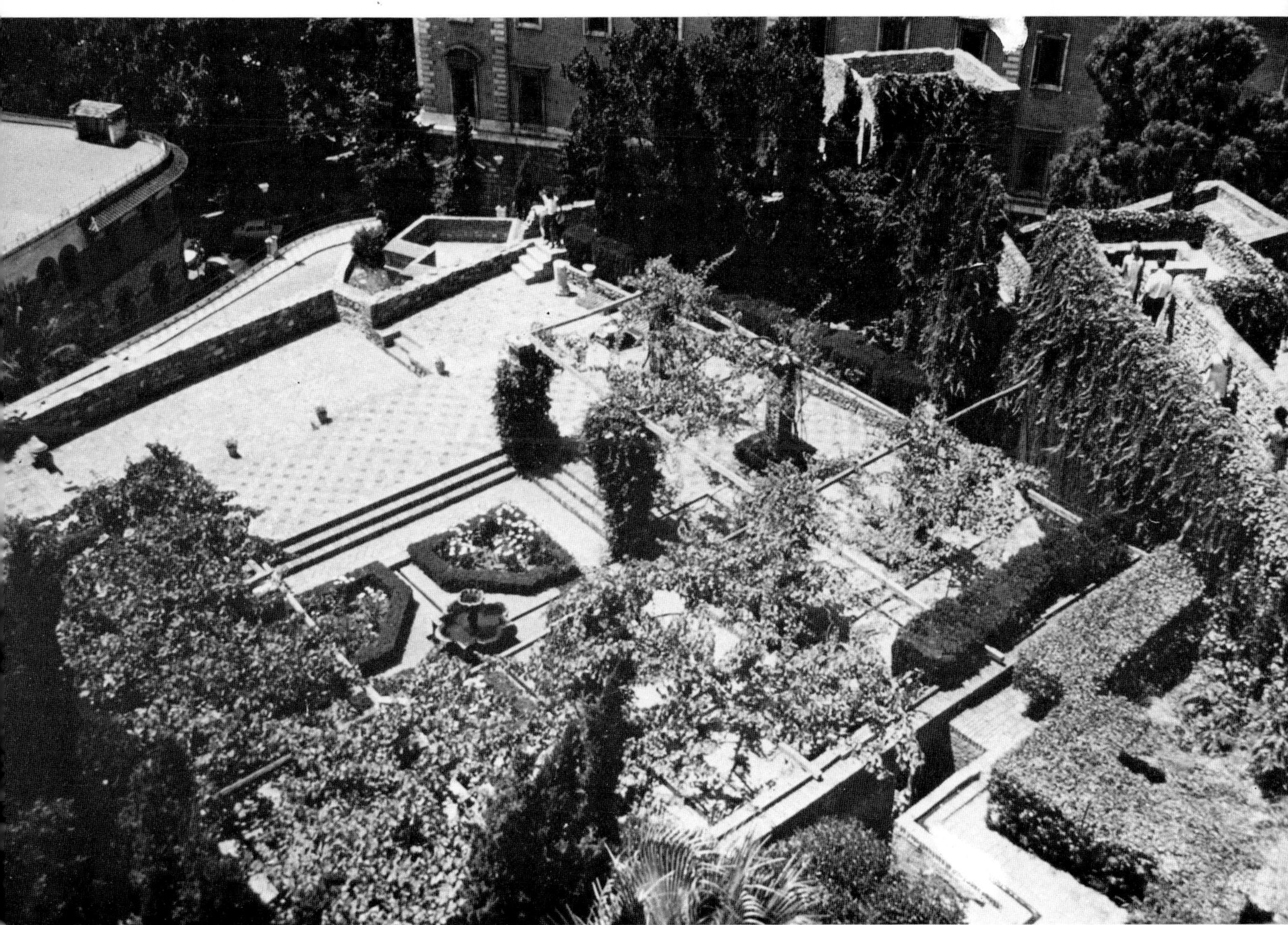

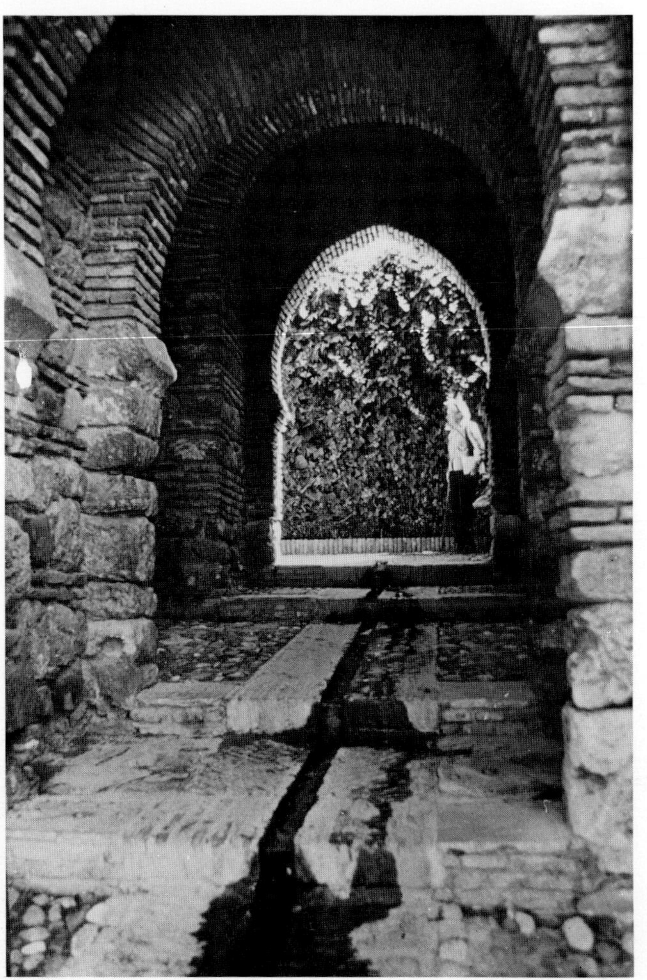

Alhambra and Generalife, and in it one can trace the earlier, more primitive forms which led eventually to the masterpieces at Granada.

As far as can be judged, the water forms in the Alcazaba never approached the refinements of those of the Alhambra and Generalife. The water channels still maintained much of their functional character as open conduits, and sometimes meander up and down the walks and through steps and porticos in a quite inconsequential manner. But the arrangement of the changing levels is masterly, and the use of partial or complete enclosure to create surprise and anticipation, is often as successful as in the structure of the Generalife.

72

A portico under the central tower leads to the upper part of the gardens. Notice the narrow water-channel that comes down through the centre of the steps.

73

Gibilfaro, Malaga, Spain. Commenced in the eighth century A.D. it is built on the site of earlier Cathaginian, Greek and Roman ruins. Now in its turn ruinous, Gibilfaro echoes forms of a similar period from Central Asia and Northern India . . . an interesting illustration of the cultural integration achieved by Islam from the Western Mediterranean to the borders of China.

74

Gateway and walls of the Purana Qila in Delhi, India. Built by the Sultan Sher Shah in the mid-sixteenth century, details of the fortress are similar to those of Gibilfaro.

75

Stone grille in Humayun's tomb which was built in Delhi, India, in the 1550s.

76

Carved stone grille in the Alhambra, Granada. The Muslims achieved coolness and privacy by the use of exquisitely carved stone screens; an architectural detail which they used from one end of the Islamic Empire to the other.

Wandering along an enclosed area between high walls at the entrance, one passes through an arched doorway constructed in a combination of stone and brick, with exquisite detail. Once within, attention is directed to a mosaic floor of great beauty; then, within seconds, one passes out into a terrace with an open vista embracing Malaga harbour, framed by the Sierra Mountains on one side and the sparkling Mediterranean on the other.

One of the surprising aspects of the whole Arab culture is the unity of thought and design concept, from one end of the Empire to the other. The architectural form, the arrangement of water-play and water channels, the techniques and patterns used in the exquisite paving and wall decorations, are almost identical from Spain around the Mediterranean to Central Asia and India. Among the most evocative of these details are the crenellations which surmount towers and walls of the Gibilfaro. Unlike those of medieval Europe which have squared tops, the Arab crenellations are pointed. This characteristic silhouette is seen outlined against the sky in Malaga and again, thousands of miles away, in Agra and Delhi. The lovely tracery of the grilles and the fine patterns of paving formed with small upright stones – so characteristic of the Arab gardens of Spain – occur in similar materials and patterns on the bridges of far-off Isfahan.

As one would expect due to climate and the materials available, interesting regional variations have taken place. The strong unity of ideas established by Islam among its nine million adherents is however more noticeable. This is one of the reasons why the surviving Muslim landscapes in Spain and India, however ruinous, are so important in tracing the history of garden art; and why the Alhambra and Generalife in Granada (the best preserved) are so valuable historically.

THE ALHAMBRA AND GENERALIFE IN SPAIN

The Alhambra was commenced by Mahammet I of the Nasred dynasty in the mid-thirteenth century and completed, together with the Generalife, in the next century. The Alhambra is therefore the oldest surviving garden in the Western world.

The Alhambra and Generalife are widely recognised as the highest peak reached by Muslim garden art in the West. More widely illustrated, written about and discussed than any other, generally they are considered in isolation and their significance in the history of landscape design is usually ignored.

The Alhambra was built as a fortress, a watch tower to overlook the plain and the town of Granada at its base. Poised high above the town, it crowns a ridge that projects into the Vega from the Sierra mountains. Granada is situated on the edge of the Vega, a high plateau in the snow-capped Sierra Nevada mountain range, and had been occupied since the eighth century when the Muslims first conquered Spain.

The Alhambra was a military fortification, and a hill was the easiest and most effective site for a fortress in that period. But the Arab builders, with consummate artistry, made the powerful group of towers and battlements seem a part of the natural landscape – an extension of the steep bluff on which they stand. Both the scarp and the brickwork of the buildings are the same dusty rose colour. When illuminated by the western sun, they glow and sparkle against the cold white and grey of the snow-capped mountain backdrop. The effect is unforgettably beautiful.

The approaches to the Alhambra today are framed in a dense forest, through which a winding road leads up to the present entrance gates. This approach is quite out of character with the initial concept of the building as a fortress: originally entry must have been by a series of controlled, enclosed gateways similar to the Alcazaba-Gibilfaro complex at Malaga. This is confirmed by one of these porches which remains about halfway up the forested mount, still imposing in its half-ruinous dignity though quite overgrown with trees.

77

Plan of the Alhambra and Generalife in Granada. This superb Moorish complex was built as a fortress on a high scarp overlooking the town. The builders, with consummate artistry, made the powerful group of towers and battlements seem at one with the natural landscape – an extension of the steep bluff on which they stand.

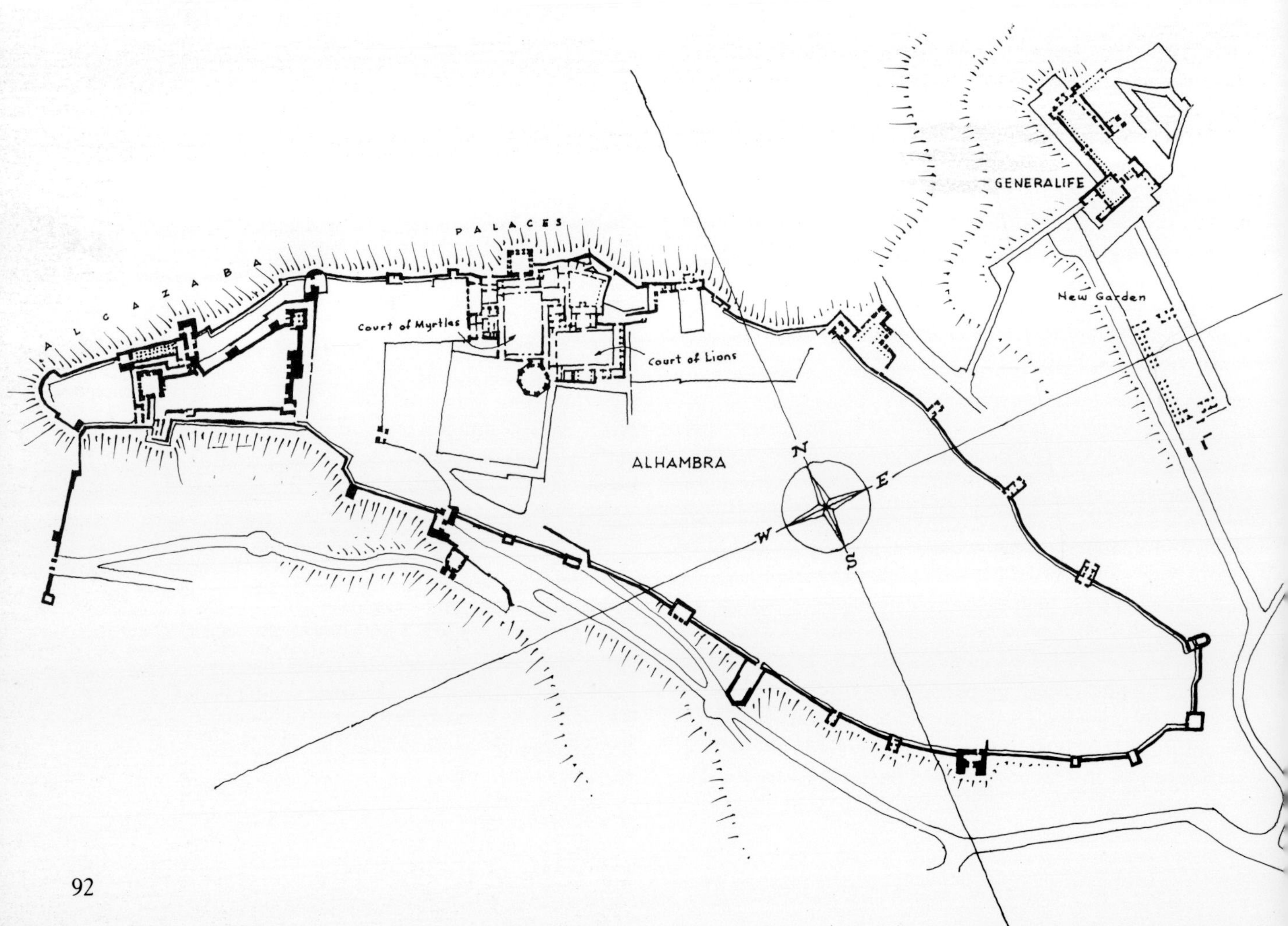

78

Pebble paving on the upper terraces of the Generalife in Granada. Similar paving was used in Isfahan, the capital of Shah Abbas, in Persia, over three thousand miles away.

79

The Alhambra. Court of the Myrtles. There is an ineffable lightness and gaiety in this restrained court with its reflecting pool, small fountains and arcaded terminals to the long axis. It is in strong contrast to the austere grandeur of the exterior of the fortress.

The fortress of the Alhambra, now partially in ruins but in process of restoration, at first sight gives an impression of severe defensive enclosure. Once within, however, and after having passed the heavy additions of Christian monarchs the sombreness is dispersed by the delicacy and refinement of the architecture and the superbly proportioned courtyards.

A magnificent reception chamber leads to a series of fully-enclosed courts; the two finest being the Court of the Myrtles with its large rectangular pond; and the quite delightful Court of the Lions. The Court of the Lions, imbued with a lightness and gaiety which we have seldom seen equalled, is surrounded by four graceful arcades in each of which centrally-placed fountains feed narrow water channels which flow down to terminate at the central Fountain of Lions. This is a rare use of sculptured animal form by the Moorish Muslims – and carved, we surmise, by 'Persian' craftsmen, for the character of the lion is reminscent of those created by Darius at Persepolis, and of those used as column bases in the Chehel Sutun in Isfahan built by Shah Abbas as late as the seventeenth century. The lions themselves have an ageless quality, they are friendly, bubbling little creatures, with none of the terror associated with their wild counterparts.

We found the Alhambra to be a superb landscape concept by reason of the juxtaposition of beautifully proportioned open spaces (courtyards) with enclosing areas of fine buildings; and also because of its subtle association with the surrounding countryside. The latter quality is achieved in a number of ways: by a series of changing views which range from grand open panoramas stretching far away to the distant horizon; down to intimate glimpses of the courts and gardens of the Alhambra itself. Delightful open balconies are provided, allowing surprise 'viewing points' of the terrain.

The long pool in the Court of the Myrtles brings in the open sky by reflection, and enhances the delicate arcades in the same manner. The whole is scaled down to human dimensions by the exquisitely sculptured stone basins with

80

The Alhambra. Court of the Lions. A rare use by the Moors of animal forms. Probably the product of Central Asian craftsmen, by whom the lion has been used in sculpture from very early times. These are friendly little animals.

their central jets, located at each end of this Court. The planting of the Alhambra is now minimal and probably was more extensive under the Moorish occupation.

After the inspiring experience of the Alhambra, we reluctantly left it to climb the steep hill road which leads up to the Generalife, wondering how this could possibly be anything but an anti-climax – despite the many pictures we had seen of its beautiful gardens and fountains ... but once within the Generalife, the whole image changed. The Alhambra seemed sombre by comparison.

The Generalife was the residence of the ladies of the court. Its land-form has the quality beloved by landscape designers. Arranged on a sloping site, the design is experienced in an episodic manner, revealed in stages as the spectator moves up through the garden area. Water and water play is the dominant theme.

The garden takes the form of an ascending series of courts and terraces. The courts are enclosed and vistas controlled by pavilions and planting. The effect of these garden courts is still quite splendid, despite the fact that the whole of the plant material must have been frequently renewed. In this process, one feels that over the centuries, some of the simplicity of the original pattern has been lost.

However, despite these modifications which in the whole have been made in sympathy with the basic design, the experience of moving up through the Generalife is most exciting. Highlights include an avenue of high jets playing gaily on the long axis of one of the large courts ... and walking up a closely-pleached stairway, cool and shaded even on the hottest day, with the sound of tumbling water all around: one becomes aware that the gentle sound is caused by cascades of water which are rippling down the stone handrails on either side. How refreshing it is to trail fingers in this ice-cold water!

From each terrace are different views, until on the highest terrace, framed in cypresses and magnolias, there is a glimpse of a distant dream-like Alhambra with a misty Granada far below.

The visual links between the Generalife, and Granada and the Alhambra, are one of its important design contributions to be emulated by the villa gardens of the Italian Renaissance in later centuries.

The design principles and details exemplified in this garden, more than any other influenced the renowned Renaissance gardens of Italy. The Generalife was completed

81

The Gardens of the Generalife are located across a narrow valley, and high above the Alhambra. The Generalife was for the ladies of the court. The garden takes the form of a series of ascending courts and terraces, enclosed and controlled by pavilions, arcades and walls. Charming vistas and glimpses of the Alhambra and the town of Granada are obtained. This is the famous Fountain Court framed by an arcaded entrance.

82

Water play was the joy of the Muslims. Here water cascades down the balustrades of a stairway which links the upper terraces of the Generalife.

in the fourteenth century and ideas based upon it were introduced to Italy by the Prince of Aragon and the Spanish Popes.

The Muslim gardens of Spain possess many of the landscape qualities summarised at the end of our previous sections on China and Japan, yet their form is completely different and have been unified with the architectural element of the landscape composition in an entirely new way. The garden pavilions and palaces are so perfectly integrated into the composition that it is impossible to distinguish where landscape ceases and architecture begins.

They too, have been deliberately designed with dimensions in both space and time. In the Generalife and the earlier Alcazaba at Malaga, one is gradually led through a predetermined progression of special experiences which provoke anticipation, suspense and surprise. An impression of great space is achieved in little compass, spaces from level to level being arranged with constantly changing axis so that new views and vistas are progressively revealed – often far beyond the extent of the enclosed landscape, by visual borrowing. And always the unity of the whole design is kept in mind by the designer, who relates the scale to man himself. These qualities of design, as well as the superb details of water play, paving, planting and architectural screening allow the Generalife, the finest of the surviving gardens of Islam, few equals in the formal gardens of the civilised world.

The Spaniards love and respect the Alhambra and the Generalife and we believe that much of the spirit of Islamic gardens survives in the people today. This is well illustrated by the quite delightful more recent additions at the Generalife that we have illustrated and by the lovely open spaces of present-day Malaga.

83

A long vista to the 'new' garden court of the Generalife. It retains the spirit created by the Moors. The design of this court is reminescent of the garden carpets of Persia and Northern India of the sixteenth and seventeenth century.

THE MONGOL EMPIRE

Returning to Central Asia, we find events were taking place in the thirteenth century which were to have repercussions that we are still experiencing today.

When Genghis Khan united all the North-Eastern Tartars living in felt yurts (tents) into a mobile cavalry army of incredible mobility, discipline and stamina, the bow and arrow was the most effective long-range weapon devised by man; and the Mongols (as they now called themselves) were the finest archers in the world. Being nomads, they were completely mobile and accustomed to carrying all their needs with them on pack horses. Genghis Khan led a nation on horseback, hundreds of thousands of devoted subjects who were brilliant cavalrymen and superb archers, and were eager to follow him to the end of the world. Once he had learned the techniques of siege warfare, which he did during his early conquest of North China, his armies became invincible; and with them he carved out the largest Empire the world has seen.

The Europe-oriented history which we learn concerning this period presents Genghis Khan as an unmitigated villain, a destructive force who set back the course of civilisation, and contributed nothing of permanent value to the progress of mankind. But could such history, presenting as it invariably does, the viewpoint of the conquered nations, perhaps be prejudiced?

It is true that when Genghis Khan first unified the Tartar tribes into a nation and a powerful military force (1206–1211 A.D.), they were still semi-barbarian nomads with no written language. Their economy was a pastoral one. They had no use for settled areas, either cities or agricultural lands, except as a source of booty and they did not hesitate to destroy whole cities and their populations, pillaging the countryside and returning it to grazing land from its former agricultural usage. Genghis Khan was absolutely ruthless in his treatment of those who opposed him or stood in his way. Terror was one of his most effective weapons. It is this aspect of the Mongol conquest which is represented in Western historical accounts, and also in those of China. Alexander the Great used exactly the same terror tactics in Asia and is called 'The Great' in all our history books as a consequence.

One should recognise that Genghis Khan had other qualities which enabled the Mongol Empire to have permanence. He was a superb organiser, and a talented innovator who was able to assimilate the more advanced techniques of the lands he conquered, and adapt them to his own ends. He was able to combine the mobility and endurance of the Mongol cavalry with the most advanced military techniques which had been already developed in China, conquered in 1211 A.D.

Once the Mongols had completed their initial conquests, they established an unparalleled system of communication between the eastern and western extremities of their empire. An organisation of post horses and trading posts was established from China almost to the Mediterranean.

Traders were encouraged and furnished with everything they needed to conduct their business expeditiously. As a result, trade flourished in all parts of the vast Empire. Restrictions which had been placed on merchants by the feudal monarchs ceased. Merchants were a mobile group, without national loyalties; and the Mongols used them to help penetrate and finally subdue such feudal empires as that of Khwarizm, then the most powerful in Central Asia.

Under the Mongols travel and communication became safer. It was said that a beautiful girl carrying a gold dish on her head could walk from one end of the Empire to the

84

Gayumart, the First King, in the Mountains. A mid-fourteenth century painting from the Shahnama manuscripts. This Central Asian painting shows how the Mongols introduced naturalistic Chinese idiom into the Islamic world. The bamboo, curiously shaped rocks and informally arranged plants are all clearly of Chinese origin.

other in perfect safety. The former separation between Eastern Asia and Europe was broken down.

Another characteristic of the Mongol leaders which assisted the interchange of ideas was their tolerance concerning religious issues. Traders and merchants of all nations and creeds were given equality of treatment in an almost modern way – quite unlike the methods and attitudes adopted by Christian and Muhammedan monarchs who were their contemporaries.

This freedom of thought and movement permitted the Polo brothers to make their initial visit to China in 1271, followed by that of Marco Polo, who was to stay in China at the court of Kublai Khan for seventeen years. When the Polos returned to Venice in 1295, Venice had become the wealthiest and most powerful City State of Europe. Marco Polo brought back with him arts and techniques which were then completely unknown in Europe, though they had been practised in China for many centuries. Printing, gunpowder and the compass were three of these, the effect of which had wide repercussions. Chinese ideas and techniques of garden design and landscape painting were also brought through Central Asia to the West.

CHINESE INFLUENCE ON THE MONGOLS

For countless centuries before the conquest of China, the Tartar hordes of North East Asia had established a close, though intermittent, association with the Chinese, their neighbours. To them China was the centre of the world; a place of untold wealth; fair game to them when they could organise enough strength to invade North China and carry away rich booty.

The Tartars would carry back to their horde skilled craftsmen and artisans as slaves along with their booty. This practice was greatly extended by the Mongols under Genghis Khan. As the wealth and power of the Mongol leaders increased, they needed scholars and administrators to help manage their estates. Engineers were required to build siege engines, such as battering rams and catapults; to build dams to divert rivers and so deprive besieged cities of their water supply.

During his initial invasion of China in the early thirteenth century Genghis Khan took an intense personal interest in the quality and abilities of these captives. After the fall of Peking to the Mongols, the vast treasures there accumulated were sent to Genghis Khan; and along with them, 'useful men', catalogued by name and profession.

> One day Genghis Khan, examining these new arrivals, was struck by a tall man with a long black beard. He was catalogued as Yeliu-Ch'uts'ai, sage and astrologer, a scion of the Liao family who were traditionally opposed to the ruling Imperial house of Kin.
>
> 'The House of Liao and the House of Kin have always been enemies,' said Genghis Khan. 'I have avenged you.'
>
> 'My father, my grandfather and myself were servants of the House of Kin,' answered Yeliu-Ch'uts'ai. 'I should be a liar and a hypocrite if I were to cherish hostile feelings towards my father and my Emperor.'[6]

The courage and integrity of Yeliu-Ch'uts'ai pleased Genghis Khan and he decided to take him into his service as soothsayer and adviser. Thereafter Yeliu-Ch'uts'ai accompanied Genghis Khan upon all his campaigns to the West. He became his chief adviser and 'prime minister'. After Genghis Khan's death, Yeliu-Ch'uts'ai by brilliant diplomacy, managed to separate the administration of the huge Mongol territories from the war machine, using the Yasak (code of laws) laid down by Genghis Khan, as his main weapon to persuade his successors.

Yeliu-Ch'uts'ai was not only an able administrator but like all Chinese scholar-officials, he had a deep interest in the arts and sciences. Through his wisely wielded power, many of the cleverest and most talented citizens of the conquered races were brought into his new administration. Yeliu-Ch'uts'ai and men of his kind were responsible for the influence of Mongol regimes upon the arts of Central Asia. Professor Ipsiroglu in his *Painting and Culture of the Mongols* has expressed it in this way:

> In the countries occupied by the Mongols the Chinese were renowned as the most skilful masters in the world in all the products of human aptitude. Their talent for painting was proverbial in the East. Ibu Battuta relates how he visited the Imperial palace in Peking with one of his companions: when he passed through the painters' market in the evening, he saw his own picture and that of his companion painted on paper and glued to the wall. This is said to have been done on the order of the Emperor. By his order, a picture was made of everyone who passed through his country. If a foreigner should take flight because of a crime that he had committed, his picture was sent into all the provinces, and on its evidence he could be found and arrested.[7]

85

***The Battle of the Crows and Owls.* 1370 A.D. Here again the Chinese vocabulary of landscape idioms is fully utilized. The atmospheric effect and the treatment of rocks, fire, mountains and trees can all be clearly traced to Sung China.**

This art of painting is the most helpful to us today in research into landscape and garden design of this period. The inter-action of painting with garden design (which we have already noted in our chapters on the gardens of China and Japan) accounts for the importance of paintings, in which one can also examine replicas of gardens and landscapes that have long ago disappeared. This has already been demonstrated very clearly by the Forty Scenes of the Yuan Ming Yuan, which are all that remain to us of that famous Chinese garden. It is the miniatures of Central Asia that tell us most about the landscape and garden influences introduced there by the Mongols.

But before we examine some of these, we must comment further on the somewhat misleading nomenclature that is currently used among scholars, writers and collectors. Almost all significant art forms which have developed in Central Asia since the rise of Islam, are assumed to be Persian or derived from Persia . . . Persian gardens, Persian miniatures, Persian pottery, to name the three arts most relevant to our study.

It is true that since the time of Cyrus the Great, Persian culture has considerably influenced that of Western Asia, much as Greek culture has influenced that of Europe, and the Chinese culture that of East Asia. But to call the arts of Central Asia 'Persian' is to ignore all the other cultural influences that preceded Persia's greatness, were contemporary with it and came after it. What we call 'Persian' art forms today are a composite of every important culture that has had an impact upon Central and Western Asia.

The whole painting of Central Asia was profoundly changed by the Mongol Invasion. This has already been analysed by Professor Ipsiroglu:

> We are dealing with works that arise from the interaction of Eastern and Western currents of culture, and [they] therefore show in a great or less degree a unique mixture of influences. In their style these pictures are unmistakably dependent on the great Far Eastern and Central Asian traditions of painting which the Mongols carried westward. The Western share is rather confined to the iconography of the pictures. The Near East at this time had a highly developed literature in Arabic and Persian, and the paintings of the Mongol period drew its favourite themes from the works belonging to this literature. In this way the foundation was laid for the Islamic illustration of books. The illustration of the Persian national epic the *Shahnama* [*The Book of Kings*] by Firdausi, done about 1300 A.D., marked a decisive turning point in the development which was to lead away from pre-Mongol Mesopotamian art to the new Mongol style.[8]

The cultural influences introduced by the Mongols would have been accompanied by a very strong infusion of Mongol blood into all the different nationalities who inhabited Central Asia.

The ideal of Mongols (who saw themselves as an elite, equivalent to the knights of Europe and the samurai of Japan) was stated by Genghis Khan in these terms: 'The greatest joy a man can know is to conquer his enemies and drive them before him. To ride their horses and take away their possessions. To see the faces of those who were dear to them bedewed with tears, and to clasp their wives and daughters in his arms.'[9] With such an ideal, the resulting progeny, of mixed blood, must have been considerable. The slanting eyes and other Mongol characteristics that are so typical of the miniatures of the Mongol period would very often have also occurred in real life. It is said that three decades after his death, direct descendants of Genghis Khan were estimated at ten thousand.

From careful study of the many thousands of Mongol-style miniatures which were painted in the succeeding centuries, we can obtain an interesting picture of the landscape-design trends which prevailed throughout the Central Asian areas controlled by Genghis Khan and his successors. Let us look at some of them.

Our first miniature is a mid fourteenth-century painting from the Shahnama. It shows how the Mongols introduced natural Chinese idioms into Islamic art. The bamboo, the curious-shaped rocks and informal arrangement of plants are all clearly of Chinese origin. Another, *The Battle of the Crows*, 1370 A.D., again shows the Chinese vocabulary of landscape idioms fully utilized. The atmospheric effects, treatment of rocks, fire, mountains and trees can all be clearly traced to Sung China.

Our next miniature dates from the first half of the fourteenth century. Though the painter is a Muslim, the subject is a romantic one and is set in China. Prince Humay, from Central Asia, is received by Princess Humayun in the garden of the Emperor of China. You will notice the stream wandering informally around a lawn, its banks decorated with flowers, trees and shrubs, also planted informally.

The Garden of the Fairies follows this in time, dating from the beginning of the sixteenth century. Both the fairies and the garden are unmistakably of Chinese origin; and the artist shows a remarkable familiarity with the detail of Chinese garden-making.

A further miniature in the series is another scene from real life. Painted in the late sixteenth century, it shows Fidawsi, author of the Shahnama (*circa* 1,000 A.D.) in a garden with the Court poets. Here we see the now-familiar meandering stream, edged with water-washed stones. The garden is framed by an informal arrangement of the two trees most favoured by the Muslims, cypress and flowering prunus; bulbs and small plants fringe the stream and appear in the lawn. The informality is heightened by the posture of one of the poets who has draped one arm gracefully around the branch of a flowering prunus.

Summer Landscape our last in this group is now only a fragment of a group of landscape paintings dating from the middle of the fourteenth century. Paintings like this would have come to Venice with Marco Polo after his travels, and thus played an important part in Renaissance painting.

Significant in all these garden pictures extending in time over three centuries, is the fact that the detail in them bears little resemblance (except in the plant material used) to the formal gardens we associate with the Islamic culture.

86

Prince Humay is received by Princess Humayun in the garden of the Emperor of China. **This early fourteenth-century miniature underlines the cultural exchange that was taking place between Central Asia and China during the thirteenth and fourteenth centuries. It was painted by Khawadju Kermani who worked in Herat, Afghanistan (1291–1352 A.D.).**

87

The Garden of the Fairies **painted in the early sixteenth century. This Central Asia miniature shows a remarkable familiarity with the details of Chinese garden-making.**

88

Fidawsi with the Court Poets. **The Central Asian garden portrayed is composed of an informal arrangement of the two trees most favoured by the Muslims – cypress and flowering prunus. Bulbs and small plants fringe the stream and are sprinkled on the lawn.**

TAMERLAIN

After the collapse of Mongol rule in Central Asia military struggles developed between rival Emirates. During these engagements in the second half of the fourteenth century a Baghatur (military leader) named Timur came into prominence. Daring, ambitious and astute, he after many adventures and vicissitudes, gained control of the key city of Samarkand. Timur aspired to emulate the great Genghis, making his code of laws, the *Yasak* his guide. Like him, Timur possessed outstanding qualities of military genius. In a series of campaigns, he gradually gained control of the whole of Central Asia. Timur, the Lame, often known as Tamerlain, was not only a military genius but also a statesman. He encouraged the arts and Samarkand became the cultural centre of the Central Asian world.

چون عارض تو ماه نباشد روشن
عنصری گفت
مانند رخت گل نبود در گلشن
فرخی گفت
مژگانت همی گذر کند از جوشن
عسجدی گفت
مانند سنان گیو در جنگ پشن
فردوسی گفت

89

***Summer Landscape.* A fragment from the Satay Albums. A pure Central Asian landscape painting with all the qualities of perspective which the Chinese had developed through the T'ang and Sung periods. It dates from the middle of the fourteenth century.**

Timur took considerable interest and delight in the creation of gardens and parks and by the time of his death in 1405, the whole of Samarkand was surrounded by spacious garden parks. These pleasure places included the Northern Garden; Garden of Eram; Garden of Paradise; Plane Tree Garden; Garden of Heart's Ease; New Garden; Garden of the Glory of the World; Garden of the Image of the World; Garden of the Black Throne; Long Garden; and Garden of the Black Hill.

Judging from accounts written by Clavijo, ambassador in Samarkand for the King of Castile and Leon, the gardens of Samarkand were immense. Their main framework appeared to be formal, but within this framework there must have been very considerable informality, for '. . . in the direction of Kesh, Timur's birthplace, lay the Green City, or Shahr-i-Sabz, in which the Palace of the Black Throne was situated. One of the builders of the palace lost his horse in the garden and it grazed there for six months before it was found.'[10]

We can obtain some idea of the details of the gardens from miniatures depicting Timur and his Court in actual occupation. An even clearer indication of detail may be seen in a miniature of one of Timur's successors, Abu'l Ghazi Husayn Bayqara, who ruled at a new centre, Herat, in present Afghanistan. Herat became the most important centre at this time in Central Asia. The miniature we have reproduced is by Bihzad, an acknowledged master of the art.

The layout of the part of the garden illustrated, though level, is quite informal in character, with a meandering stream, flowering trees and shrubs fringing the water, and gay colourful smaller plants scattered about in the lawn. It is interesting to compare the informality of detail of the gardens in these miniatures with one painted in the second half of the sixteenth century in Mughal India. The theme is an ancient one showing the Persian hero Rustam with his mistress in a garden. The garden is typical of those built by the Mughal rulers in India. All 'structural' informality has disappeared; though the plants are still arranged freely and permitted to grow naturally.

Early in the sixteenth century another Baghatur, Barbur, came into prominence in Central Asia. During his early exploits and adventures he visited Samarkand and Herat and was greatly impressed by their gardens and parks. As he acquired power and influence he was finally able to carry out a successful invasion of Northern India where he overthrew the Sultanate in Delhi and became the first of the Mughal rulers in India.

90

***Husayn Bayqara in his garden.* A Central Asian miniature painted by Bihzad, an important artist of the Herat school. There is no sign of formality in this garden with its meandering stream, flowering trees and shrubs fringing the water, and gay colourful smaller plants in the lawn. Husayn was one of Timur's successors.**

91

***Rustam in a Garden.* A Mughal miniature of Rustam, a famous Persian hero portrayed in the Shahnama, the Book of the Kings. This miniature was painted in the sixteenth century. The formality of this garden scene is in sharp contrast to the other paintings we have been examining. It reflects the strong tendency towards formality, beloved by Barbur, which became characteristic of the Mughal gardens in India.**

THE OTTOMAN TURKS

Before moving to India we will deal briefly with an Islamic force that developed in Western Asia during the Mongol domination of Central Asia. During the twelfth and thirteenth centuries a Muslim kingdom under a Seljuk dynasty had survived in Anatolia. This was sandwiched between Byzantium and the invading Mongols under Genghis Khan and his sons. Finally the Seljuk kingdom collapsed and was replaced by that of the Ottomans, formerly a small Turkish principality within it. The Ottoman armies penetrated deeply into Europe and at the time of Timur they were also challenging his power in Central Asia.

Beyazid I the fourth Ottoman sultan defeated the Crusaders at Nicopolis in 1396. He was nicknamed 'the Thunderbolt' because of his speedy successes against hostile armies, but he met his match when he was defeated by Timur at Ankara in 1402 and was deposed. The Ottoman state revived under his successors and his great grandson Mehmed II captured Constantinople in 1453, renaming the city Istanbul.

The Islamic culture established by the Ottomans was notable for its garden art, its architecture, its superb ceramics and its paintings. Like their counterparts in other Muslim lands, the Ottoman gardens were enclosed paradises 'consciously devised for relaxation and contemplation, with every suggestion of coolness and peace after heat, noise and dust – coolness of water and peaceful retreat in the shade of trees or tent'.[11]

There was no division between architect and garden designer under the Ottomans. Both their mosques and palaces contained superbly organised enclosed and open garden spaces. The finest Ottoman architect was Sinan, who completed most of his work under Suleyman I (The Magnificent). Sinan designed the Suleymaniye complex at Istanbul which included a fine mosque, a Theological College, a soup kitchen, a hospice and a hospital and the Sultan's Tomb. These were framed and linked by garden courts. He also designed a number of other important mosques in Istanbul.

Sinan built additions to the Topkapi palace which became a glorious accumulation of buildings, gardens and art treasures. It continued to develop as the palace, harem and administrative headquarters of the Ottoman sultans for many centuries and is now one of the world's most exciting museums.

From the Satay album of miniatures in the Topkapi collection come the *Summer Landscape* and *Gayumart the King,* discussed earlier in this chapter. An interesting survival of Sinan's work at Topkapi is his ten double-domed kitchens which we have pictured from an adjacent garden court. Though essentially practical, the domed chimneys have a vertical rhythmic quality that echoes the great trees of the court and their design has a lightness of touch that is unusually pleasing. Sinan's masterpiece is the Selimye mosque at Edirne built for Selim II (the Sot), the son of Suleyman the Magnificent. The mosque is surrounded by some gardens.

Due to the Ottomans' preoccupation and passion for gardens and flowers, and due to the favourable climate of Istanbul, the palace buildings were usually quite unpretentious and sat in their gardens like summer houses or kiosks. The gardens themselves were less formal than those associated with Central Asia. They did not use the characteristic four-river rectilineal divisions associated with Persia, also used most effectively in the Court of the Lions at Granada in Spain.

Under the Ottomans, Istanbul continued its time-honoured role as the meeting place of the cultures of the East and the West. That spirit still pervades Istanbul to the present day and makes the Republic of Turkey a most exciting country to visit.

92

Sinan also worked on the buildings and grounds of the Topkapi Palace. This photograph was taken in the grounds of the Palace, looking towards the famous many-domed and many-chimneyed kitchen designed by Sinan.

93

The Ottoman Turks were for centuries, the go-between who linked Central Asia and China with the European world. They succeeded the Byzantine Empire. Constantinople (now called Istanbul) and Venice were the most important cities of exchange and both prospered greatly. In Turkey, architect and garden-designer were one: Sinan, the master-architect, worked under Suleyman I, the Magnificent (1548–1557) and his successor. Shown here is Sultanahmet Mosque with its surrounding gardens. It was designed by pupils of Sinan.

CHAPTER 5
INDIA AND THE MUGHAL GARDENS

Although India's contribution to the gardens and landscapes of the world has undoubtedly been considerable, it is difficult to assess.

The civilisation which grew up around the rivers of the Indian sub-continent could be the oldest continuous one the world has seen. It is customary to assume that the Aryan invasion which took place about 1500 B.C. destroyed the Indus culture, but history is full of instances of nomadic invaders being absorbed by the culture they appear to overcome. The authors believe it is more likely that Hinduism – the religion which has given unity to India through the centuries – had its roots in the ancient Indus culture.

If this were so, then the beginnings of Indian civilisation go back to the third millenia B.C. But the history of India is not documented in the way most other civilisations have been. This is due in part to the Indian attitude to time, derived from the Hindu religion which has been the guide to Indian thinking as far back as 1500 B.C. and probably much earlier.

94

View from a houseboat on the Dal Lake, Kashmir. Some of India's most beautiful gardens were built on the shores of the Lake. Kashmir was used by the Mughal Emperors as a summer retreat. To the Hindus, the rose-petalled lotus flower symbolises Brahama's prayer.

Our Western concept of a continuous progress through time from the past through the present to the future, is quite foreign to Indian throught. To the Hindu, what is happening now, has happened before and will happen again. Life is a constantly revolving, endless cycle, in which he has always participated and will continue to do so – starting in his past cycle of lives, and continuing in his present one and in those into which he will be reincarnated in the future. The recording of historical events in a time sequence becomes less important when viewed through this philosophy.

Another way in which the background of India differs from that of other civilisations is that, due to the caste system of the Hindu faith, the Indian population has been more fragmented than that of other civilisations. Though the population of India was one hundred million when the Roman Empire was taking shape, it has usually taken the form of a great number of petty states, with the Hindu religion as the unifying factor.

Geographically it was the great wall of the Himalayas, the Hindu Kush, the Arabian Sea, and the Indian Ocean, which gave India her unity. Countless invasions and intrusions took place through the deep river valleys that provided access through the mountain barriers. But up to the twelfth century, the geographic, climatic and cultural forces of India were too strong for the invaders. They either

95

In the Ajanta murals, dating from 400-700 A.D., gardens are depicted in the palace grounds.

retired; or were driven out, like the Persians, Alexander and Genghis Khan; or they were absorbed into the hierarchy of the Hindu caste system.

Cultural ideas flowed out of India through the mountain passes of the North and later by sea, influencing those of other civilisations in ways that have seldom been properly acknowledged. Buddhism is the most important example, which arose in the sixth century B.C. as a powerful challenge to the Hindu religion and caste system. As a religion Buddhism achieved remarkable initial success both within India and abroad: later it succumbed to Hinduism within India. However during its peak of development, its influence was carried far beyond the Northern passes into Asia Minor, Central Asia, China and Japan. Buddhism also travelled across the Bay of Bengal to South-East Asia. Its concepts have affected the whole of the civilised world.

Gardens and flowers were dear to the Hindus, and played an important part in Indian cultural life. Some indication of this is given by Constance Villiers Stuart in her *Gardens of the Great Mughals*: 'From very early times flowers and plants have been admired and cultivated in

of semi-precious stones. The carved screens around the outer area of the tomb have an almost unbelievable delicacy, throwing enchanting patterns of sunlight and shadow on the pavement within. The garden is a simple four-square one, similar to the very early gardens typical of Central Asia.

Inlays on the red sandstone of the gateway seem to indicate a touch of humour: wine bottles are used prominently in the design. Nur Mahal's husband Jahangir loved his wine, and is shown in a miniature, drinking even while he embraces Nur Mahal.

Shah Jahan, the next of the Emperors, married Mumtaz Mahal, daughter of Asaf Khan, his Prime Minister; thus making the bond between the rulers and the family of I'timud-ud-Daulah even stronger. Jahan had evinced a deep interest in garden design before coming to the throne, and this broadened during his reign. We have listed his gardens and monuments but shall have to confine our comments and illustrations to those which survive today.

An early contribution by Shah Jahan – his Black Pavilion in the Shalimar Bagh in Kashmir, on which he had collaborated with his father – we have already mentioned. Other surviving works by Shah Jahan are the Chasma Shahi and the Chenar Island on the Dal Lake. The Chenar Island is a delightful focal point in the changing views experienced from the various gardens and vantage points which fringe the Lake.

Chasma Shahi was disappointing to us – though it is much admired by many other garden lovers. The outlook from the site is a fine one, and the abruptly changing levels are of considerable interest: but for us, the beauty of the garden itself has been destroyed by inappropriate additions and variations which have been made by later generations.

Shalimar Bagh in Lahore has also suffered in this way, as well as at the hands of predators, especially the buildings: though its layout and water play are still of considerable interest. We prefer the relative simplicity and refinement of detail of the Black Pavilion in Kashmir, the Forts at Agra and Delhi, and the Taj Mahal.

One of the special contributions of Shah Jahan was his use of white marble as the most prominent building material in his projects. It had already been introduced by Nur Mahal in her father's tomb, but Shah Jahan developed it in

117

The entrance to I'timud-ud-Daulah's Tomb is in red sandstone with wine bottles as a decorative motif. Jahangir loved his wine and perhaps Nur Mahal had a sense of humour.

118

In this miniature, Jahangir embraces Nur Mahal in a garden. He was very fond of wine too! Notice that he is holding out his glass to a servant for a re-fill.

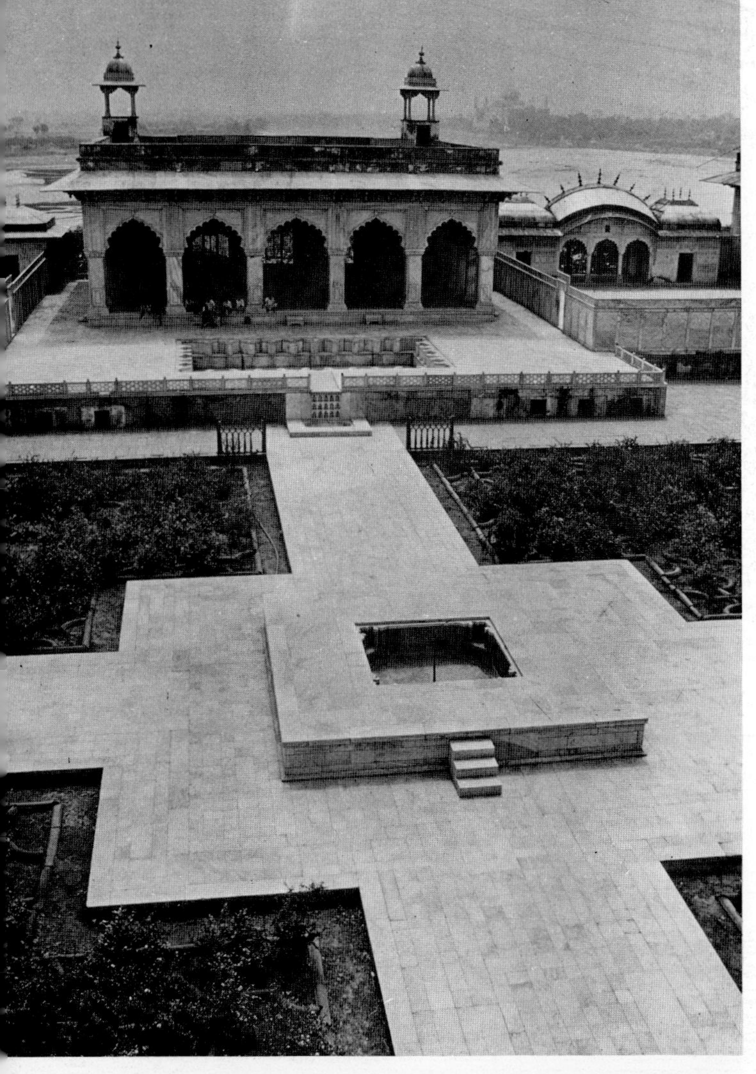

his buildings and landscapes to a perfection that has never been surpassed.

It is charmingly used in his additions to the Fort at Agra, especially in the Anguri Bagh and the Khas Mehal which adjoins it. Here Shah Jahan spent his declining years as a prisoner of his son Aurungzeb. The delightful pools and basins, adorned with fountains, which link the Anguri Bagh with the Khas Mahal, lose much today by the absence of water. Some indication of how beautiful they must have looked in their prime is given by a more recent water parterre in the Bari Mahal Lake Palace at Udaipur.

(The marble parterre in Anguri Bagh is derived from forms developed by the Rajputs; an excellent example survives in an Island garden, part of the Ambar Palace at Jaipur. There is also one, designed by Jahangir, in the Jamandar Lake Palace garden at Udaipur.)

The finest of the creations of Shah Jahan is the Taj Mahal. The main vista has been so often depicted, that it is one of the best-known and widely admired combinations of building and landscape in the world. Yet it is still a wonderful and surprising experience to visit the Taj Mahal. The approaches to the main entrance gate, the gateway itself, are an inspired introduction to the main vista. Red sandstone, the chief material used, is relieved by marble facings and details. These are familiar because of their wide use throughout Agra. But they also serve to make the sudden revelation of the vista down to the main Taj pavilion, come as a complete surprise. This is still effective, though pictures

119

Shah Jahan used white marble as his most favoured material in his palaces and garden structures. It is delightfully employed in his Anguri Bagh additions to his grandfather Akbar's Fort at Agra, the interior of which he re-designed. During Shah Jahan's declining years, he was imprisoned by his son Aurangzeb in the Fort, where he could look over the Jumna River to his beloved Taj Mahal. The Taj can be faintly seen on the horizon in this photograph.

120

Charmingly sculptured pools adorned with fountains link the garden and pavilion of the Anguri Bagh. But unfortunately, today they lack their most important element – water.

121

This water parterre in the Bari Mahal Lake Palace, Udaipur, gives an idea of how these decorative pools look when they are still in use. Though of a later date, this garden is obviously inspired by the earlier Mughal gardens.

122

Vista to the Taj Mahal through the archway of the entrance gate. Early morning is the best visiting time.

of the vista have made it so familiar to us. How can pictures create the elusive, dreamlike quality of the original? It must be seen before one can fully experience its lightness and delicacy – the ethereal floating quality that seems to impress all observers.

It is hard to account for the complete lack of the coldness which we generally associate with white marble . . . but we personally think that, even at a distance, warmth is lent by the inlays of semi-precious stones, and the slight bas-relief sculptural designs that decorate its surface.

The most disappointing quality of the Taj is the present condition of its garden. Informal planting of trees and lawns are distressing and inappropriate. It is to be hoped that a sympathetic restoration of the gardens to their traditional form will one day take place.

The major undertaking of Shah Jahan was the removal of the seat of government from Agra to Delhi. He chose a site on the banks of the Jumna river and in 1638 commenced building a massive Red Fort as his new headquarters. With its mighty walls, towers and battlements it was designed to accommodate five thousand persons and took eight years to build. In addition to the Red Fort Shah Jahan built a superb mosque, the Jama Masjib, one of the finest in India, which was to be the spiritual and religious centre of the new city.

A fine boulevard led from the main gate of the Fort bisecting the new city which was to occupy about six hundred hectares. Down the centre of this boulevard flowed a delightful canal flanked with beautiful avenues of shade trees. The boulevard was called Chandni Chowk (the moonlight market) and was terminated at its far end by Fatehpur Mosque built by one of the wives of Shah Jahan. Along one side of the Chandni Chowk a lovely garden was built by Begum Jahan Ara, a daughter of Shah Jahan.

123

Still full of wonder and surprise is a visit to the Taj Mahal, Shah Jahan's masterpiece, a memorial to his beloved wife Mumtaz Mahal. Red sandstone, widely used throughout Agra, is the chief material of the entrance gateway. This serves to make the sudden revelation of the ethereal white marble vista to the main pavilion, come as a delightful surprise.

124

***Shah Jahan riding in his Garden.* This Mughal painting gives an excellent idea of the planting that existed in the Mughal gardens in their prime.**

125

The Red Fort, Delhi built by Shaha Jahan adjacent to his new city of Shahjahanabad. Within the Fort are a series of charming pavilions from which are superb views down and along the Jumna River.

126

Looking across the great court of the Red Fort to a group of pavilions. They contain a delightful series of fountains, water basins and water chutes in white marble. The pavilions have a superb outlook over the Jumna River.

Constance Villiers-Stuart tells us, 'Fergusson, in his *Indian Architecture* says that the whole conception of the palace fort, with its entrance built to look straight down the Chandi Chauk (the moonlight market) with its trees and long canal full of running water, forms the finest approach to "the most magnificent palace in the East – perhaps in the world".' Constance Villiers-Stuart describes the gardens of the Red Fort in the following way:

> The entrance to the more private apartments is through the great court of Divan-i-Am (Public Hall Audience), behind which were originally several small garden courts, in front of various buildings Bernier saw these zenana quarters during the King's absence from Delhi, and says that 'nearly every chamber has its reservoir of running water at the door; on every side are gardens, delightful alleys, shady retreats, streams, fountains, grottoes, deep excavations that afford shelter from the sun by day, lofty divans and terraces, on which to sleep coolly at night. Within the walls of this enchanting place, in fine no oppressive or inconvenient heat is felt.
>
> Within the palace walls there were also two larger gardens, called respectively the Life-giving Garden and the Mahtab Bagh or Moon Garden. Looking at an old plan of the place before its partial destruction in 1857 showing the positions and names of these two gardens, one cannot but be struck afresh with the practical imaginative beauty of Indian garden-craft. These gardens formed two separate enclosures treated in one design: the first was a square of about five hundred feet, the second garden-court was the same length and about three hundred and fifty feet across. The larger of the two was laid out more particularly as a water garden. The centre was occupied by a big bathing tank with a baradari (a pavilion) surrounded by fountains in its midst. Four canals radiated from this reservoir, two of them being filled at their far ends, by streams running in through two charming little marble water pavilions. These buildings still exist, and were called the Bhadon and the Sawan, from the fact that their sheets of water falling over recesses for lights suggested the showers and lightning of the rainy season. Along the terrace walk on the ramparts ran a water parterre with a fountain in each of its little beds; this finished on the north side in

127

The Pearl Mosque or Moti Masjid, built by Aurangzeb in the Red Fort. He probably employed workmen trained by his father, Shah Jahan.

another larger building called Shah Burj. Here there is a lovely fountain basin and a deeply carved white marble waterchute.

One must have passed a long hot summer in the Indian plains to realise the full delight of this well-named garden – the joy of the life-giving dewy mornings, of the vivid transparency of the fresh opening flowers, and of the swim in the fountain-sprinkled pool; or the vast relief of the one cool hour before daylight dies, when the grey haze steals over the fields below the river terrace where the fountains play and creamy marble glows suffused with magic life. This was the Daylight Garden; while beyond seen through its central gateway, lay the Moonlight Court – dark trees, and a white night garden full of perfumes.[6]

As a direct result of the building of The Red Fort and the removal of Shah Jahan's court to Delhi, the seventh city of Delhi grew up on each side of the Moonlight Market boulevard, between the Red Fort and Fatehpuri Mosque. It reached its zenith during the early period of the reign of Aurangzeb who deposed his father Shah Jahan in 1658. From that time onwards it declined as did the power and influence of the Mughals.

Thirty-two years after the death of Aurangzeb, Shah Jahanabad was sacked and plundered by a Persian adventurer Nadir Khan and the inhabitants were put to the sword. He took away with him almost the entire wealth that had been accumulated by the Mughals including the Peacock Throne, priceless jewels like the Koh-i-Nor diamond, fine works of art, thousands of books and manuscripts and five hundred masons and carpenters.

Later under the protection of the British it regained some of its grandeur. But then came the Indian Mutiny, and the citizens of Shahjahanabad (now called Delhi) played a prominent role in trying to throw off the British yoke. After the defeat of the mutiny in September, 1857 when the British Army entered the city from Kashmir Gate, the mood was of revenge and reprisal: '. . . the city itself was sacked by the British Soldiers . . . the *Bombay Telegraph* reported: "all the city people found within the wall were bayoneted on the spot, the number was considerable, as you may suppose when I tell you that in some houses, 40 to 50 persons were hiding".'[7] From then on Shahjahanabad was ignored and neglected by the British. Though Delhi

128

A fountain in the Red Fort. White marble was used for the water play that cooled and decorated the buildings and courts.

became the capital of India, when New Delhi the seat of British Imperial Government was constructed no attempt was made to merge the new city with the old. The only changes made in Shahjahanabad were for the worse.

Ahmed Ali in his novel *Twilight at Delhi* describes these: '... The gutters which were deep and underground from the times of the Mughals to this day were being dug and made shallow and dirty water flowed very near the level of the streets ... worse than all the changes was the disfiguring of the Chandri Chowk whose central causeway was demolished and the expansive peepal trees, which had given shelter to the residents and the poor from the scorching rays of the sun, were cut down.'[8]

Today the Indian Government is concerned about what remains of the pavilions and gardens of the Red Fort. The arrangement of palaces, pavilions, and water parterres along the river terraces of the Fort are being sympathetically restored. They look impressive when viewed from the River and one is reminded of the fact that Shah Jahan would appear on the terraces before his subjects congregated on the river flats below; and that the river flats were also used for military reviews and elephant fights, a favourite entertainment of the Mughal Court.

But when we move across the Fort and look out upon Shahjahanabad it is a different story. Jagmohan, Vice Chairman of the Delhi Development Authority in the preface to his book *Rebuilding Shahjahanabad* sums up the views of many Indians today.

> ... I have sometimes been repelled by its congestion, its slums, its overgrown trade, and its apparent lack of pride. I have often grieved over the fate of about half a million people, jampacked into two square miles of area. Yet I have been charmed by its vast and strange antithesis, by the romance and tragedy of its past, by its milling crowds, by the pulsation and vigour of its life in the day time and by the poetry of its broken silence in the midnight. Its numerous monuments, old buildings, chhattas, colonnades, and its street patterns have excited and stimulated my imagination and brought to me the vision of the old life, its style, charm and grace.[9]

His book then outlined a fine, imaginative plan to restore and rehabilitate this ancient city. Let us hope that in the future it may be carried out.

Gardens of the Great Mughals by Constance Villiers-Stuart, an Edwardian classic, is still the best introduction to Indian gardens. Beautifully written, it is also illustrated by the author, slightly but delightfully, with those gentle amateur watercolours which our parents and grandparents loved to paint.

Constance Villiers-Stuart wrote and painted with insight, passion and enthusiasm. She was fighting to save the best of the Mughal gardens, just as we in Australia have had to fight to save representative colonial buildings. She had another object as well: New Delhi, the monumental headquarters of the British Raj, was about to be planned and built, and she was determined that it should reflect, in some way at least, the best of the Mughal tradition, and she succeeded. Sir Edwin Lutyens was undoubtedly influenced by Constance Villiers-Stuart when he created the neo-Mughal gardens of the Vice-Regal Palace. Certainly the most important landscape contribution to India made by

the British Raj, these were taken over by India on the departure of the British, and are now the gardens of the presidential palace.

Until Constance Villiers-Stuart wrote her book, of all the world's gardens, those of India with their background were the least known. In recent centuries, they had been subject to considerable aesthetically distressing mutilation. When Britain conquered India, the English or Natural Landscape School was dominating the thoughts and actions of the British landed gentry, from whom most of the military and civil leadership were drawn. These men, with the best intentions, tried to graft English landscape ideas on to the grounds and approaches to the great Mughal Palaces and tombs. The results have been, in many cases, unfortunate, to say the least. Even today, many of the Indian gardeners who are working in India, were also trained in the English garden traditions.

Our hope for the future is that the indigenous landscape architectural movement which is growing in the new India, will gain sufficient influence in time to stop some of the catastrophes which are still taking place: and that these professional Indian landscape architects will finally restore, sympathetically, the best of these masterpieces of landscape architecture to the splendour and grandeur which they possessed in the Mughal period.

Recently a most valuable contribution to knowledge and understanding of the Mughal gardens has been published: *The Gardens of Mughal India* by Sylvia Crowe, Sheila Haywood, Susan Jellicoe and Gordon Patterson.

PERSIA

Meanwhile in Central Asia a new dynasty, the Safavid, had replaced that of the Timurids. The greatest of the Safavids, Shah Abbas, fostered the arts, particularly architecture and garden making and constructed a new capital city at Isfahan in Persia.

The building of the new city of Isfahan was commenced in 1598 and was sited on the banks of the Zayandeh River, where a small settlement, and a Royal Palace and its gardens already existed. By 1670 the French jeweller Chardin was able to record that Isfahan 'had 162 mosques, 48 religious schools, 1,802 caravanserai (caravan hostels), 273 public baths and at least 600,000 inhabitants.'[10]

During the reign of Shah Abbas the interest of Europeans in Persia increased. A British Embassy visited the country in 1627, this being only the second ever to go to Persia. Many other countries also sent representatives to the court, including the Russians; between whom and the British, diplomatic competition was already developing. It was during this period that the general nomenclature which described all the arts of Central Asia as 'Persian' received considerable impetus.

At Isfahan the huge Imperial Square still exists, with the Mader-i-Shah Mosque as its most important focal point. The main gateway to the Square, the Ali Qapu Gate, is intact and some of the mural decoration is fine.

Unfortunately the scale and grandeur of the Square itself have been spoiled by the recent introduction of a long rectangular pool surrounded by a hedge and balustrade. Some magnificent vistas at ground level have been ruined, so that it is hard to visualise that Shah Abbas and his nobles used to play polo on the Square, and that it was the scene of great parades, tournaments and other popular assemblies. The Great Square, which is actually a rectangle nearly three times as long as it is broad, is terminated at its northern end by an enclosed market place. The latter is much frequented today by both Isfanese and visitors.

Of the gardens of Shah Abbas, the best preserved and most interesting which survives is the Chehel Sutun, at one time physically linked with the Imperial Square. Like the

129

Early in the seventeenth century another exciting garden development was taking place in Persia. Shah Abbas had established a new capital at Isfahan. A view down on to the garden of the Mader-i-Shah (the religious school of the Mother of the Shah) shows the central canal lined by chenars and with a secondary decorative reflecting pool.

130

The dignified entrance to the Masjid-i-Shah which is a focal point set at the top of The Great Square.

Square, the site is completely level and the arrangements of the garden court are quite formal. In the centre of the garden is a tall pavilion of considerable beauty. It has a high, three-storied open porch, supported by graceful soaring timber columns; the entrance foyer, also three-storied, is open to the porch, but otherwise fully enclosed. This foyer leads to a magnificent banquet hall with murals depicting scenes of the seventeenth-century court.

The combination of full enclosure, partial enclosure, and open porch, creates a delightful unity between pavilion and garden. An early lithograph by Flandin shows a view to the garden from the pavilion in the nineteenth century. In this drawing, the vista is closed by planting: at present it opens on to a long rectangular pond. The existing planting is linear, with plane trees as the dominant theme, and that these follow tradition is indicated by some huge logs in one corner of the garden – relics of the original plane trees. The whole precinct is fully enclosed by a garden wall, punctuated by decorative apses which terminate some of the vistas.

Also fairly well preserved in Isfahan, is the interesting garden in the main court of the Madrasa Madir-i-Shah, completed in 1714 as a religious school. The two-storied open-apsed enclosure to this garden is very lovely, and a handsome mosque closes the southern side. The courtyard is a simple four-square, with a long pool on the east-west axis, flanked by plane trees. Broad marble pavements break the simple rectangle into four lawn areas, some of which are now planted informally with standard roses.

Just to the east of this court, and originally forming part of the Madrasa Mader-i-Shah, is the modern Shah Abbas Hotel. The original building stands on one side of the main garden court, otherwise the hotel is designed in a modern, yet traditional style which is highly successful. We found it a comfortable and enjoyable headquarters, partaking of the atmosphere of the old-time caravanserai. Our description of Isfahan would be unfinished without some reference to the bridges which span the Zayandeh River. Two are contemporary with Shah Abbas; the third appears much older. The seventeenth-century structures are impressive in scale; massive in construction. The restrained simplicity of their outline is reminiscent of some contemporary architecture.

131

The Great Square, Isfahan. Long view to the Ali Qapu Gateway with the Masjid-i-Shah Mosque closing the vista. The simplicity and impressive scale has not been improved by modern additions.

132

The Chehel Sutun garden with its stately central pavilion was once linked physically with the Masjid-i-Shah.

133

The Chehel Sutun pavilion connects most successfully with the garden, as this nineteenth-century lithograph by Flandin shows. The outline of the Masjid-i-Shah can be seen just beyond the garden precinct.

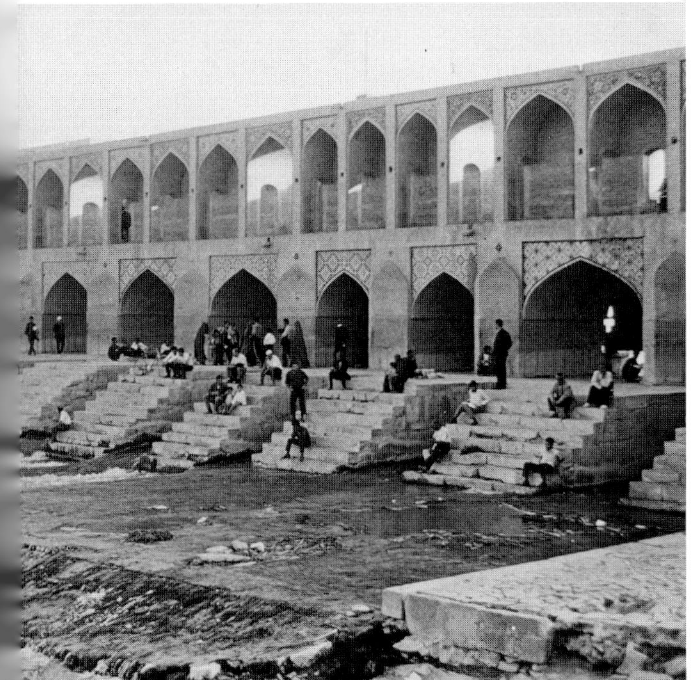

134

The approach to Isfahan was over this superb bridge that spanned the Zayandeh River. Lord Curzon, Vice-Roy of India, remarked, when he visited Isfahan: 'One would hardly expect to have to travel to Persia to see what may in all probability be the stateliest bridge in the world.'

Ssez y fery et
hurtay·
Et maintesfois
je escoutay
Se je orroye leans nulle ame
Le guichet qui estoit de charme

Front reluisant sourcilz voultis
Lentreoeil si nestoit pas petis
Ains fut assez grans par mesure
Le nez eut bien fait a droiture
Les yeulx eut vers comme faulcone
Pour faire envie a toutes hommes

CHAPTER 6

MEDIEVAL EUROPE AND THE ITALIAN RENAISSANCE

THE MIDDLE AGES

To most Western historians it appeared that the fall of Rome signified the end of the progress in the arts and sciences; that there followed a cultural blank of several centuries, which they liked to call The Dark Ages, before progress began again with the birth of the Italian Renaissance in the fifteenth century. They have also believed that the main source of inspiration for the Renaissance was a renewed interest in the long-forgotten cultures of Greece and Rome.

Expounded by Western historians until recent times, this concept grew out of the circumstance that the countries of Europe were constantly in a state of war with Islam from the seventh century. To Christian Europe, the Muslims were bitter enemies, ignorant, benighted heretics; and the idea that anything could be learned from the hated Saracen, was anathema.

This blinded most European scholars to the fact that the cultural advances made during the period from 3,500 B.C. to the seventh century A.D. in science, literature and the arts, had been absorbed by the Muslims from the countries they had conquered; and that this process had been assisted by the immense literature produced on these subjects, first by the Egyptians and afterwards by the Persians, Greeks and Romans.

This literature fell into the hands of the Muslims when they conquered Egypt and occupied Alexandria in the seventh century. The knowledge was absorbed into the new Islamic culture, which extended from Spain and North Africa across Asia to China; and which later, in a new form under the Mongols, embraced all China and part of Central Europe as well. Despite the Crusades this superb new Islamic culture did come to medieval Europe. It was both brought back by the Crusaders and deliberately sought by European Arabists.

> In the Middle Ages oriental studies (as they are called) were the only means of access to the most advanced science existing and many of the medieval translators from Arabic were natives of the British Isles; including Abelard of Bath who, working in Sicily and Syria in 1126 turned into Latin the astronomical tables of al-Majiriti and other mathematical translations. In this and the succeeding centuries came several English Arabists who worked mainly in Spain.[1]

135

A 'troubadour' with singers in a medieval garden, an illustration from *Le Roman de la Rose.* The spouting animal heads of the fountain are perhaps an echo from the Alhambra.

Most European scholars of the Renaissance and later, could not see things in this historic way. They were quite unable to understand the enormous contributions made to human knowledge by Islam and China. They were even unable to see that Roman and Greek ideas did not cease to exist with the fall of Rome but continued quite vigorously for several centuries in the East Roman Empire. Centred in Constantinople, where Christianity established its powerbase first under the Emperor Constantine in the fifth century A.D., this Empire transmitted Greek and Roman ideas to Europe through the re-conquest of the West by the Emperor Justinian. His East Roman Empire, soon to be known as the Byzantine Empire, embraced most of the Mediterranean in 562 A.D.

The schism that developed between Western Christianity based on Rome, and Eastern Christianity based on Constantinople, put even Byzantium beyond the pale. The very terms 'Far East', 'Orient' and so on, exemplify that fundamental insularity of outlook which it is so difficult for Europeans, even those who have the best intentions in the world, to discard. 'Europo-centrism' is widespread among scholars today – and shows itself in many ways – Europe being regarded as the centre of civilisation, as the vital nerve-centre from which all other cultures radiate.

This is why Greece and Rome, European countries and therefore among the 'goodies', are generally regarded in the West as the source of all Western culture by many people. At the time of which we are now writing China was too distant and unknown even to be considered as a source, and the great English scholar Francis Bacon, referred to it as 'obscure and inglorious'.

Yet the cultures developed by Islam and China had a profound effect on the Renaissance in Europe: and especially on landscape design and garden art. For this reason, we must examine in some detail the early developments that lead to the Renaissance.

The history of medieval Europe, so often misleadingly described as The Dark Ages, was by no means completely a dark age. Christianity consolidated and spread as a unifying force and superb gothic cathedrals were built as places of worship. New national states took shape, that were to play a decisive role in the future of the world. Independent City Republics appeared in Italy, and a little later in Flanders, Germany and Russia.

It is true that during the early medieval era, landscape design and garden making did become a lost art. The Christian monasteries, which alone in Europe carried on classical literature and scholarship, turned inwards. Affairs of the world were regarded as sinful and ugly. The thoughts of the monks were directed to things of the spirit and the expected future in Heaven.

The new feudal aristocracy was composed of military leaders who controlled their lands by force of arms. They were frequently illiterate; skilled only in the art of war. Europe was distracted by thousands of petty tyrants, no longer amenable to the restraints of law; perpetuating with impunity excesses of oppression and cruelty. Incest, murder and rapine were ordinary and familiar actions.

But gradually as trade and commerce grew new States were formed, and the merchants and guilds built free fortified cities. As a result of this more settled condition, an interest in garden art was rekindled. This was practised in small courts behind the high walls and battlements of the feudal castles or within the secluded precincts of the monasteries.

Inspiration came from tales that merchants and crusaders brought back to Europe from the East. They described beautiful 'Paradise gardens' which were common in the Muslim lands. Troubadours crossed the Pyrenees from Spain to France bringing tales of romance, the scenes of which were set in courtly gardens surrounded by the loveliness of flowering fruit trees, roses and singing birds. In this way, Arab garden culture overcame austere Christian prejudice and became the fashion in Europe towards the end of the medieval period. In the words of Eleanor Sinclair Rhode: 'Every illustration of a medieval or Tudor garden, every book in the whole range of medieval sixteenth and seventeenth century literature, whether English, French, Italian or Dutch, shows the dominant influence of the East.'[2]

The medieval garden closely followed Eastern precedent. The four-square plan with a central fountain became widespread in the internal cloistered courts of the monasteries. In herb gardens the chessboard arrangements of beds was adopted from Eastern counterparts, the dividing canals were often no longer needed for irrigation. But as late as 1572 Thomas Hyll points out that in Elizabethan times, beds were still sometimes watered according to the Eastern fashion.

The medieval garden also followed the Eastern precedent of combining use and pleasure, in the planting of orchard trees combined with flowers in the grass between. Oriental influence was apparent in the bathing pools which were used as a visual feature in many medieval gardens – though with the very different climate, one doubts if these were much used for bathing. These new 'Western' Paradise gardens are delightfully illustrated in manuscript paintings of the period, perhaps the best known of which is *Le Roman de la Rose*.

The main flow of ideas from the East came through the surviving East Roman Empire, later called the Byzantine Empire. Important streams came from Spain, across the

136

This Paradise Garden from the fifteenth century discloses its Eastern origin in the title.

137

Most of the medieval gardens were behind high walls in castles or monasteries. The Palace of the Popes at Avignon is typical. Behind the walls are a number of open courts.

Pyrenees to France, and eastwards to Italy. Another stream of influence was through Sicily and the Kingdom of Naples in Southern Italy.

The City Republics of Venice and Genoa in Northern Italy and Naples in the South, were the European go-between through which most of the knowledge was distributed. Quite naturally, they gained the most from it, and were the first to be influenced by the new knowledge from the East. It was in these city states (later to include Florence and the Papal State of Rome) that the Italian Renaissance came into flower.

VENICE

Venice became the most powerful, independent and prosperous of these new City States. She had a virtual monopoly of trade with Byzantium, due both to her strategic position across the trade routes from East to West, and to her island site which made for easy defence. She had her own navy and an efficient army of mercenaries and so controlled the sea route to Asia.

The pursuit of wealth by the Venetian merchants was completely ruthless. She was often at war with other City States of Italy, particularly Genoa. Her spiritual links with Rome were tenuous. To Byzantium she gave nominal allegiance. In the early thirteenth century Venetian power was greatly increased when she was able to exploit the power-vacuum created by the collapse of her erstwhile partner, the Byzantine Empire. Colin McEvedy describes what took place:

> The Empire Byzantium existed in a state of stagnant anti-climax for another quarter century, and when the expected end came it was a stab in the back from the fourth Crusade (1204). The villains of the piece were not the ignorant crusaders, who blindly cut out the heart of the dying Empire, but the Venetians, whose sly manipulations contrived the final perversion of the enterprise. Having begun by making the crusaders pay for their passage by taking for Venice the Dalmation town of Zara (1202) they ended by seizing all the islands that lay on the trade routes they now monopolized.[3]

Venetian citizens used the new wealth these acquisitions brought, and their subsequently increased leisure, to adorn and beautify their city. They engaged in a conscious programme whose purpose was to make Venice the finest city in the world.

Quite deliberately they developed the central city square of St. Marco around the cathedral and old campanile, and echoed St. Marco's magnificence with a number of secondary urban city open spaces. Artists and sculptors and other craftsmen whose work contributed to the adornment of the city, became honoured citizens.

A little later in the thirteenth century, when Venice was reaching the zenith of her power, the Polo family made their famous visits to China. These visits gave a most significant stimulus to the growth of the Renaissance. Marco Polo was a Venetian citizen, son of Nicolo Polo, a scion of a noble family with a seat on the Council which ruled the Republic. Nicolo and his brother Maffeo first journeyed to China as early as 1260, returning in 1269. In 1275 they made a second visit, taking the young Marco with them. Marco became a trusted administrator under the Emperor Kublai Khan, travelling throughout China on business of the court. After twenty years in China, he returned to Venice with a tremendous admiration for, and a thorough working knowledge of, all things Chinese.

Three very important innovations that Marco Polo brought back with him from China were printing, gunpowder and the magnet. They were to completely revolutionise the fields of literature, warfare, manufacture and navigation in Europe. In the words of Francis Bacon:

> It is well to observe the force and virtue and consequence of discoveries. These are to be seen nowhere more conspicuously than in those three which *are unknown to the ancients,* and of which the origin, though recent, *is obscure and inglorious,* namely printing, gun powder and the magnet. For these three have changed the whole face and state of things throughout the world, the first in literature, the second in warfare, and the third in navigation; whereat have followed inevitable changes in so much that no empire, no sect, no star, seems to have exerted greater power and influence in human affairs than these mechanical discoveries.[4] (Our italics.)

But as we have noted, Bacon, like most Renaissance scholars, gives no acknowledgement to China, the country of origin of all these inventions.

Marco Polo brought back to Europe information of great consequence to the arts.* And to the Venetians' desire to make their city the finest in Europe, he contributed much which was to guide them in their city planning. He described in remarkable detail Hangchow, the Sung capital taken over by Kublai Khan: 'At the end of three days you reach the noble and magnificent city of Kin Sai [Hangchow], a name that signifies "The Celestial City" and which it merits from its pre-eminence of all others in the world in point of grandeur and beauty, as well as from its abundant delights, which might lead an inhabitant to imagine himself in paradise'.

The city was frequently visited by Marco Polo who carefully and diligently observed and enquired into every circumstance respecting it, all of which he has recorded in his notes.

*Marco Polo's information about the art of food preparation as practiced by the Chinese, completely changed the food style of Italy. Spaghetti, canneloni, vermicelli, risotto, ravioli are the Italian equivalents of Chinese long soup noodles, spring rolls, short soup noodles, Sai Foon and fried rice ... yet today they are regarded as typically Italian and their origin is forgotten.

'According to common estimation, this city is a hundred miles in circuit. Its streets and canals are extensive, and there are squares or market places, which being necessarily proportioned in size to the prodigious concourse of people by whom they are frequented, are exceedingly spacious.' Polo then went on to describe the city planning in a wealth of detail: taking sixteen pages of close type, he covered layout, sanitation, communications by road and water, bridging, marketing, architecture, social structure and behaviour patterns, administration, trade organisation, manufacturing processes, and finally land-forming by artificial lakes and hills and the widespread use of gardens.[5]

From the point of view of landscape design in Europe, the most important innovation that came to Venice from China was landscape painting. Kublai Khan had inherited the culture of Sung China when it was at its peak, with landscape painting as its finest contribution. What Marco Polo had to tell, and show, helped give rise to the Venetian and Tuscan Schools of painting, that were later to influence all Europe.

In Marco Polo's time the Byzantine Greek painters were regarded as the great masters of painting. (As we have already discussed, these artists received considerable stimulus from Islamic and Mongol sources.) But now the painter Giotto went back to nature, re-establishing the dignity and beauty of living things. Petrarch the poet

138

Venice from the air. The harmonious quality of the buildings of Venice is clearly revealed when viewed from above. The Doge's Palace and St. Marco Square are right centre.

139

There is a strongly Eastern atmosphere about the buildings that line the canals of Venice. Even the dome of Santa Maria della Salute takes one's mind back to the mosques of Islam.

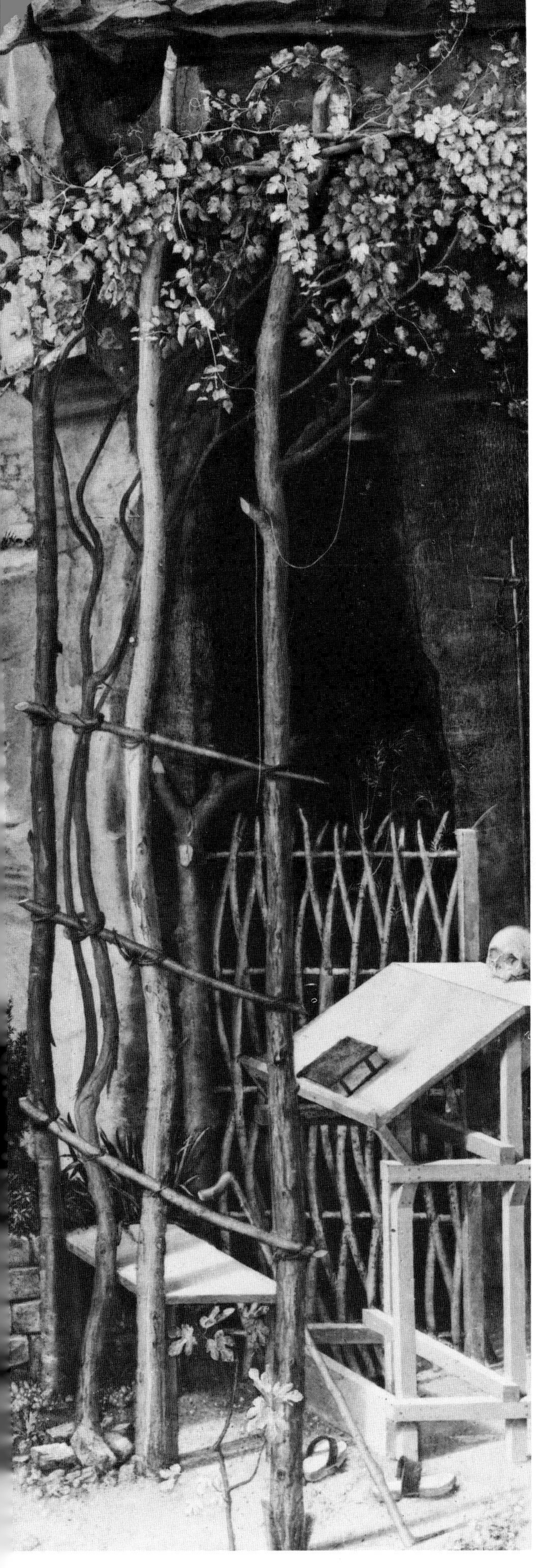

140

St. Francis in Ecstasy **by Giovanni Bellini. Like most of the landscape background to early Renaissance painting, the landscape in this picture was influenced by Chinese painting. In the detail shown here, the leaves of the trees illustrate their obvious origin in the bamboo.**

rejected the Christian concept of the corruption and ugliness of the world.

These painters and writers had their problems, because they were still earnest Christians. Petrarch, in pursuit of natural beauty as inspiration for his poetry, is said to have been the first fourteenth-century scholar who climbed a mountain to admire a view. A compulsive reader, he had with him his favourite book, St. Augustine's *Confessions*. Dipping into it while resting at the top of the mountain, he read: 'Men go about to marvel at the heights of mountains, at the huge waves of the sea, at the broad estuaries of the rivers, and forsake their own souls.' Petrarch tells us he started guiltily, all his joy in discovery gone. He never climbed a mountain again!

But the painters persisted. Flesh-and-blood human beings were depicted with real landscape backgrounds; until finally the Venetian painter Giovanni Bellini became intrigued with the concept of landscape painting as a thing in itself. A fine tribute to this special landscape quality of these early Renaissance paintings has been written by the poet W.B. Yeats:

Quatro cento put in paint
On backgrounds for a God or Saint
Gardens where a soul's at ease;
Where everything that meets the eye,
Flowers and grass and cloudless sky,
Resemble forms that are or seem
When sleepers wake and yet still dream,
And when it's vanished still declare
With only bed and bedstead there,
That heavens had opened.
Gyres run on
When that greater dream had gone
Cabert and Wilson, Blake and Claude
Prepared a rest for the people of God,
Palmer's phrase, but after that
Confusion fell upon our thought.[6]

The full impact of this early Renaissance painting on landscape design did not occur for several centuries when, through the French landscape painters Claude and Poussin, it became an inspiration for garden designers in England. But this is to anticipate our story: we are still examining the early developments which led up to the Renaissance in Italy.

The next stage in the unfolding of the Italian Renaissance was to take place in Florence.

FLORENCE

In 1433 Cosmo de Medici, the head of a powerful banking family in Florence, was exiled to Venice. He was most stimulated and inspired by what he found there.

One of the world's first true democracies, the free city of Florence was successful some years previously in defending itself from an invasion from the north by the tyrant Giangaleazzo who was based in Milan. The Florentines were inspired in their struggle by reading about the historic democracies of Greece and Rome. Once the threat of invasion was removed, Florence enjoyed a flowering of the various arts, seeking inspiration from Greek and Roman precedents.

In 1434 Cosmo de Medici was invited to return to Florence by the Signoria (the governing body of the city). He gave new leadership and considerable financial support to the cultural upsurge taking place there. In the succeeding years three generations of Medici enjoyed this position of leadership in Florence; the most famous of whom was Lorenzo the Magnificent, grandson of Cosmo. Under the patronage of the Medici all the arts flourished. Ghiberti, Donatello, Brunelleschi and Michelangelo excelled in sculpture; Masaccio, Pollaivolo, Francesca, Botticelli and Leonardo da Vinci as painters; Alberti and Michellozi led a school of architects.

Though ideas from China and the East had sparked off the Renaissance in Italy, Christianity still maintained a strong hold on men's minds and the clergy still played a leading role in society. Only a few daring spirits ventured beyond the limits set down by the Church and they, like Gallileo, were constantly frustrated by Christian dogma and finally were forced to succumb to ecclesiastical dictation.

The works of classical Greece and Rome being native to Europe, and having an emotional rather than an intellectual appeal, were more acceptable to the Church; and the sculptors, artists and architects were free to seek inspiration from these sources. As a result, Western scholars assume that the art of landscape design and garden making was also derived from classical precedents. What is forgotten by them, or perhaps just not understood, is that the strong flow of landscape ideas and garden inspiration that we have outlined, had been coming to Italy from the East for many centuries.

The formal Islamic garden culture fitted well with the forms of Greek and Roman architecture. This is the reason the inspiration for Renaissance gardens came from Muslim sources rather than from China. China's influence on European gardens did not mature until centuries later.

Italian gardens of the early Renaissance period were most strongly influenced by a Muslim garden tradition which came, paradoxically, not from the east geographically but from the west – that is, from Spain, which had been conquered and occupied by the Muslims many centuries previously.

One of the Italian gardens of this early Renaissance period that made a tremendous impact extending far beyond Italy itself, was Poggio Reale in Naples. It was built in the middle of the fifteenth century. At that time, Italy was not the unified country we know today: Naples was then under the domination of Spain. Aragon had conquered Naples in 1442 and for sixteen years, Naples was a part of the Kingdom of Aragon. When in 1458 it was made a kingdom again, the royal house of Naples was Aragonese.

Alphonso of Aragon, when he was Crown Prince, built the Poggio Reale; in it he incorporated the most advanced Islamic garden design which he knew from the royal gardens of Spain, which had been taken over from the Muslims. Poggio Reale was full of water devices derived from the Muslim gardens: water was used decoratively in cascades, water stairways, fountains and canals. Water was also used as a humorous device: at unexpected moments, sprays would suddenly spurt out, flooding the whole Court and courtiers, much to the amusement of those 'in the know'. 'The Spaniards brought with them the water stairway, the cascade and a positive passion for water in the garden.'[7]

When Charles VIII of France conquered Italy in 1495, he was greatly impressed with the Poggio Reale and endeavoured to emulate it in France, taking there the design ideas, including this infantile one of practical jokery which was to be much employed subsequently in the royal gardens of France, including Versailles.

The influence of Spain had already extended further throughout Italy when in 1455 Alfonso's private secretary, the Spaniard Alphonso Borgea, was elected Pope. This resulted in a great inflow into Italy of Spaniards who were equally familiar with the Alhambra and the Generalife at Granada, then a Royal garden; and they quite naturally also transplanted design ideas and water devices from these beautiful gardens of their homeland.

Financial advisers to the Holy See in Rome were the Medici family of Florence, who intermarried with the Borgea family; so garden ideas from Spain soon reached Florence from this direction as well.

In 1458 Lorenzo de Medici employed the architect Michelozzo Michellozzi to design for him a villa in Feisole outside Florence, as a rural retreat. It bears a strong resemblance to the Generalife in Granada. It occupies a steeply sloping site, the garden built in three terraces with the villa on the highest level. Like the Generalife, its terraces command superb views of the surrounding countryside. The garden courts are rectangular in shape and are laid out in a formal way. The Villa Medici is in a very good state of preservation today.

Such Muslim influences on the design of Italian gardens of the early Renaissance period are clear. Yet despite this very obvious kinship between the gardens of Italy and the earlier ones created by the Muslims in Spain, Derek Cliff-

141

Villa Medici at Fiesole. 'It bears a strong resemblance to the Generalife in Granada. The villa and its formal gardens are superbly related visually with the countryside beyond.

142

The Villa Medici from its main terrace. The high defensive walls of the medieval period have disappeared, replaced in this case by equally high retaining walls to support the terraces.

ord, in the introduction to his otherwise excellent work *A History of Garden Design* writes: 'For all practical purposes the history of gardening as an art begins at the Renaissance.'[8]

The theory that the Italian Renaissance gardens were derived from Greece and Rome is almost universal and has lone gone unchallenged. Mr G.A. Jellicoe, a most important landscape design authority who has made a superb contribution in the field of landscape architecture, subscribes to this view. In this study, *The Italian Gardens of the Renaissance,* he writes:

> Classical Roman planning upon which it (the Renaissance villa garden) is based technically, had pointed the way to an organisation of space which

> appropriately expressed the Roman sense of law and order. It is, however, to pre-Alexandrian Greece that the Italian garden owes its real origin. Although the Roman developed the technique of garden making through his villas, it was the Greek, who did not make gardens, who evolved the philosophy.[9]

He elaborates his theory a little later in the same essay:

> Geographically, the gardens of Italy are fairly evenly distributed northwards from Naples. As with the sister arts, the highest achievements centre on Rome, Florence and Venice. Each of these three great States made a separate contribution to garden art. It may be said in principle that the garden art of Rome was a kind of climax to the contribution of antiquity to the Western civilisation, the ultimate significance of which is seen in the Villa Lante at Bagnaia; that Florence illustrates man poised between the ancient and modern world as we know it today; and that Venice and the Venetian mainland are the spring board of the future.[10]

These quotations imply that the vast panorama of landscape design and garden art that had unfolded outside Europe prior to the Renaissance, was of little consequence to European designers.

We believe, on the other hand, that the gardens of Italy were derived from the Muslim gardens of Spain (which had been brought directly from Central Asia) and form a continuity in development which was natural and inevitable. In our opinion Mr Jellicoe, in outlining his arguments for the classical origins of the villa gardens, has reversed the order of historic development. We believe that the Renaissance started in Venice, then moved to Florence and reached Rome considerably later. Let us now examine the villa gardens of Rome and the arguments concerning their origins.

ROME

The earliest of the villa gardens of Rome was the Villa Madama. Built early in the sixteenth century, its original designer was Raphael. It has been frequently modified, but the basic structure remains and it bears remarkable similarity to the Villa Medici in Fiesole, built fifty years earlier. This villa, which we have just described was clearly inspired by the great Muslim garden of the Generalife in Granada. The Villa Madama is on a sloping site overlooking Rome and, as with the Medici villa and the Generalife, is terraced along the hillside.

The Villa Madama has been sympathetically restored by the Italian government and is now used to accommodate important State visitors. Because of its recent restoration, it is not overgrown like some of the early villa gardens. Its parterre and alleys may probably be closer to the original form than many of the other historic Italian gardens.

The best-known of the villa gardens of Rome, and perhaps the most typical of the Italian gardens of the Renaissance, are the Villa d'Este in Tivoli and the Villa Lante in the little country town of Bagnaia some forty miles north of Rome. Let us first consider these two renaissance villa gardens as Mr Jellicoe sees them – that is, as the direct products of classical inspiration.

Mr Jellicoe considers that the design of the villa gardens is derived from earlier Renaissance painting. In establishing the relationship between painting and garden, he first analysed the painting by Perugino, *Christ giving the keys to St. Peter,* in the Sistine Chapel: 'Behind the foreground figure is a great patterned space containing a domed building anchored to the earth by four porches penetrating the sky. On either side are classical triumphal arches, as it were, guarding the central building. There are no boundaries, and the landscape appears to contain all the splendour of human aspiration in time, namely, identity with a glorious past, leading to identity with the revolving universe itself.'[11]

The Villa d'Este he describes thus: 'It is overwhelmingly impressive, not only for its architecture, its disposition, and even its somewhat robust and crude detail, but also for the sound of its waters, which, to the visitor walking about it, varies like the tones of a gigantic organ. The true greatness of the Villa de'Este however, lies in *the fact that it is an indirect translation of Perugino's picture into reality, causing a sense of fulfilment to follow that of wonder.*'[12] (Our italics.)

Transferring to the Villa Lante, Mr Jellicoe continues: 'Finality and perfection in pure classical garden planning were reached in the curious and original Villa Lante at Bagnaia, about forty miles north of Rome. Begun a few years after the Villa d'Este, by Vignola and Guilio Romano, Lante has been felt by many to be the most contemplative of all gardens. It contains the elements of the Perugino picture, the place of the domed buildings being taken by the

143

Villa Madama, Rome. Designed originally by Raphael, it has been frequently modified and recently restored, but the basic structure remains. It is now used by the Italian Government to house important State visitors.

144

Looking from the upper floor of the Villa Madama to the parterre, tank and countryside beyond.

parterre, and Giovanni de Bolognia's fountain, and that of the classical arches by square twin houses.'[13]

We find unconvincing the way in which Mr Jellicoe selects certain architectural elements in the Perugino picture, and relates them to those in the gardens. Whereas the Islamic and Central Asian influences in the gardens of Villa Lante and Villa d'Este are everywhere clearly apparent, and require no exercise of the imagination to understand the connection.

Taking first the Villa Lante: the beautiful symmetrical plan, with its ascending terraces and descending water-play, is identical in conception with 'Persian' and Mughal gardens of Asia. But there is a reversal in the movement-pattern. In the typical Mughal gardens of Kashmir (which were based on earlier Central Asian prototypes) it will be remembered that the garden is entered from below and the terraces are gradually revealed step by step as the visitor moves up through them, culminating on the highest terrace with its backdrop of snow-capped mountains; and from the higher terraces was revealed a vast panorama terminated by the Dal Lake far below. Nishat Bagh is a typical example.

At Villa Lante, the major spectacle is experienced at once, in the main parterre and the Fountain of the Moors; then this focal point is re-experienced from above as the spectator moves up through the terraces.

145

Two delightful Cupids are poised above a little pool in a relatively informal precinct beyond the main avenues in the garden of the Villa Madama.

146

***Christ giving the key to St. Peter* by Perugino. 1503 A.D. 'There are no boundaries and the landscape appears to contain all the splendour of human aspiration of the time: namely, identity with a glorious past leading to identity with the revolving universe itself.'[11]**

147

This engraving of the gardens of the Villa d'Este in Tivoli near Rome, done in the sixteenth century by Duperac, shows the extreme formality of the original plan. We feel that time has been kind to the gardens: topiary has now been almost excluded and the giant cypresses which are the theme tree grow naturally and quite informally.

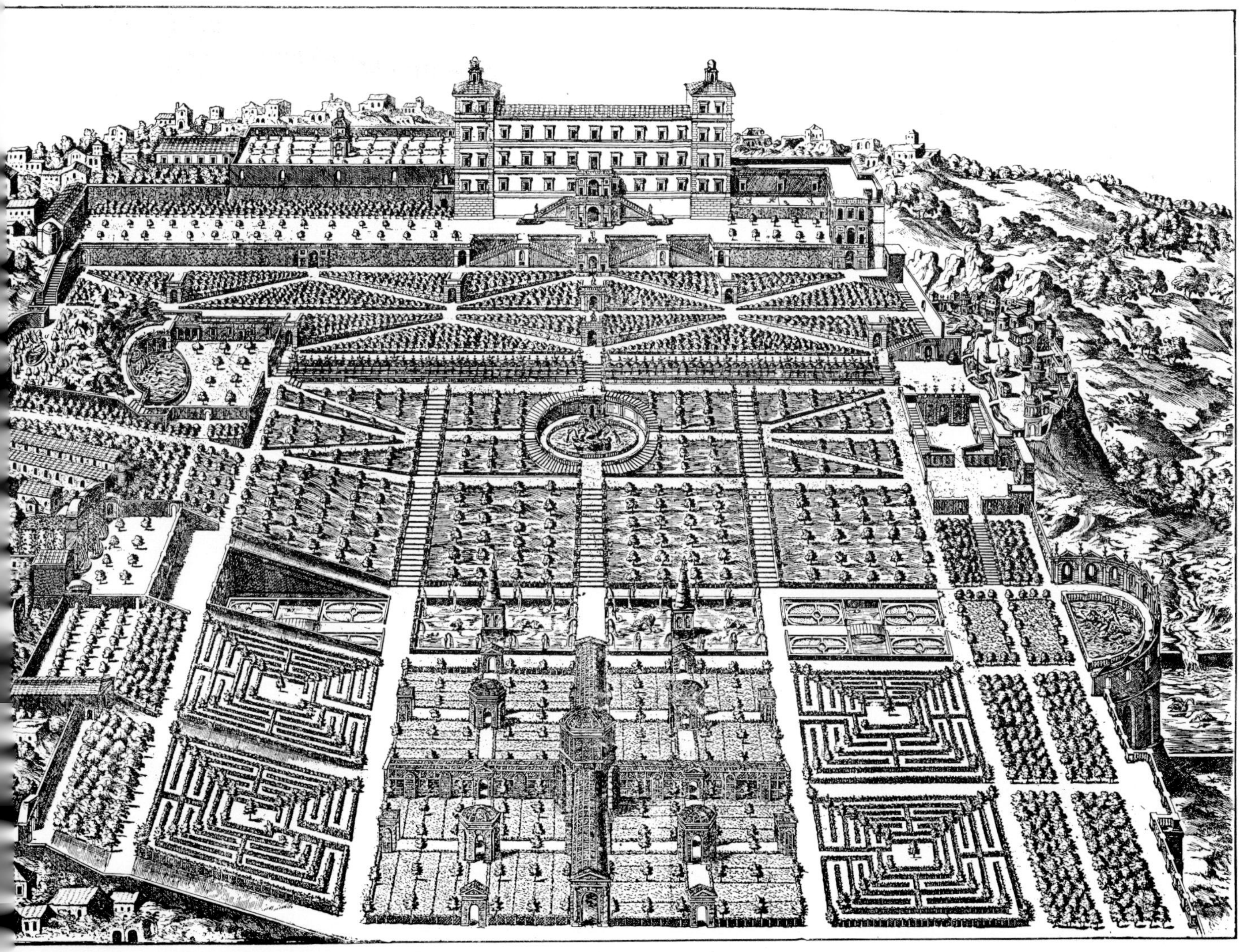

148

Terrace walk of the Hundred Fountains, Villa d'Este. The Villa and gardens were designed for Cardinal Hippolito d'Este by Pirro Ligorio in 1550. The whole is a superb water-garden, created by vast quantities of water diverted from the River Arno. It is a joy to wander through it in the daytime; and at night it becomes an enchanted place, with all the main fountains illuminated.

The Villa d'Este reverses the plan of the Islamic prototype in yet another way: here one enters the garden from above, the main climax of the Dragon Fountain is gradually revealed as the spectator moves down through the garden. A secondary climax, the Water Organ, is not seen until one reaches the lowest and final terrace; and it is brilliantly placed to one side, so as to close a magnificent cross-vista of reflecting pools.

So the Renaissance villa garden grew out of the medieval one which was itself inspired by Eastern precedents, especially the gardens of Islam. But with the growth of the City States in Italy which heralded the Renaissance, the flow of ideas from Muslim sources in Spain, Central Asia and the Orient, became a flood. The triumph of Christianity in Spain placed the whole vocabulary of the Moorish gardens at the disposal of the new garden-makers; and the conquests of the Mongols in Asia made available for the first time vast cultural resources from Central Asia and China. The Eastern influences distinctly appear in the overall plan and garden form, which can be directly traced to Central Asia, while the major water forms and water-play are clearly adopted from the Moors in Spain.

But the gardens of Renaissance Italy show great creative ability and are quite different from those created previously in the Muslim countries. In the arid countries where the Muslim gardens were built, water was scarce and very precious and its functional purpose in the garden could never be completely forgotten. In the gardens of Rome, where water was abundant, the use of water was prodigal –

149

The Dragon Fountain, Villa d'Este. This beautifully conceived focal point in the gardens is so contrived that it can be enjoyed from many levels – from above, from below and from the sides – as one moves up or down the terraced hillside.

especially in the Villa d'Este, where a whole river was diverted to provide a head of water for the fountains, and there appeared to be no limit to its use. Water was freed completely from its original functional purpose, and was employed solely for aesthetic effects. So in the Italian Renaissance gardens, we find water used with an exuberance, a joy, and an admirably consummate artistry which has never been excelled.

A second important innovation in the gardens of Rome, was the use of sculptural forms of men and animals. Such form was forbidden for religious reasons to the Muslims (though very occasionally it was used, as in the Court of the Lions in the Alhambra).

Superb combinations of water play and sculpture became focal points in the Renaissance gardens and cities of Italy. One of the delights of the Villa Lante is the use of graceful sculptured stone urns as a repeated motif up the stairs and along the balustrades. The long central water chute is made lively and gay by its sculptured framework. The vista down to the Fountain of the Moors, and going beyond to Bagnaia town, is very fine, while the central fountain itself is delightful, and an excellent example of the way in which Renaissance designers combined sculpture and water play.

Interestingly, the main theme-trees of both these Italian gardens are identical with those of Islam. The cypresses of the Villa d'Este repeat the theme of the Generalife and the Bagh-i-Eram; and the great plane trees of the Villa Lante recall the gardens of Persia and Kashmir (in India these plane trees are called Chenars). But in this case there was a classical precedent as these two trees were also popular in Roman times.

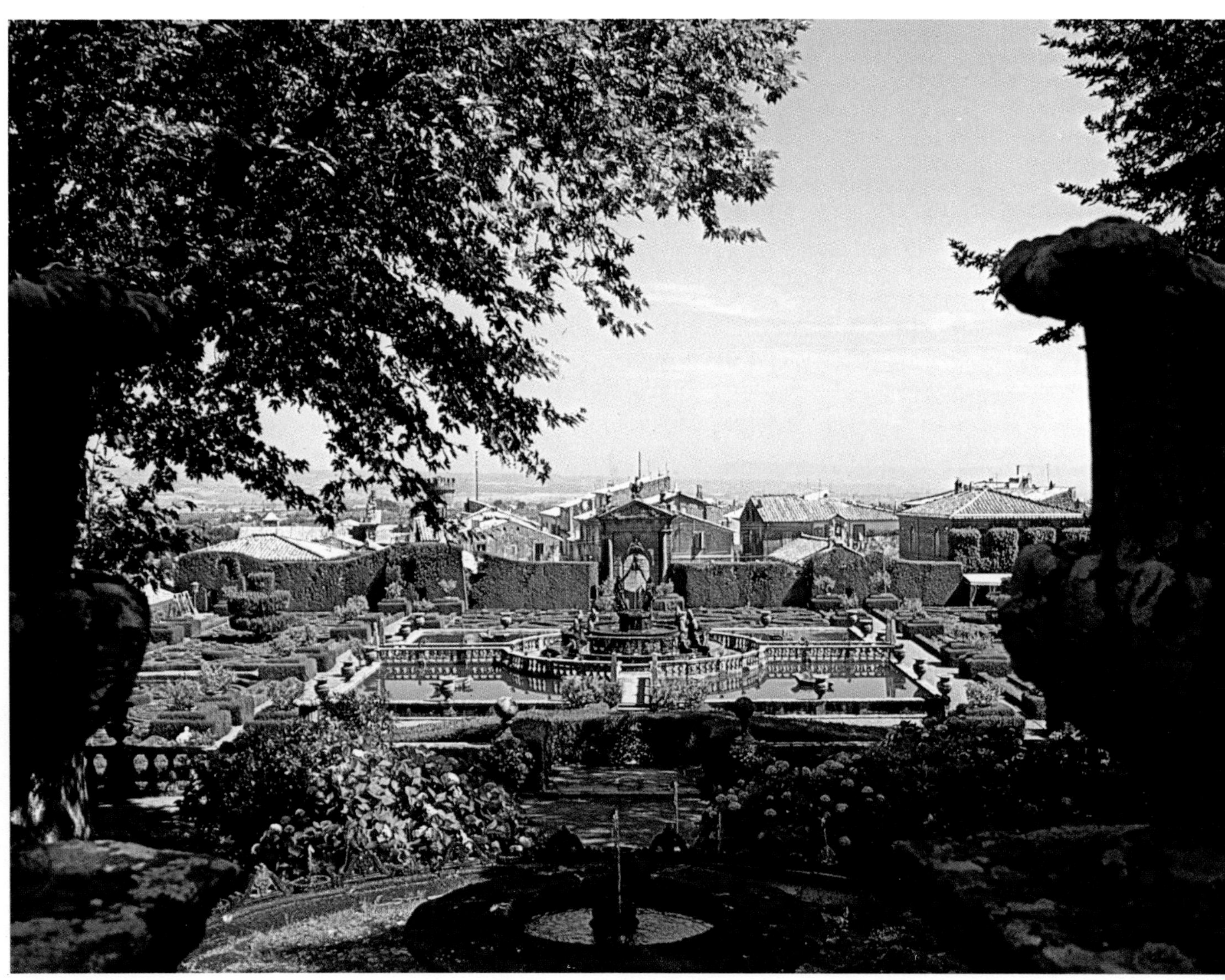

150

The Water Organ which terminates a cross-vista of reflecting pools on the lowest level of the garden of the Villa d'Este. This fountain is a fitting climax to a glorious garden composition which is developed down an unusually steep site.

151

There were many beautiful villa gardens built at the time of the Renaissance in Italy. Villa Lante is acknowledged by most to be the finest. Here we look past the twin pavilions over the quadrado, the *tour de force* of the garden, to the town of Bagnaia beyond. The view is superbly framed by plane trees – the theme tree of the garden.

A not-so-desirable technique which the Italians did take from the gardens of the early Romans, was the use of topiary. Most of the garden designers of the Renaissance were architects and sculptors. They adopted topiary with enthusiasm as a formal extension of their architecture, on a horizontal plane. Trees and plants were usually cut and clipped into mathematical figures, as can be seen from early engravings and from many surviving examples.

We have no love for topiary and consider that its abandonment has enhanced the attractions of some of the Renaissance villa gardens such as the Villa d'Este.

About the same time as the Villa d'Este was being constructed in Rome *c.*1550, a quite different villa was being built on a low hill near Vicenza, in the territory of the Venetian Republic. Called the Villa Rotonda, it was designed by the architect Palladio. Inspired by 'landscape painters' such as Giovanni Bellini, Palladio projected the design of his villa out into the natural landscape. This made it is a forerunner of the natural school of landscape gardening which however, would not come to perfection until two centuries later. But at least the natural landscape, though for long not to be incorporated directly into garden design, was recognised as having aesthetic value in itself . . .

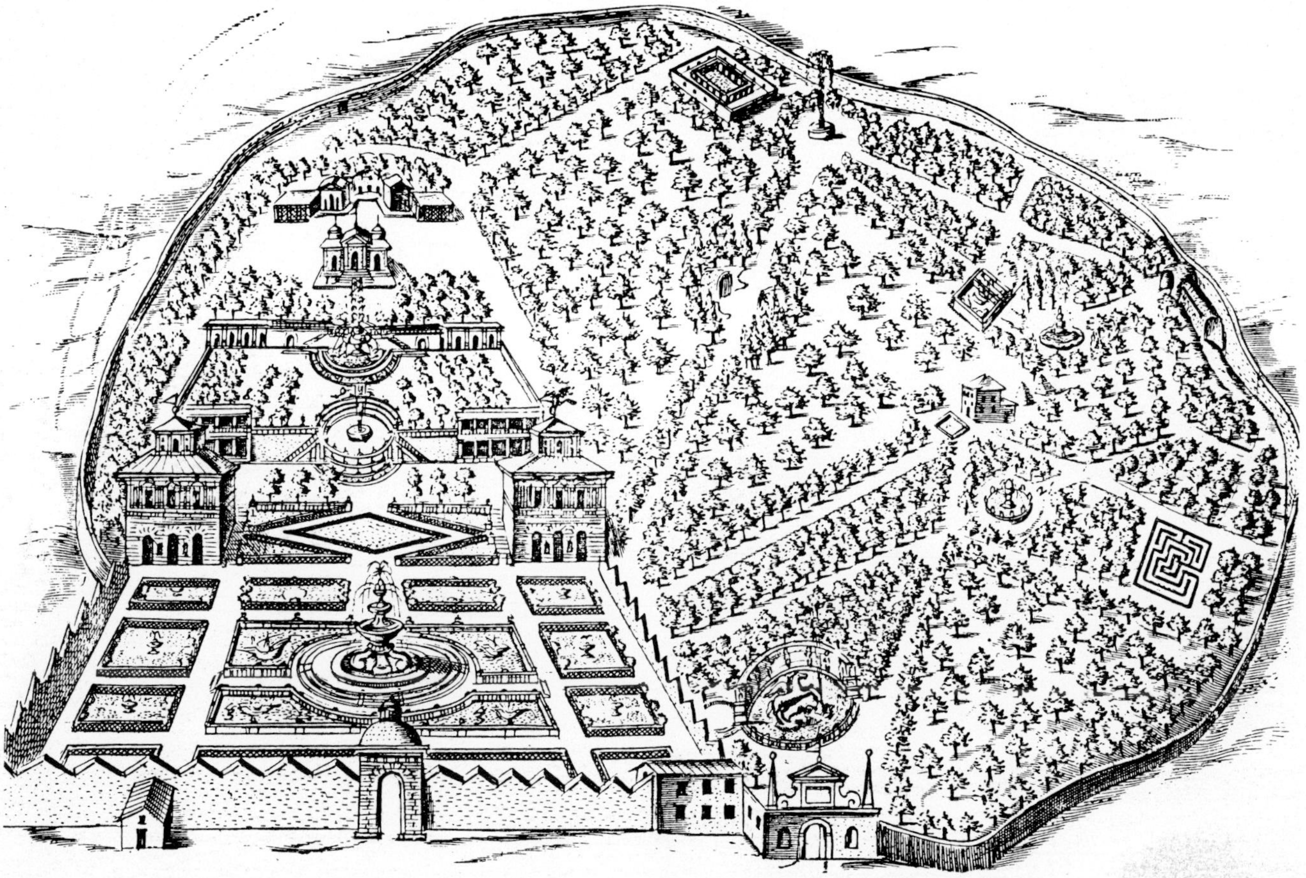

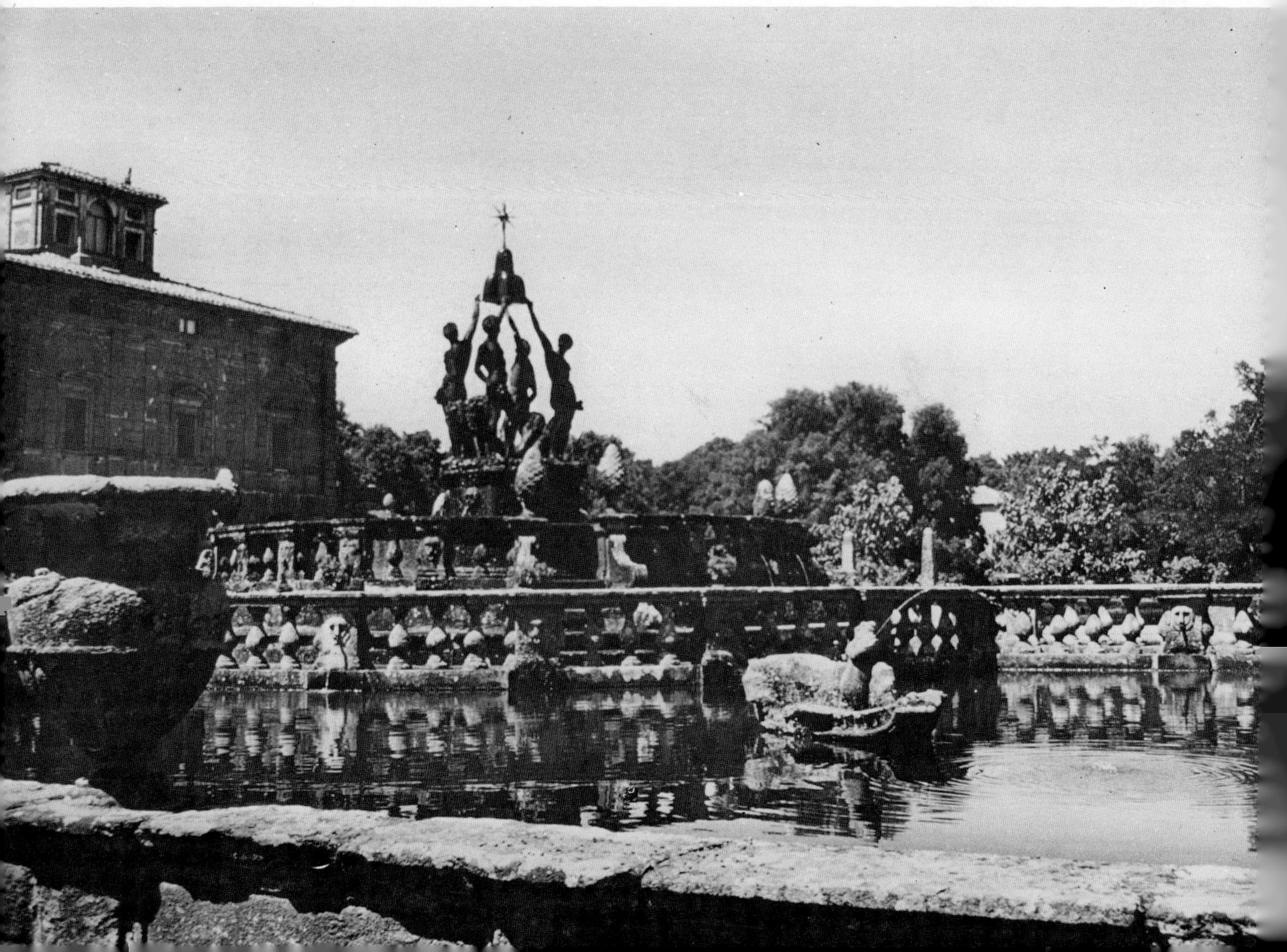

152

An engraving of the gardens of the Villa Lante. The beautiful symmetrical plan with its ascending terraces and descending water-play is identical in conception to the 'Persian' and Mughal gardens of Asia. This garden was designed by Vignola and Guilio Romano.

153

Villa Lante. View across the quadrado to one of the twin pavilions that flank the approach to the top of the garden.

154

Sculptured urns give both strength and lightness – like ballet dancers – to the terraces and stairways of the Villa Lante. Here they combine effectively with the spreading plane trees in a cross-vista above the pavilions.

155

Villa Lante. The water channel in the upper garden is a happy combination of sculpture and water-play.

RENAISSANCE OPEN SPACE

Another landscape form to which the Renaissance gave special significance and additional quality, was the city square. A contribution of immense consequence is made by Venice with the Piazza San Marco and its Piazzetta, the latter leading to the lagoon-like entrance of the Grand Canal. Piazza San Marco is surely one of the finest urban open spaces in the world.

San Marco Square as it is today, was created quite deliberately from a much smaller area, hardly larger than the present Piazzetta – 'the result of a long series of agonising decisions, constantly aiming at perfecting the squares.'[14] The free-standing Campanile was achieved only by pulling down the whole of what constituted the library and re-building it further south. The Campanile is delightfully echoed by the strong vertical note of San Georgio Maggiore built on an island in the lagoon, and which terminates the water vista visible from the San Marco Piazzetta.

Edmund Bacon in his *Design of Cities* points out that all the less important squares throughout the city were finally developed to be complementary to San Marco, so that all the citizens should feel an affinity with it, strengthened by their local experience.

The influence of the East on the creation of San Marco Square is undoubted. The merchant traders of Venice brought back to their city news of the magnificent urban spaces which they had seen in the East, and which were quite unknown in medieval Europe. (The contribution of Marco Polo must not be forgotten.) This knowledge was gradually assimilated and adapted to the needs of the Venetians' own city.

156

A morning scene in San Marco Square. The magnificent free-standing Campanile is 'the result of a long series of agonising decisions'.[14] All the buildings in the complex harmonise beautifully though they belong to many different periods and styles.

157

To the Grand Canal from the St. Marco Piazzetta. The Doge's Palace on the left has a superb facade fronting on to the Piazzetta. Notice how the Campanile on the Island beyond, echoes the main Campanile of St. Marco.

158

The Renaissance in Italy produced many fine examples of well-designed and organized urban open space. This is the Piazza della Signoria in Florence.

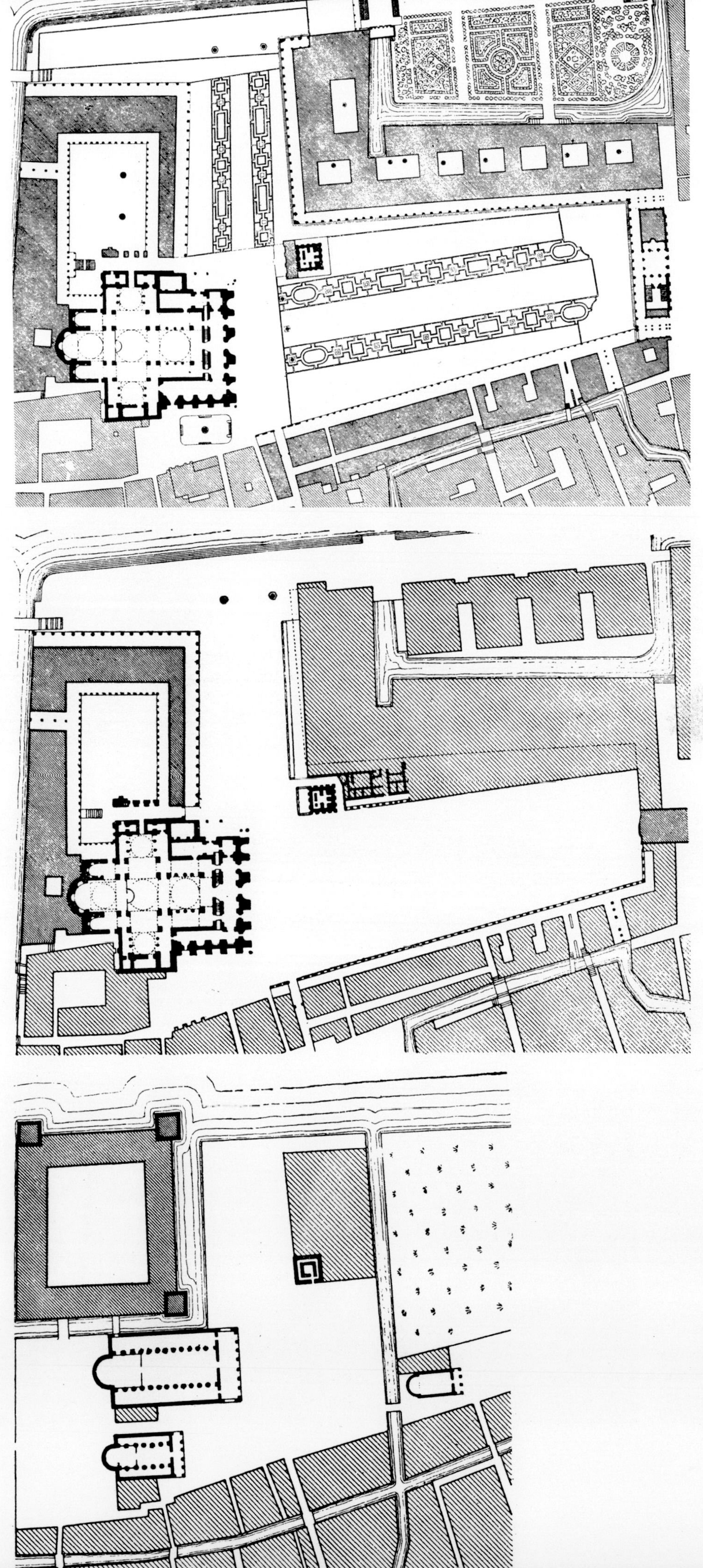

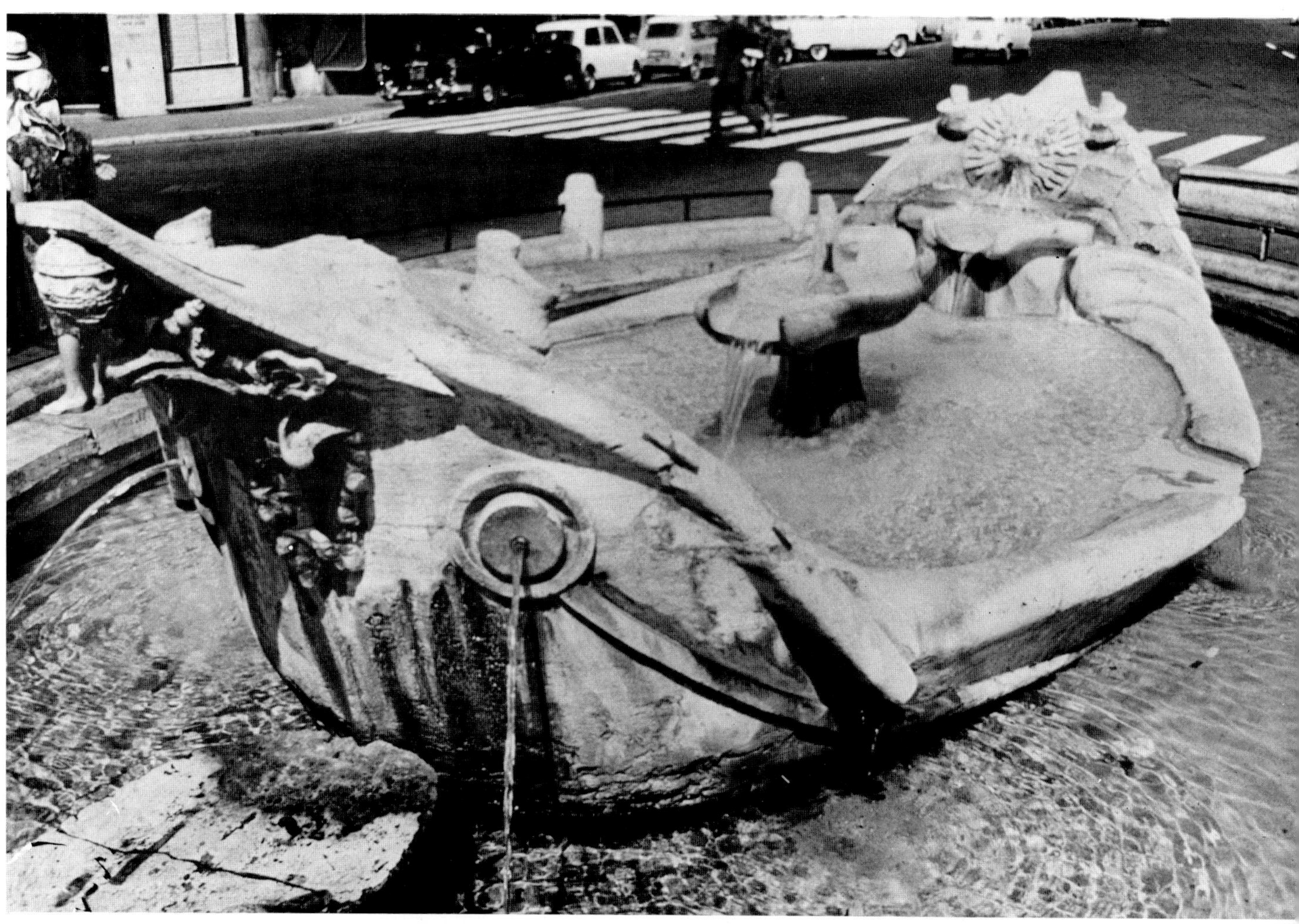

160

The Barcaccia, designed by Bernini the Elder, is in the Piazza di Spagna at the foot of The Spanish Steps in Rome. Though the boat is of stone, it appears to float in the surrounding pool. The central jet was probably higher when it was first constructed, as it would then have the appearance of a mast and sail.

159

These plans from *Design of Cities* by Edmund Bacon illustrate clearly the painstaking care and unusual expense that went into the creation of the masterpiece of St. Marco.

Living in the second half of the twentieth century, we find it difficult to appreciate fully the tremendous impact of such new ideas on people of the early Renaissance period. For two or three generations or more today, we have had access to knowledge of the art, the science, the way of life of every country of the world. Through books, films, radio, TV and newspapers, we in the West have come to know the masterpieces of other lands, and it is not necessary to travel to them *in situ* to experience them. If we do, we are already so familiar with them that their actual presence can no longer evoke the surprise and create wonder in us as it could in medieval man.

Superb city squares were developed in Florence and the other city states, and also in Rome, especially during the Baroque period. Fountains became important adornments to these squares. This was particularly so in Rome, which became a city of fountains. They ranged in scale from small, delicate creations such as the Fountain of the Bees by Gianlorenzo Bernini, to the very large concept of the Trevi Fountain.

Probably the best known and most popular of all the fountains of Rome built during the Baroque period, is the Trevi Fountain. This was designed by Nicolo Salvi. The sculptural group seems to grow up out of informal water-washed stone that fringes a large pool at its base, forming a most satisfying link between it and the architecture behind.

The Barcaccia boat fountain at the base of the Spanish Steps was designed by Petro Bernini, father of the more famous Gianlorenzo (Bernini the Younger). The latter was most prolific. Among his designs is the Fountain del Tritone in the Piazza Barberini within sight of the Fountain of the Bees. Today the square is swamped by vehicles, parked

161

Close-up of the Fontana del Tritone (Tritan Fountain), one of the finest designed by Bernini the Younger to decorate the squares of his beloved Rome.

and moving, so that the former relationship between the two fountains is obscured. The magnificent proportions of the Piazza Barberini are no longer impressive, and the beauty lost in a seething mass of motorcars.

Two other fountains designed by Bernini have been more fortunate: these are in the Piazza Navona, where vehicular use of the square is restricted and much of the space reserved for pedestrians. The scale of the centrepiece, Fontana de Fiumi, is finely proportioned in relation to the square itself. Flat sheets of water which pour from the mouth of the dolphins, made a delightful detail. Another fountain modelled by Bernini, Fontana del Moro, uses reed-like trickles which present an amusing contrast to the fountain's centrepiece.

Another significant Renaissance contribution to spatial design, which influenced landscape architecture both in gardens and in urban settings, was the handling of changes of level. It is a far cry from the heavy, solid sloping ramps of Queen Hatchepsut to the graceful steps and stairways seen in many Italian terraced gardens. But a supreme achievement is the Spanish Steps in Rome. This flowing open space of constantly changing levels achieves a grand scale which yet retains human proportions.

The fanciful Bacaccia Fountain by Bernini the Elder can be seen at the bottom of the steps. The Fountain was made in 1629, but the Steps were not completed in their present form until the beginning of the eighteenth century.

When the authors last climbed the Spanish Steps in 1969, hundreds of Italians and visitors thronged the area. Impromptu singing and guitar-playing were taking place at different levels, the atmosphere was gay and informal. Modern youth had brought this centuries-old precinct to life again. The experience was joyful and unexpected.

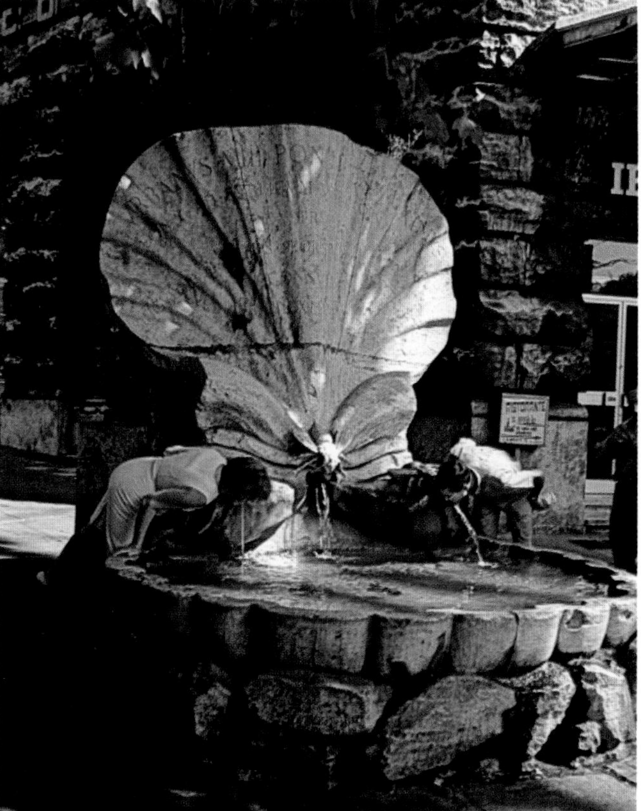

162

The combination of sculpture with the play of water was one of the finest contributions of the Italian Renaissance in the field of landscape design. Bernini the Younger made an outstanding contribution to the public squares in Rome. This is the Piazza Barberini viewed across the square to the Fontana del Tritone. Busy motor traffic and commercial signs now obscure the beauty of the Piazza.

163

Fontana della Api (Fountain of the Bees) in the corner of the Piazza Barberini, Rome. A delightful little fountain by Bernini the Younger, obviously a favourite drinking place for people of the district. Ray found the water delicious.

164

Piazza Navona looking over the Fontana del More to the centrepiece of the Fontana dei Fiumi. Fortunately most of this square is a pedestrian precinct so that one can view it comparatively free from motor vehicles. It is a lovely square, adorned by three fountains: Fontana More on the south, by pupils of Bernini; and on the north, the Fountain of Neptune, a modern addition.

165

A close-up of Fontana del More. Fine trickles of water contrast amusingly with the gushing streams of Fiumi.

166

Fontana dei Fiume, the centrepiece of the Piazza Navona.

167

Detail of the Fontana dei Fiumi. The sparkling, gushing, translucent water is consumed by the stone Dolphin gambolling in the pool below.

168

Fontana di Trevi, a popular gathering-point for visitors to Rome who wish to return and enjoy its glories again. The sculptured figures seem to emerge from the massive rock base. It was designed by Nicole Salvi.

169

Trinita de Monti, better known as The Spanish Steps, Rome. A glorious flowing open space of changing levels. One of the most popular assembly points for visitors to Old Rome. The umbrella'd flower stalls add animation to the scene.

170

Halfway up The Spanish Steps, this scene shows how much they are appreciated today. Masterly handling of changing levels was one of the qualities of Renaissance designers.

THE DECLINE OF THE RENAISSANCE IN ITALY

The growth of the city states in Italy and the emergence of a 'capitalist'-type democracy in Florence, with its freedom of thought and emphasis on the powers of man in an expanding universe, had effects far beyond the shores of Italy. A new approach to history, science and the arts developed, not dependent on God-given revelation and miracles. Based on humanistic principles, exact, critical, it spread from Italy to the Netherlands, Germany and England, becoming the basis of the Reformation and a new Age of Enlightenment.

The Papacy became alarmed and so did the national states of Spain and France, which had become the most powerful in Europe. France, previously united by Louis XI, and now led by his son Charles VIII, had a ruling class and powerful army which had been almost untouched by the Renaissance. Prompted by Lodovico il Mora of Milan, Charles decided to advance his claim to the Kingdom of Naples, and invaded Italy in 1493 with Lodovico il Mora as an ally.

Florence was in decline. Lorenzo the Magnificent was dead, succeeded by his son, a weak young man; and a Dominican friar, Savonarola, was leading a powerful counter-reformation. Florence, Naples and Rome were suspicious of one another and Florence, being isolated, was easily overcome and occupied by the French army in 1493, this leading to the sack of Rome in 1527.

Venice and Genoa were also declining in power due to the opening up of new sea routes to the East in 1486 and the discovery of America in 1492, both of which had a catastrophic effect on their trade supremacy.

After the fall of Rome, Italy became subject first to Spain and then to France; and Italy's contribution to the Renaissance gradually declined. Weakened politically, the Catholic Church struggled to reassert its spiritual and temporal supremacy. With the Council of Trent in 1583, the Counter-Reformation became effective in France, Spain and Italy; the Papal State regained much of its power; and the spirit of democracy and independent enquiry was ruthlessly suppressed by the Inquisition. The Late Renaissance artistic movement called Mannerism and Baroque was a consequence of this new situation.

MANNERISM AND BAROQUE

The garden most expressive of this movement is a large park near Bomarzo, named Villa Orsini after the family who built it and who were strong supporters of the Church. The garden is a most revealing one as it shows the attitude of the Counter-Reformation to the influences both of China and ancient Rome. The park of the Villa Orsini is peopled by primitive giants shown as intent upon the destruction of Christian order. Sacred turtles and dragons (symbolic of China) combine with Greek statues and a Roman centurian being attacked by an elephant. The effect is macabre. Classically-inspired buildings are thrown askew. 'A Christian tempietto on high ground alone gives assurance of salvation from these terrible forces.'[15]

171-72

Strange creatures in the garden of the Villa Orsini, near Bomarzo, belong to the Counter-Reformation. We believe the garden is allegorical, glorifying Christian dogma and decrying the influences from the Orient and the classical past that gave rise to the Renaissance. A sacred turtle and dragons (symbolising China) combine with a Greek statue and a Roman Centurian, attacked by an elephant. Classically-inspired buildings are thrown askew by a group of giants. 'A Christian tempieto on high ground alone gives assurance of salvation from these terrible forces.'[15]

A number of other interesting villa gardens were built throughout Italy during the period of Mannerism, including the Boboli Gardens of the Pitti Palace, the Villa Capponi and the Villa Gamberaia in Tuscany; and the famous island complex of Isola Bella on Lake Maggiore. Many excellent illustrations and descriptions of them are readily available in existing publications, so we shall not elaborate on them here, as they do not belong to the main stream of garden design.

One garden idiom which came to fruition in Italy in this period was the grotto, which flourished in Italy at the beginning of the sixteenth century and quickly spread to France. Grottoes often served as theatres until these were deliberately designed in garden form. A common characteristic of grottoes is the grotesque ornament. Grottoes were sometimes designed as separate structures but often were in ground-floor rooms or under terraces. A Chinese prototype of the grotto is described by Hsi-Ma Kuang in his garden of the eleventh century.

CHAPTER 7
THE NAVIGATORS

The flow of East Asian ideas by land which were brought to Europe by Marco Polo, introducing printing, navigation and gunpowder, and thus in part giving rise to the Renaissance, tended to peter out in the fifteenth century.

The land route to China, made relatively easy by the control of Central Asia and China by the Mongol Empire of Genghis Khan and his immediate successors, was disrupted by the fragmentation of the Mongol control which occurred after the death of Kublai Khan. China freed herself from the Mongol yoke by the establishment of the Ming dynasty. Central Asia separated into three: the Empire of the Golden Horde in the North West; the Empire of the Ilkhans in the South West; and the Eastern Mongols driven north by the Ming Chinese.

The Ilkhans were converted to the Islamic faith, but Islam itself was in a condition of disunity. A Turko-Ottoman Emirate had over-run the Eastern Mediterranean, destroying the remnants of the Byzantine power, and crossing the Hellespont, to pose a serious threat to Europe. Northern India was first controlled by a series of short-lived Sultanates. Then, by one of the curious quirks of history, pressure on Europe was partially relieved by the rise of Timur (Tamerlain) in Central Asia.

In Europe itself, quite independent of Italy, far-reaching changes were taking place. On land, Isabella and Ferdinand had completed the expulsion of the Moors from Spain; Henry the Navigator carried the Crusade against the Moors by sea around the coast of Africa; Vasco da Gama rounded the Cape and established a sea route to India (1486), and Christopher Columbus discovered America (1492).

Thus by the end of the fifteenth century the loss of the land link with East Asia and India was compensated by two sea links; the one pioneered by the Portuguese via the Cape and India (closely followed by the Dutch, English and French); the second to the Philippines via America, controlled by Spain. Cultural ideas from India and China now came by sea to Europe, especially Portugal, to play a new role in the development of landscape design and garden art.

Central Asia also made a contribution. Clavejo represented Castille at the court of Timur, sending back detailed descriptions of the gardens built at that time in and around

173

The gardens of Portugal have a special character due to the fact that the Portuguese were the first great navigators of Renaissance Europe. Quinta Fronteira. A close-up of the sculpture and murals. A stairway leads to a promenade above the tank, where sculptured portraits of the Kings of Portugal are arranged in niches. The tank in these Portuguese gardens came from India.

Samarkand. Later Portuguese, French and English navigators and administrators reported in a similar way, from India at the time of the Delhi Sultanate and during and after the reign of Akbar the Great.

The most significant landscape developments following the Italian Renaissance took place in Portugal, Spain and France. Though there was considerable interchange between these countries from the time of the medieval troubadours, each of these three countries received considerable independent influences which were the result of differences in historical background, and variations in the tempo of their internal political changes.

Spain never became completely modern nor learned to think or believe in a non-medieval way. France, on the other hand, notably under Louis XIV, became the cultural centre of the European world, receiving inspiration from Italy and Spain and also from India and China. Portugal, due to her initiatives in navigation, made the most immediate significant contributions. So we shall go to Portugal first.

PORTUGAL

For Portuguese garden designers, Islamic garden art was a living tradition. Portugal had been a Moorish province from 711 A.D. until the eleventh century and even today, Moorish fortresses are some of the most impressive and important historic monuments in Portugal. Her southern areas had not been re-conquered until 1139 A.D. when the preponderance of power in both Spain and Portugal was in Christian hands.

So that in Portugal in the late fifteenth century the Islamic garden culture was the indigenous one, and the classical influences from Italy were exotic and foreign. A third important stream of ideas came to Portugal from India and the Far East, brought by the Portuguese navigators who were the European pioneers into these regions by sea. As a result, Portuguese gardens of the sixteenth century are unique. They adopted from India large bodies of formal water closely associated with buildings. These were called tanks in India and they are still called tanks in Portugal today. The best surviving examples are a group of small palaces or villas in and around Lisbon. These include the Quinta Bacalhoa, the Quinta dos Torres and the Quinta Fronteira.

The earliest, Quinta Bacalhoa, has a large tank situated some distance from the villa separated from it by a long parterre. The tank is open on two sides; on the third, a long pavilion opens on to the water; a high wall closes the fourth side. The strong Indian influence is obvious and is emphasised by the coat-of-arms, dated 1565, of the father of the original owner – the Duke of Alboquerque, who played a prominent role in the Portuguese penetration of India. The villa was commenced in the fifteenth century and was later presented to the King of Portugal. It has recently been sympathetically restored by the present owner, Mrs Stoddart, a wealthy American.

Built in the sixteenth century, Quinta dos Torres has a large square tank directly associated with the main facade of the villa, so that this is reflected in the pool. In the centre of the elevated pool or tank is a delightful little pavilion. The whole concept of this composition is clearly inspired by the Islamic garden designs in India, though the pavilion's detail is classical.

The Quinta Fronteira is a small palace, originally as now, belonging to the Marquis of Fronteira. At Fronteira the use of the tank and the placing of reflecting pools directly in front of buildings, though new to Europe, are, as we have found, characteristic of Indian gardens. There are many other details of Fronteira which show eastern derivation; one of which is the extensive use of azueljos or coloured tiles, which are from Islamic sources but in this instance, clearly derive from the Moors.

The word 'azulejos' is of Arab origin. 'Tiles indeed are everywhere in the Peninsula, but they are thicker ... in Portugal. They came with the Arabs from Asia Minor where this sort of pottery was common with the Persians, and the choice of colour after centuries of naturalisation in Spain is that of the Eastern Bazaar.'[1]

174

Quinta Bacalhoa near Lisbon. Across the 'tank' looking to the unusual triple pavilion which links directly with the water. Built by a son of the Duke of Albequeue, it illustrates how he brought this device of relating buildings to water, from India back to Portugal. The word 'tank' used in Portugal to describe these water-bodies, came from the same source.

175

Quinta Bacalhoa. Looking through the arcaded water pavilion, over the 'tank' to the garden and orchard beyond.

176

Quinta dos Torres, Portugal. Here we find a large tank directly associated with an important facade of the villa. A delightful central pavilion seems to float on the water. Quinta dos Torres was built in the sixteenth century.

177

The Sahehon-i-Dari, Udaipur. An Indian pavilion used in a similar way to that of the Quinta dos Torres. Water falls in a curtain from the dome of the pavilion and fine jets spray into the pool from around its edges.

178

Quinta Fronteira. An elegant small palace belonging to the Marquis of Fronteira. Both the palace and the gardens are beautiful. A high garden terrace commands a view of Lisbon and here we look from this terrace over a delightful tank adorned with sculpture and murals of Azueljos (coloured tiles). A hint of the view to Lisbon is seen on the left of the picture.

179

A small decorative pool on the upper terraces of Quinta Fronteira, Lisbon. An Indian idiom in Classical guise.

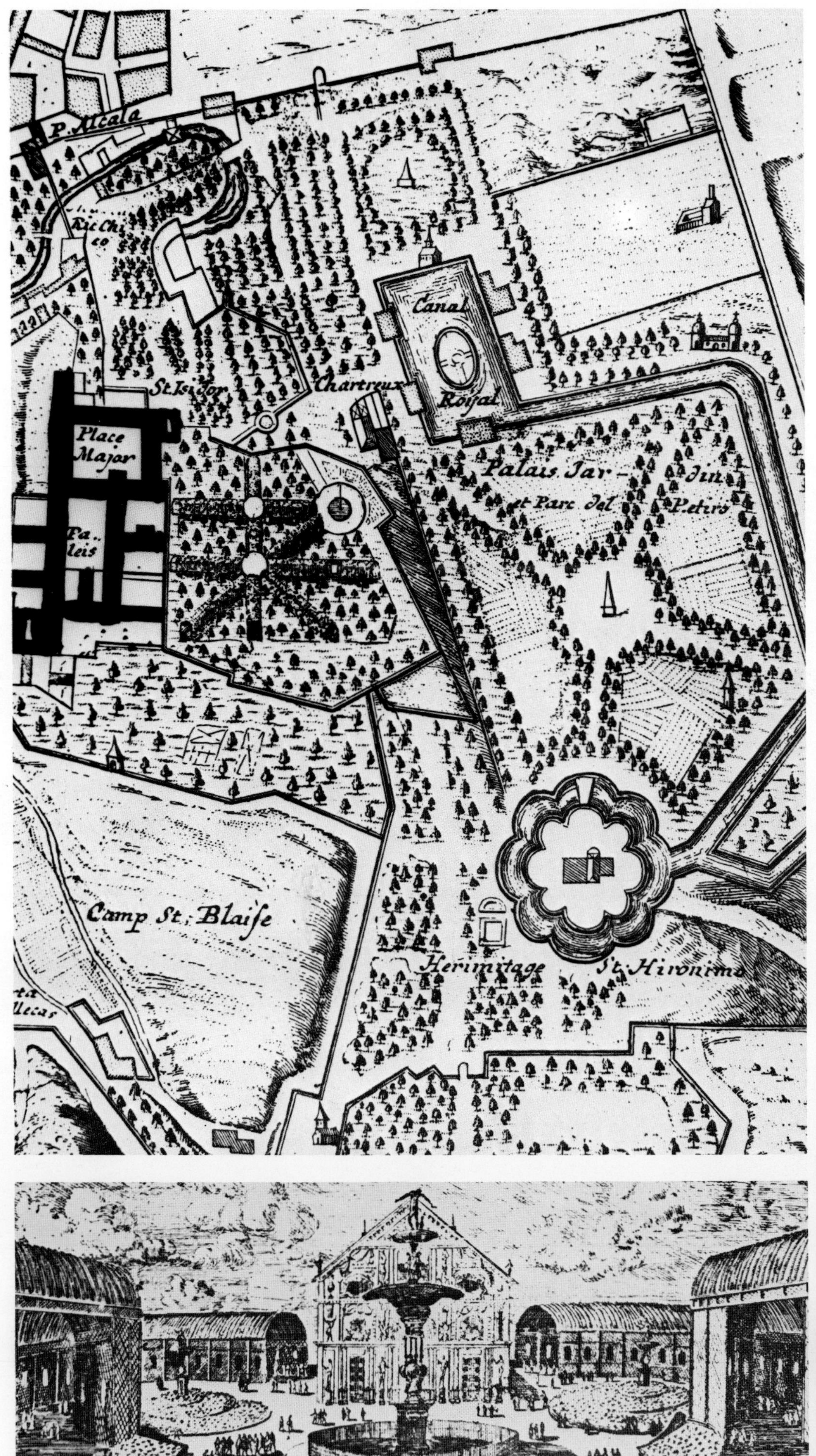
P. Alcala
Canal
Roÿal
St.Isidor
Chartreux
Place
Major
Pa..
leis
Palais Jar
din
et Parc del Retiro
Camp St. Blaise
Herimitage
St. Hironimo

SPAIN

By far the most influential Renaissance garden built in Spain was Buen Retiro, created by Count Duke Olivarez, favourite and minister to Phillip IV. Into one garden complex Duke Olivarez combined all the various idioms and influences which had been developed in Europe. He was considerably influenced by Italy but also drew on the garden examples from Portugal outlined above, and on the early Moorish traditions of Spain itself. It was this universal quality of Buen Retiro that made it so influential in Europe at the time; though in its overall form, it appears to have lacked unity of concept. The plan of Buen Retiro has little apparent order. A contemporary account describes the gardens: 'The heads of pinks show bright, with basil all round about just as if the earth were clad in red and blue gauze, in oriental fashion. Here too are streams clear as mirrors, paths sown with rose and jasmine, leafless pinks and shining purple hues, meadows where Arabia bestowed her lilies. There is no imaginable beauty that this garden lacks.'[2] The little that survives today is one of Madrid's public parks.

The principal designer who assisted the Count was an Italian, Cosimo Lotti; but the garden differs from those of the Italian Renaissance in many important respects. The Italian villa gardens were mostly 'week-enders' for the owners to escape from the cares of the city or from the summer's heat. Buen Retiro was both a town house and a park, containing all that the owner required. One of its hermitages even contained a small scientific laboratory for the use of the Duke, who was an amateur scientist. The 'theatrical garden' was said to have been born here; much of Calderon's work being first performed at Buen Retiro. This idea was extended by Le Nôtre at Vaux-le-Vicomte and Versailles some time later in France.

Another most interesting detail at Buen Retiro was that 'on one side of the park certain areas were like open country with meadows and trees keeping the simplicity of country life'.[3] Perhaps an early attempt at a 'natural' garden?

The Renaissance in Spain was short-lived and with the death of Calderon and Velasquez, the counter-Reformation set in and the initiative quickly passed to France.

180

Plan of the garden of Buen Retiro, Madrid. The garden was very influential in Europe in the seventeenth century but little remains today. A contemporary account describes it in its prime: 'Here too are streams clear as mirrors, paths sown with rose and jasmine, leafless pinks of shining purple hues, meadows where Arabia bestowed her lilies. There is no imaginable beauty that this garden lacks.'[2]

181

The Hermitage of Saint Paul in the Buen Retiro, the largest of the many in the gardens. Its centre-piece was called The Triple Narcissus Fountain. Little remains of the garden today.

182

An early engraving showing a general view of Buen Retiro with enclosed parterres in the foreground and plantations beyond.

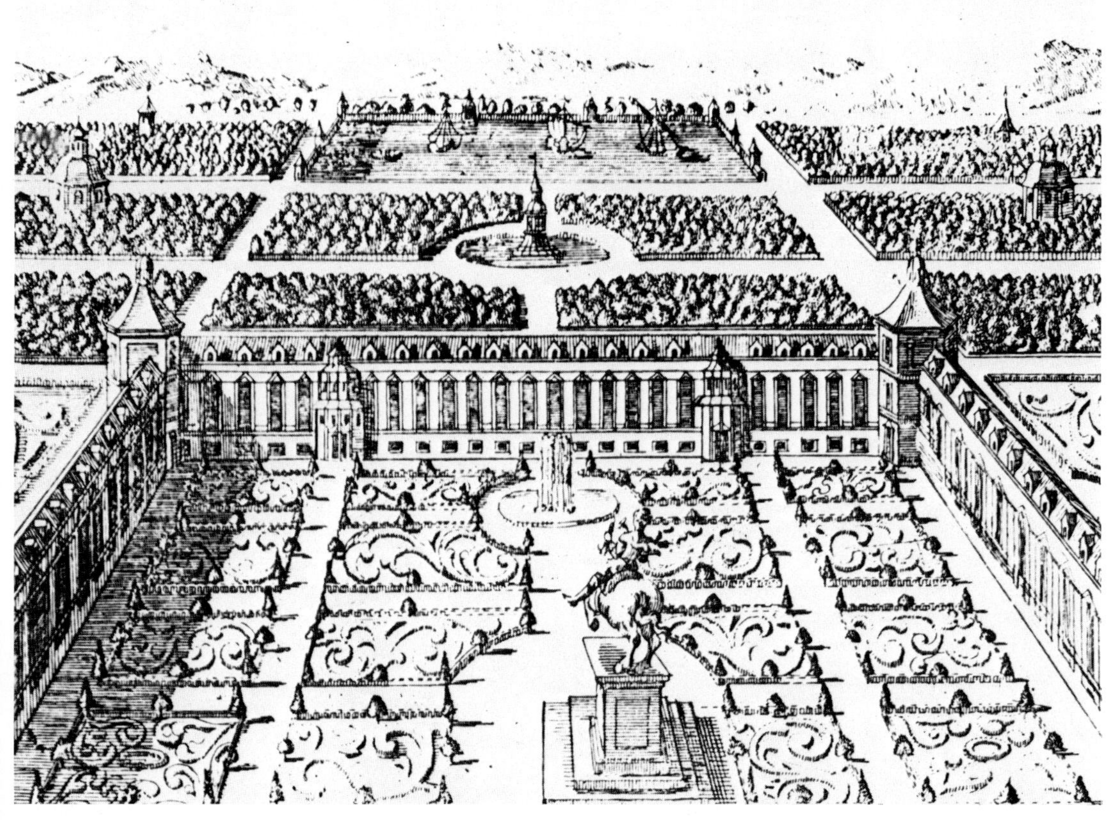

FRANCE

The seeds of the French Renaissance came from the invasion of Italy by Charles VIII at the end of the fifteenth century. He advanced triumphantly to Naples in 1495 and at once became enamoured of the gardens there, especially Poggio Reale. He determined to repeat them in France and took back twenty-two Italian artists and forty tons of *objets d'art* – a movement which later resulted in Leonardo da Vinci and Benvenuto Cellini going to Paris. Charles set his artists to work on beautifying the grounds of his castle at Amboise. But he did not realise that it was the spirit of the Renaissance, not the detail, which was important. It was the beginning, however; and a little more than a century later, Cardinal Richlieu built his great vista garden, the Château de Richlieu, establishing the basic form of what was to become the most significant French contribution to the Renaissance garden.

The idea of a vista garden was new to Europe then, though it had already been used extensively in Central Asia and India. The vista garden as it developed in France brought a new unity and scale to the formal gardens of Europe; which was strengthened by a separate movement towards unification of one of its most important features, the *compartiments de broderie*, or parterres. As the name 'broderie' implies, they were developed from the embroidered designs, in this case on silks. How these designs came to Europe from India and China is well illustrated by the following instruction by the directors of the East India Company in London to one of their factors in 1681:

'This for a constant and general rule, that in all flowered silks you change ye fashion and flower as much as you can every year, for English Ladies and they say ye French and other Europeans will give twice as much for a new thing not seen in Europe before.'[4]

'Designers of embroidery turned freely from silk to parterre and parterre back to silk, and used flowers more freely on silk than they ever did on the ground. The *compartiment de broderie* is closer to the Tailor of Gloucester's waistcoat than to an herbaceous border.'[5]

These *compartiments de broderie* became huge affairs in the French vista gardens of the mid-seventeenth century, flanking the axis of the main vista.

The new vista garden reached its zenith both in scale and unity at Vaux-le-Vicomte and Versailles, both designed by the doyen of French garden architects, Andre le Nôtre. Of these two, Vaux-le-Vicomte is much the superior as a work of garden art. It has a freshness, vivacity and humanity of

184

Aerial view of Vaux-le-Vicomte, the finest of the famous vista gardens of France. It has a freshness, vivacity and humanity of scale that is lacking in its great rival, Versailles.

185

Flower urns, furnished with geraniums, were a welcome note of colour on the grey, drizzly day when we made our visit to the gardens of Vaux-le-Vicomte.

183

An engraving of the Château Richlieu, the first great vista garden in France.

scale which the larger garden lacks. Its creator, Nicolas Fouquet, was finance minister to Louis XIV.

A man of great wealth, taste and fashion, Fouquet brought together a superb team to create Vaux-le-Vicomte. Louis le Vau was the architect, assisted by Charles Le Brun, painter and decorator. But his master stroke was to have the judgement to select Andre le Nôtre as his garden designer.

The main building is surrounded by a moat, used successfully as a decorative element and creating a pleasing link with the past. A large circular pool with its high central jet is happily related in scale and placement to the château, forming a more satisfying initial focal point than does the Fountain of Neptune at Versailles.

A high terrace on the left side of the main vista, caused by the ground originally falling across the site, prevents the somewhat distressing 'shooting gallery' effect which often occurs in vista gardens and is present at Versailles. All the details are well conceived. The statuary is of a high order; a group of lions being particularly fine. Much of the success of Vaux-le-Vicomte must be attributed to the taste and judgement of Fouquet. The garden was a living thing; plays by Molière were performed in it; La Fontaine was another of the coterie of brilliant spirits of the age whom Fouquet attracted around him.

But his garden masterpiece was to be Fouquet's downfall. He could not resist the temptation to invite Louis and his Court to a fête in the garden. Louis at first refused to

186

The main vista at Vaux-le-Vicomte seen from the terrace of the château. Large numbers of people were needed in the vast French display-gardens to overcome the stunning, overpowering effect of their scale.

187

Sculpture in the garden of Vaux-le-Vicomte is selected with much better judgement than at Versailles. This lion and lioness possess a warmth and vitality often lacking in garden sculpture.

188

The main parterre of Vaux-le-Vicomte. Red brick-dust between the clipped plants emphasises the embroidery-derived pattern.

come; then, consumed by curiosity by the descriptions he had heard from others, he requested Fouquet to organise another reception at Vaux-le-Vicomte, It must have been a magnificent affair. Molière himself acted in one of his plays which was presented before the guests. There was a lavish display of fireworks, and the guests were served supper on gold plate.

But Louis XIV had not the generosity of Shah Jahan. He had already set in motion action to destroy his minister. He left the reception before it was finished; and within a

189

The parterres at Versailles are less successfully arranged than those of Vaux-le-Vicomte. They have a restless quality and tend to distract from the main vista rather than enhance it.

month, Fouquet was in prison charged with peculation. He died there nineteen years later.

Louis took over the team of architects and artists which Fouquet had assembled to create Vaux-le-Vicomte, and determined to out-do the achievements of his deposed minister. He chose Versailles as the site for his palace and gardens. But Louis had neither the judgement nor the taste of Fouquet. Le Nôtre's concept for the garden of Versailles is undoubtedly a masterpiece of ingenuity; and because of its size and prominence, Versailles has had a greater influence than any other formal garden.

This vast display garden covering square miles and requiring the destruction of numerous French villages in its creation, was the ultimate achievement of the Renaissance garden. It could go no further. At Versailles the garden plan embraced and unified the hunting park in an entirely new way for formal gardens. Hunting rides became secondary, and tertiary vistas flowing out into forests and the countryside were brought into the plan as part of the grand conception.

But the parterres are a rather restless composition which do not relate happily to the main vista, as do those at Vaux-le-Vicomte.

The water-play, when the fountains are functioning, is fine. Unfortunately, the location is not sympathetic to water displays. Unlike the sites of Kashmir and Italy, there is no steepness to give a natural head of water. Everything had to be contrived by man, with pumps and cisterns. As a result, the fountains are not played all the time, but only on special occasions. And, as Constance Villiers-Stuart said of the Mughal water gardens: 'Nothing is more desolate than one of these great enclosures when their stone-lined tanks and water channels are dry and empty.' Though the effect at Versailles when the fountains are not playing is not so desolate, the scale of the vistas is such that, with no intermediate interest, the visitor tends to be overwhelmed by it.

Unlike many garden lovers and landscape architects, the authors find themselves inclined to be in sympathy with Saint-Simon who, writing at the time of its creation and use by Louis XIV, described Versailles thus:

> Not Asia nor antiquity could show anything more vast, grandiose and elaborate than these gardens ... To make the smallest use of them is disagreeable and

> they are in equally bad taste. To reach any shade one is forced to cross a vast, scorching expanse, and, after all, there is nothing to do in any direction but go up and down a little hill, after which the gardens end . . . Who could help being repelled and disgusted by the violence done to nature? . . . The fountains and other effects are incomparably fine, although they require a great deal of attention, but the net result is one that one admires and flies.[6]

It is interesting to notice in Saint-Simon's quotation that he was fully aware that there were large formal gardens in Asia at this time. Clifford points out, it is important to remember the purpose for which the gardens were created:

> It was primarily to be a stupendous theatre for fetes. Buen Retiro had not set an example for nothing. To achieve his end, Le Nôtre seized on one great principle – that the whole extent of the enormous garden should be visible at a gasp; accordingly, whatever variety there might be within the parts, the parts themselves were to be subordinate to the whole. If the garden was to be seen at a glance, it must be relatively narrow, but as it must be impressive by sheer size, it had also to be long. The eye of a man on the uppermost terrace can look on and on into distance, but must not be asked to move from side to side . . . the small square moated garden developed into an enormous carpet laid from the home terrace into a distance so remote that it seemed a backdrop rather than a reality . . . its major coherent purpose was to stun, not to charm.[7]

Clifford was describing Vaux-le-Vicomte but the points he makes apply with even greater force to Versailles.

The role of the leader of the cultural world in Europe, enjoyed by France during the sixteenth and seventeenth centuries, ensured that the late Renaissance formal garden movement spread to all the other nations. Already many of them had been influenced by the gardens of Italy to a greater or lesser extent.

190

Versailles. Parterres when viewed close at hand are colourful and gay with delightful flowers.

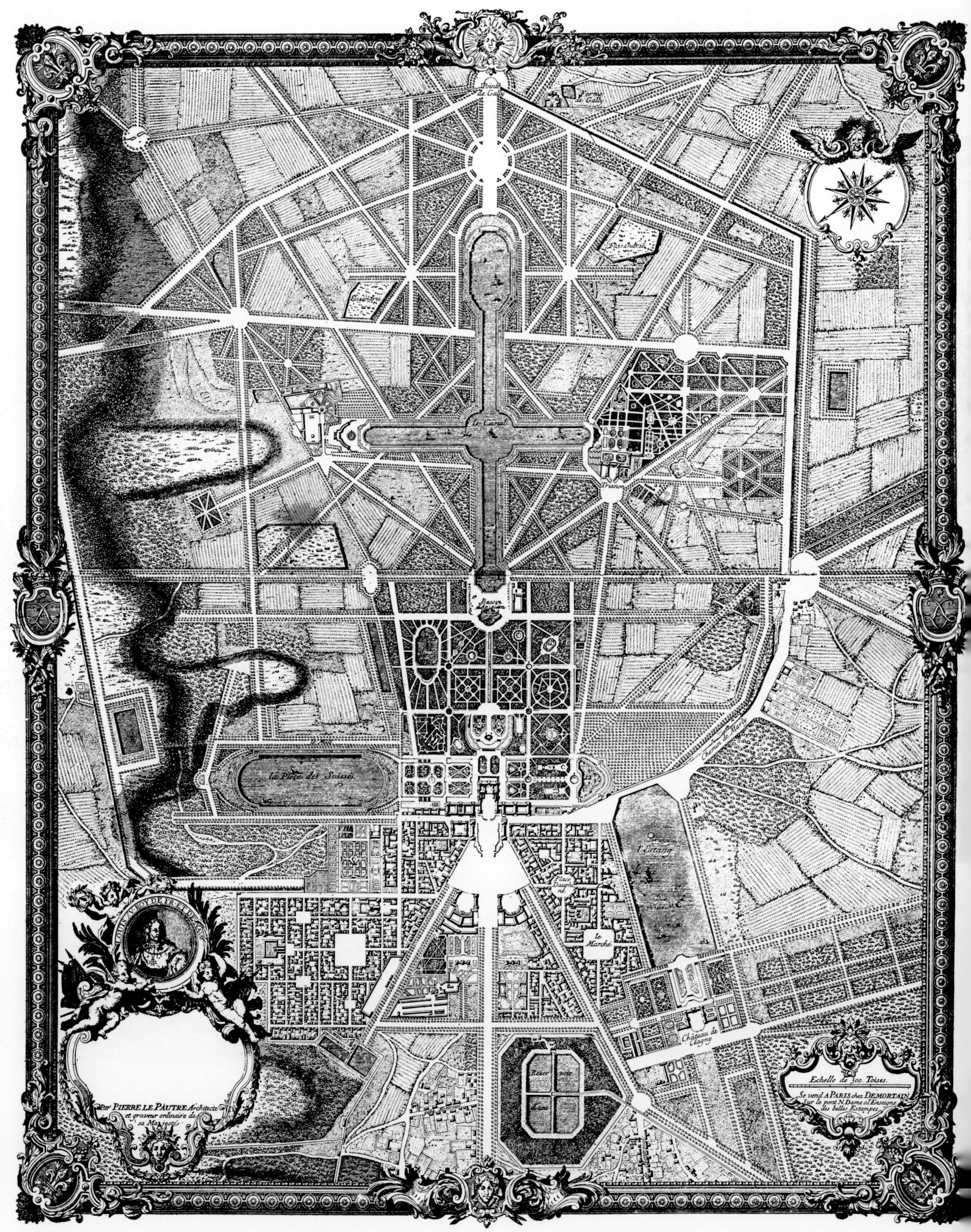
le Canal
Trianon
la Piece des Suisses
l'Etang
le Marché
Château de Clagny
Chemin de Marly
Echelle de 300. Toises.
Se vend A PARIS chez DEMORTAIN
Sur le pont N. Dame a l'Enseigne
des belles Estampes.
Par PIERRE LE PAUTRE Architecte
et graveur ordinaire de
sa Majesté

191

Plan of Versailles. The garden has embraced and unified the hunting park by a series of 'rides' or avenues. These became secondary and tertiary vistas flowing out into the forest. The scale of Versailles is enormous . . . 'its major coherent purpose was to stun, not to charm.'[7]

192

The main vista of Versailles seems to carry on into infinity. Water is a problem at Versailles and the fountains are rarely playing, which makes it difficult for visitors from abroad to see the gardens at their best. We have made three visits without being able to enjoy the water-play.

The original garden at Hampton Court, which was built in the first half of the sixteenth century (and which also led to the downfall of Cardinal Wolsey) was inspired by Italian models. However the present garden with its triple vista was designed by Andre and Gabriel Mollet, who played a prominent role in carrying French garden influence beyond its borders even to Drottningholm in Sweden and Fredensborg.

Great gardens were built in Germany, Austria and in the Low Countries: those of Germany, Holland and Belgium, in the French manner; while those of Austria were predominantly influenced by Italy. Peter the Great carried the French idiom to Russia, fine gardens being laid out around the Peterhof by Alexander Le Blond.

New forces were growing in France and Italy (even during the period of the development of the great formal gardens) which were to cause a revolution in landscape design, so profound and far-reaching that it now dominates most of our present thinking about man in the landscape. Marco Polo, and then the European navigators, laid its foundation, eliminating for all time the old isolation between 'East' and 'West'. Western thinkers were exposed to a totally new philosophy of nature much more in tune with the great scientific and physical discoveries which took place as a result of the Renaissance.

We have already touched upon this cultural revolution in our introduction to the Italian Renaissance. We shall now discuss the next stages of this movement.

193

Parterres in the gardens of Hampton Court, seen from the upper windows of the palace.

194

The influence of the great French vista gardens extended throughout Europe. This engraving of the gardens of Hampton Court illustrates the design prepared by Andre and Gabriel Mollet, who played a prominent role in carrying the influence of French gardens beyond France.

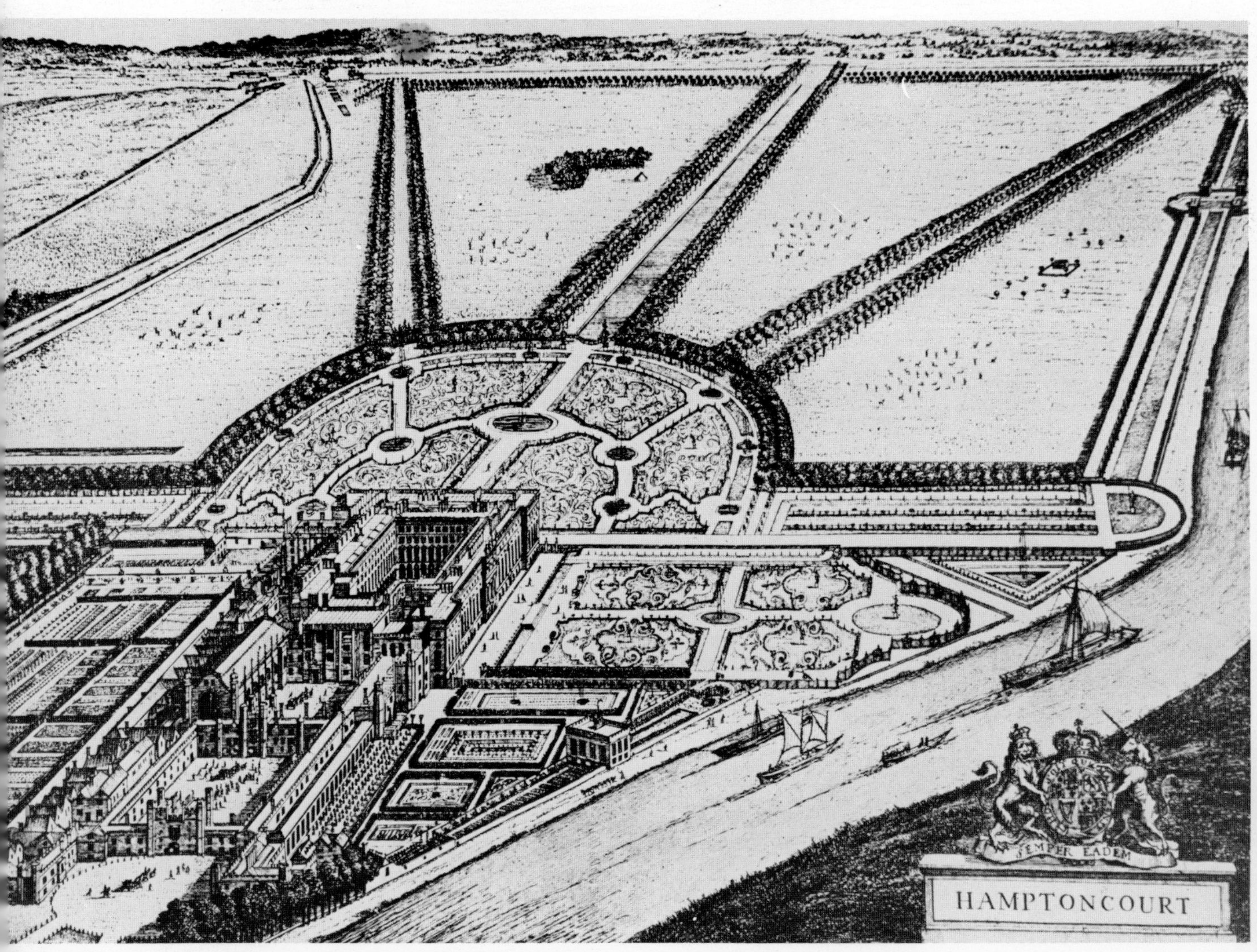

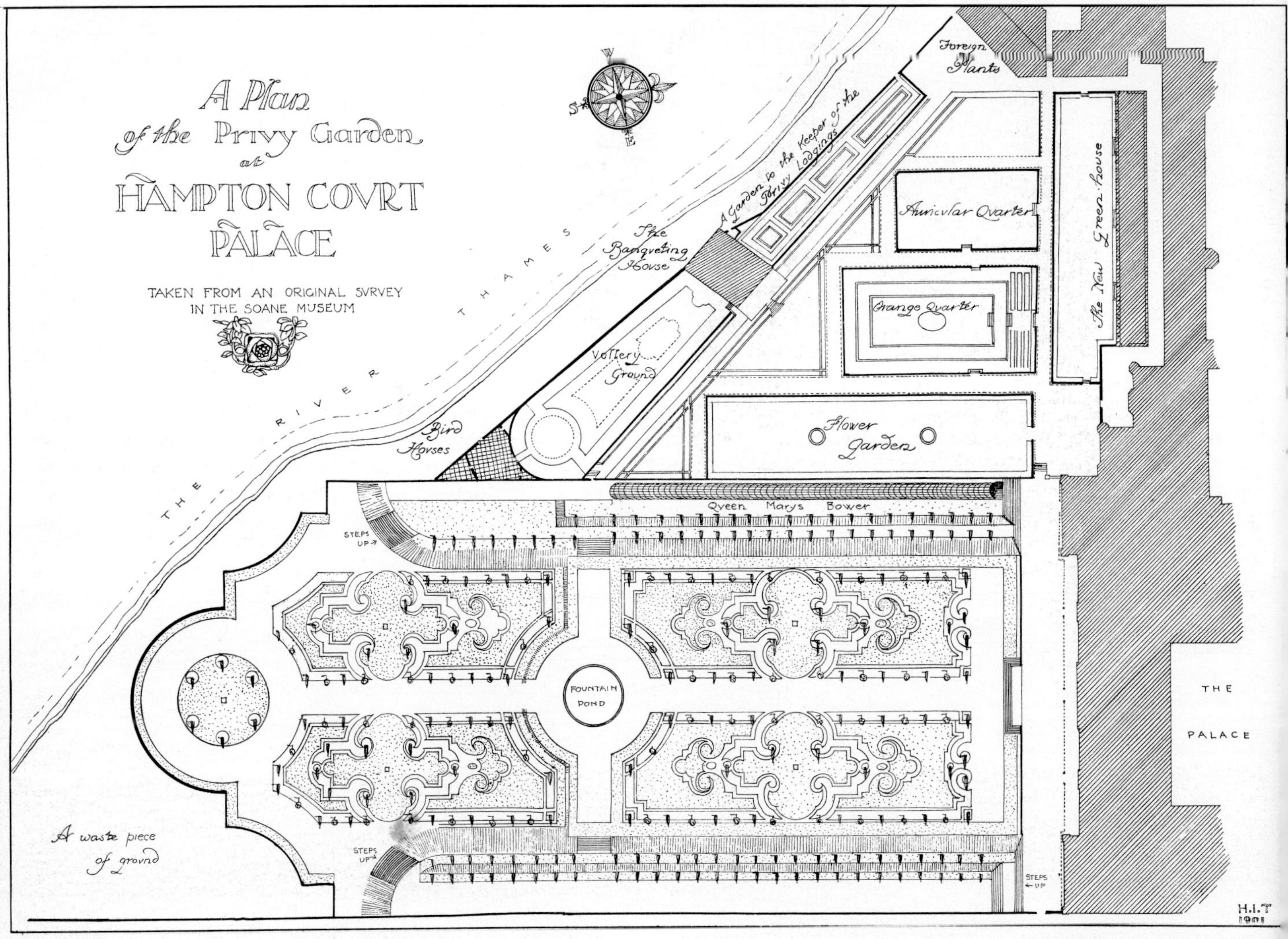

A Plan of the Privy Garden at HAMPTON COVRT PALACE

TAKEN FROM AN ORIGINAL SVRVEY IN THE SOANE MUSEUM

W S E

Foreign Plants
A Garden to the Keeper of the Privy Lodgings
Auricular Quarter
The New Green house
Orange Quarter
The Banqueting House
THE RIVER THAMES
Vollery Ground
Bird Houses
Flower Garden
Qveen Marys Bower
STEPS UP
FOUNTAIN POND
THE PALACE
A waste piece of ground
STEPS UP
STEPS UP
H.I.T 1901

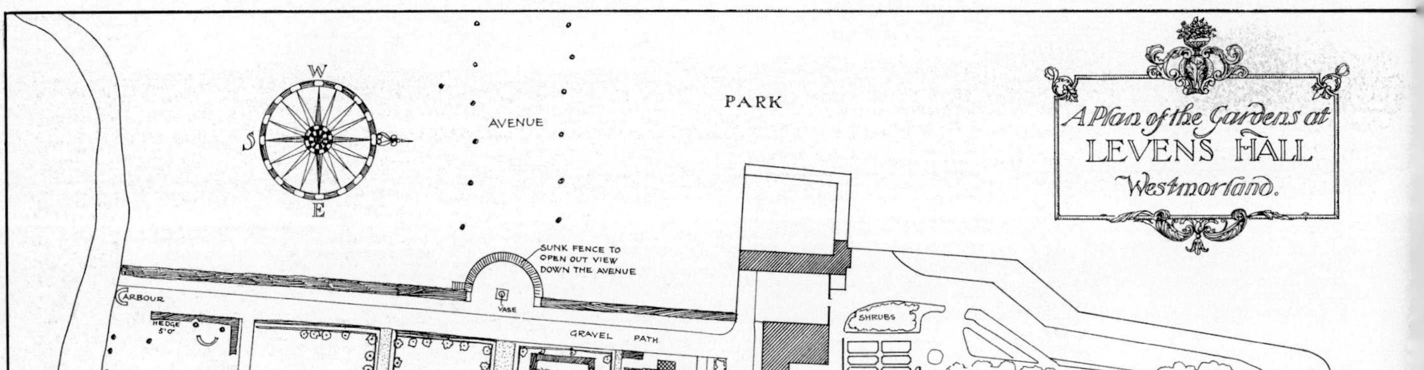

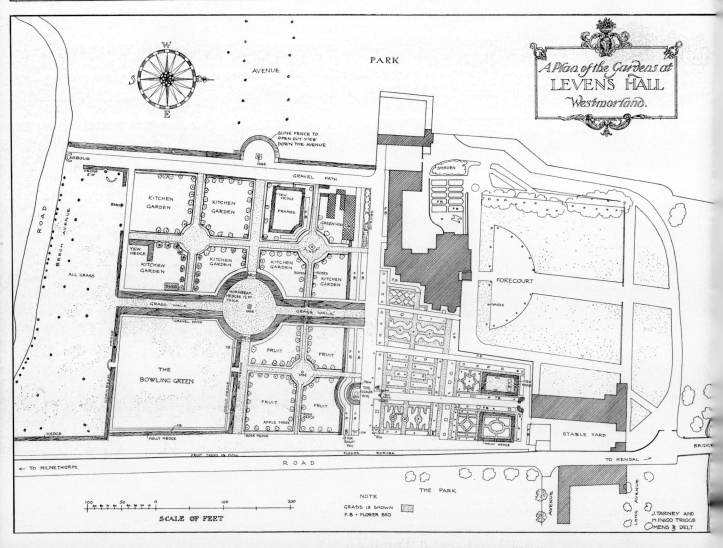

A Plan of the Gardens at LEVENS HALL Westmorland.

W S E
PARK
AVENUE
SUNK FENCE TO OPEN OUT VIEW DOWN THE AVENUE
ARBOUR
VASE
HEDGE 5'0"
GRAVEL PATH
KITCHEN GARDEN
KITCHEN GARDEN
YEW HEDGE
FRAMES
GREEN HOUSE
SHRUBS
F.B
BEECH
ROAD
BEECH AVENUE
ALL GRASS
YEW HEDGE
KITCHEN GARDEN
KITCHEN GARDEN
KITCHEN GARDEN
SUNDIAL
ROSES
ROSES
KITCHEN GARDEN
ARCH
HORNBEAM HEDGES 12 FT. THICK
GRASS WALK
GRASS WALK
VASE
GRAVEL PATH
FORECOURT
VASES
HEDGE
HORNBEAM
THE BOWLING GREEN
BOX HEDGE
HOLLY HEDGE
FRUIT
FRUIT
FRUIT
FRUIT
VASE
APPLE TREES
ROSE HEDGE
YEW
THE JUDGES WIG
YEW ARCH
YEW HEDGE
LION
YEW
B FOR BAGOT YEW
HOLLY HEDGE
HEDGE
HOLLY HEDGE
ROSE HEDGE
STABLE YARD
BRIDGE
FRUIT TREES ON WALL
FLOWER BORDER
← TO MILNETHORPE
ROAD
TO KENDAL →
THE PARK
AVENUE
LONG AVENUE

SCALE OF FEET
100 90 80 70 60 50 40 30 20 10 0 100 200

NOTE
GRASS IS SHOWN
F.B = FLOWER BED

J. TARNEY AND H. INIGO TRIGGS MENS & DELT

195

The Privy Garden at Hampton Court, as modified in the early eighteenth century by Sir Christopher Wren, George London and Henry Wise.

196

The plan of Levens Hall garden, Westmoreland, probably the finest surviving topiary garden in the world. The garden was designed by Monsieur Beaumont, gardener to King James II and Colonel L. Grahame. M. Beaumont used a ha-ha to permit an unobstructed view of an avenue beyond the enclosed garden: perhaps the first ha-ha ever used in England.

197

A view over part of the topiary garden at Levens Hall, taken 1901. A coloured photograph of the garden as it is today is illustrated in plate 18. Though M. Beaumont was supposed to be a pupil of Le Nôtre, the garden appears to be more Dutch in character than French.

198

An aerial view of the Nymphenberg in Munich. The gardens of the Nymphenberg were created by French designers, the chief of whom was François Girard.

199

An aerial photograph of the gardens of the Belvedere in Vienna, built in the early eighteenth century. François Girard, who was the principle designer at Nymphenburg, also collaborated in the creation of these gardens.

200

A parterre adjacent to the moat in Kasteel Twickel, Holland, designed in the French manner.

201

Vista to the sea from the Peterhof, designed by Alexander Le Blond for Peter the Great of Russia. Le Blond had previously worked with Le Nôtre at Versailles. He went to Russia in 1716 after the death of Louis XIV.

CHAPTER 8

THE 'NATURAL' AWAKENING IN FRANCE AND ENGLAND

As early as the beginning of Christianity, Mediterranean civilisations were intrigued by the products of 'the land of the Ceres' — to the extent that the Roman Senate were compelled to introduce stern measures to prevent the drain of Roman gold to the East for the purchase of silk.

Later influences in painting, particularly in landscape painting and poetry, reached Europe through Islam. But during the reign of the Mongol Emperor Kublai Khan in China, as we have seen, information, art and artifacts were introduced to Europe by the Polos; and finally on his return to Venice, Marco Polo wrote his comprehensive book about China, which became a 'best-seller' in Europe.

But still China was remote, strange and mysterious. Information among the tales and discoveries of Marco Polo that did not have direct application to the life of his times or the Renaissance that followed, was often regarded as a figment of his imagination or at least, as exaggeration. It was only when navigators established direct sea routes to India, China, Japan and other countries of the 'Far East' that the thirst for information, that had been created by Marco Polo, could be fully satisfied.

202

Detail from a folding screen by Tamuru Chikuo, Japan, late seventeenth century. Ming prototypes came to Europe earlier in the century and were mentioned in Sir William Temple's essay quoted in our text.

A body of Jesuit priests working in Peking sent back to Italy and France comprehensive details of Chinese life and culture. Later dispatches in the Ming and Ch'ing periods included translations of the works of Chinese philosophers Confucius and Mencius. At the same time, descriptions of gardens intrigued artists and intellectuals who found them quite different from European gardens. The Court of Louis XIV became avid for the products of China such as ceramics, painted screens, silks and embroideries. Upon these were illustrated garden scenes which gave life and reality to the descriptions sent back by the Jesuits and brought by seafaring men and merchants.

The philosophical basis for the 'Natural' garden movement which was later to take place in England was not initially developed in England, but in France. Like most true seekers after knowledge, the French artists and scholars, were pleased to acknowledge their debt to Chinese Confucianism, Taoism and Buddhism, although they did not fully understand them, and interpreted what they did grasp, in terms of the needs of seventeenth-century Europe. The French sought 'freedom of thought'. They also evinced the need for spiritual renewal in the adoption of a natural philosophy and a love of Nature and natural things. Of course they were unaware at the time that all this intellectual stimulation was finally to result in one of the most important flowerings of garden art in the English School of Landscape Design.

203

A nacre inlay box showing a water-garden with a weeping willow and water birds. Illustrations like these would have been most illuminating to European eyes.

The intellectual ferment first expressed through the Renaissance in Italy but checked there by the Counter Reformation, in the sixteenth century moved to France. Men were questioning the merit of revealed religion and seeking an explanation of life in keeping with their new vision of the world. The new philosophy in the works sent back to France by the Jesuits in China excited scholars, and in 1688 *Confucius Sinarum Philosophys* was published in Paris. Edited by Father Couplet it came from a group of Jesuit missionaries in Hangchow. It comprised the Ta Hsueh, Lun Yu and Chung Yung. A translation of Chung Yung was already in existence. Father Couplet's work was quickly translated into English.

The ideas contained in the Chinese classics were extremely stimulating to European intellectuals, containing as they did a natural philosophy of life with detailed indications of its application in everyday affairs. That these ideas were available to thinking men in England is revealed in a comment by Sir William Temple in 1685: 'Works of Confucu have lately in France been printed in the Latin tongue, with a learned preface by some missionary Jesuits under the title *Works of Confucius*.'[1] He was probably referring to the initial translation of Chung Yung mentioned above.

Under the stimulating influence of the Chinese philosophers, European man 'discovered' Nature for the first time as a physical entity. Brought into an entirely new relationship with natural things, for the first time he saw the beauty of the natural environment and developed an enthusiasm for everything that grows and blooms.

The Christian concept of 'Man in God-given form', (separate from Nature, and its master) was challenged by the idea of 'Man one with Nature' (not separate, but part of an infinitely diversified natural environment). He was only on the brink of discovery. But nature soon provided an inspiration for poets and artists and an infinite field of research for man's enquiring and scientific mind. When this was paralleled by the wonderfully exciting visual material seen on paintings, screens and porcelain, Marco Polo's 'best-selling' travel book with its earlier descriptions of the Celestial City of Hang Chow must have come to life in quite a new way.

Marco Polo had been entranced by the palaces and gardens of the Sung Emperor who had preceded Kublai Khan. Enclosures ten miles in circumference, two-thirds of which were devoted to gardens . . . he had described them in the following terms:

> The other two divisions of this estate were laid out in groves, pieces of water, beautiful gardens stored with fruit trees, and also enclosures for all sorts of animals that are the object of sport, such as antelopes, deer, stags, hares and rabbits . . . Here likewise the King amused himself in company with his damsels, some in carriages, some on horseback. No male person was

204

A similar box with a group of pavilions, informally arranged among some trees.

205

This third box, shows a man and his servant relaxing on the edge of an artificial lake.

206

Water landscape in cut silk, Ming Dynasty. This could be an illustration to Marco Polo's description of the people of Hanchow engaged in boating on the West Lake. Sir William Temple in 1685, speaking of the informal gardens of China, said: 'Whosoever observes the work on the best of the India gowns or the painting from the Far East or the painting on their best screens and porcelains, will find their beauty is all of this kind, without order.'

> allowed to be of these parties, but on the other hand the females were practised in the art of coursing with dogs, and pursuing the other animals that have been mentioned. When fatigued with these exercises they retired into the groves on the banks of the lakes, and there quitted their dresses and rushed into the water in a state of nudity, gaily swimming about, some in one direction and some in another, while the King remained a spectator of the exhibition. After this they returned to the Palace, but sometimes he ordered a repast to be provided in one of these groves, where the foliage of the lofty trees afforded a thick shade.[2]

Marco Polo also described a part of the lake that was accessible to the people of Hang Chow and used for the amusement of boating:

> Such persons who take delight in the amusement of boating and mean to enjoy it, either in the company of their women, or that of their male companions, engage one of these barges, together with every other kind of furniture necessary for giving an entertain-

> ment. As they sit at the table they have the opportunity of looking out in every direction and feasting their eyes on the variety and beauty of the scenes as they pass them, and truly the gratification afforded in this manner upon the water exceeds any that can be derived from amusement on the land, for as the lake extends the whole length of the city on one side, you have a view as you stand in the boat at a certain distance from the shore, of all its grandeur and beauty, the palaces, temples, convents and gardens, and trees of the largest size growing down to the water's edge.[2]

At the time of his writing these descriptions, the formal garden concept was so universal in Europe that readers would have interpreted them in formal terms. But now a change had occurred: European man was seeing the beauty of Nature, of trees, water and land forms in a new informal way. This new vision was confirmed by paintings and artefacts from China, while merchants and seamen were in a position to supplement the scenes in paintings and upon screens, by their eye-witness accounts, and first-hand questions and discussions could take place concerning the gardens they described. John Neuhof of the East India Company of the United Provinces, wrote a report on his travels in China in 1653-57. Published in Dutch, German and English (1669) it is described by Siren thus:

> It gave a vivid account of what the author himself had seen – partly illustrated in quite successful engravings. The publication went through several editions.

207

An early Ming dish depicting a water garden with little islands, informal plants and decorative rocks.

208

Here we have a garden scene with a large, irregular decorative rock, a carefully-shaped informal tree and a trellised vine. A group of large-leaved plantains is in one corner.

209

Greeting the Spring. Wu Pin (1573–1620 A.D.). **This section of a Ming Dynasty handscroll contains all the elements of a large informal landscape garden on the shores of a lake. Houses, courtyards and pavilions are beautifully integrated into the landscape of mountains and water.**

> He spoke of enormous hollowed out rockeries, artificial mountains planted with trees or sprinkled with playing cascades. The winding river flows by several artificial mounts made in the court; on top of them are trees and flowers planted in excellent order. Lords and persons of quality oft times spend most of their estates in making such artificial mounts in their gardens and orchards. In one of them are mazes, though not very big, yet by their strange turnings and wanderings of one walk into another, keep the water two or three hours before it can get through them all, and at last comes out by another gate.[3]

It is amusing to see how Neuhof had difficulty in finding appropriate words with which to describe this new landscape garden art in terms of the old, just as did the Jesuits in their later descriptions of the Yuan Ming Yuan, but we have no doubt that the illustrations did much to clarify the meaning of such terms as 'artificial mounts' and 'trees and flowers planted in excellent order'. No doubt The Forty Scenes of The Garden of Perfect Brightness also clarified the Jesuits' descriptions.

It was the European missionaries in China who supplied the most comprehensive details of Chinese garden art. As early as 1610 Father Nicole Trigault had published the experiences of Father Matteo Ricci, who reached Peking in 1601 after 18 years in Macao. Detailed descriptions of gardens were included in these accounts. In 1713 another Italian priest, Father Matteo Ripa engraved 36 views for the Emperor K'ang-hsi. These showed the Imperial palaces and gardens at Jehol and several copies came to Europe. Finally The Forty Scenes of The Garden of Perfect Brightness arrived, now in the Bibliothèque Nationale, Paris.

It must have been tales such as those of Neuhof and other travellers which inspired Sir William Temple to write in 1685:

> What I have said of the best forms of gardens is meant only of such as are in some sort regular, for there may be other forms wholly irregular that may, for ought I know, have more beauty than any of the others, but they must owe to some extraordinary dispositions of nature in the seat, or some great piece of fancy or judgment in the contrivance, which may reduce many disagreeing parts into some figure which shall yet, upon the whole, be very agreeable. Something of this I have seen in some places, but heard more of it from others who have lived much among the Chinese . . . Among us the beauty of building and planting is placed chiefly in some certain proportions, symmetries, and uniformities – our walks and our trees ranged so as to answer one another, and at exact distances. The Chinese scorn this way of planting, and say a boy who can tell an hundred may plant walks of trees in straight lines, and over and against one another, and to what length and extent he pleases. But their greatest reach of the imagination is employed in contriving figures where the beauty shall be great, and strike the eye, but without any order or disposition of parts that shall be commonly or easily observed, and though we have hardly a notion of this sort of beauty, yet they have a particular word to express it, and where they find it hits their eye at first sight. They say the Sharawaggi is fine, or is admirable, or any such expression of esteem. And whoever observes the work upon the best of the India* gowns, or the paintings from the far East, or the painting upon

*A general term for imports from the Far East.

their best screens or porcelains, will find their beauty is all of this kind, that, without order.

. . . But I should hardly advise any of these attempts in the figure of gardens amongst us; they are adventures of too hard achievement for any common hands, and though there may be the more honour if they succeed well, yet there is more dishonour if they fail, and it is twenty to one they will, whereas in regular figures it is hard to make any great and remarkable faults.[4]

An Englishman who, despite the warnings of William

210

***Return from a stroll in Spring.* Tai Chin, early Ming.**

211

***Listening to the Wind in the Pines.* Ma Lin. Southern Sung hanging scroll. This painting illustrates what became known as the picturesque in the English School of Landscape Gardening that followed in the eighteenth century.**

212

A most interesting hand-painted 'Chinese' wallpaper on the walls of a drawing-room at Ightham Mote in Kent. Dated *c.*1672, it shows a surprising knowledge of Chinese garden idiom. It is interesting to compare this detail of the hand-painted wallpaper at Ightham Mote with *Partridge and Sparrows,* Plate 25.

Temple, had the temerity to take up the challenge of the new landscape concepts, was Anthony Ashley Cooper, later Lord Shaftesbury. Writing in *The Moralist* in 1709, he says:

> I shall no longer resist the passion growing in me for things of a natural kind, where neither art nor the caprice of man has spoilt the genuine order by breaking in upon that primitive state. Even the rude rocks, the mossy caverns, the irregular unwrought grottoes and broken falls of water, with all the horrid graces of the wilderness itself, in representing nature more, will be the more engaging, and appear with a magnificence beyond the mockery of princely gardens.[5]

Ashley Cooper's phraseology is particularly interesting in that it expresses his changing way of thinking, for he still clings to the old vocabulary of 'rude' rocks and 'horrid' graces of the wilderness, which belong to the previous attitude of abhorrence of nature and natural things.

Later in the same paper he refers to nature as 'all loving, all lovely, all divine'.

Ashley Cooper's essay demonstrates clearly that the philosophical movement begun in France was now being accepted and developed in England, where the objective conditions were so much more favourable for it to blossom in landscape architectural form. By 1712 Joseph Addison was writing his now-famous essay in *The Spectator:*

> The Chinese laugh at the plantations of our Europeans which are laid out by the rule and line, because they say anyone can place trees in equal rows and uniform figures. They choose rather to discover the genius in trees and in nature, and therefore always conceal their art.
>
> . . . Our trees rise in cones and pyramids, we see the mark of the scissors upon every plant and bush. I do not know if I am singular in my opinion, but for my own part I would rather look upon a tree in all its luxuriance and diffusion of boughs and branches, than when it is cut and trimmed into a mathematical figure; and cannot but fancy that an orchard in flower looks infinitely more delightful than all the little labyrinths of the most finished parterre.
>
> Why may not a whole estate be turned into a kind of garden by frequent plantations, and man might make a pretty landscip of his own possessions?[6]

Alexander Pope, fifteen years Addison's junior, then took up the aesthetic fight. Not only in his writings and poems did he express his support for the new theory, he also actually built a transitional informal garden of his own at

213

Two details from a twelve-fold screen (now a wall hanging in the National Gallery of Victoria). Screens like these were common in Europe in the late seventeenth century. By the turn of the century potters in Delft and Frankfurt were already producing porcelain products decorated with informal Chinese landscape garden themes.

214

Study the Old: it contains the Present, **painting of 'The Garden of Perfect Brightness' near Peking.**

Twickenham, and assisted friends in laying out their gardens. He collaborated with William Kent, the first professional landscape gardener in England to adopt the natural style, on work for Lord Burlington at Chiswick. As the plan we illustrate clearly shows, Chiswick was essentially a transitional garden.

Pope expressed his garden ideas most clearly in his Epistle to the Earl of Burlington:

In all let Nature never be forgot'
But treat the Goddess like a modest Fair,
Not overdress nor leave her wholly bare;
Let not each beauty everywhere by spy'd,
Where half the skill is decently to hide.
He gains all points who pleasingly confounds,
Surprises, varies, and conceals the bounds.
Consult the genius of the place in all;
That tells the water where to rise or fall,
Or helps the ambitious hill the heavens to scale,
Or troops in circling theatres the vale,
Calls in the country, catches opening glades,
Joins willing woods and varies shades from shades,
Now breaks, or now directs, the intending lines,
Paints as you plant, and, as you work, designs.[7]

Why was it that the new 'Natural' movement which developed in France had little impact on the landscape there – yet when it crossed the Channel, it gave rise to a landscape revolution unparalleled in history?

The answer is partly in the objective conditions which existed in the two countries. Louis XIV's France, despite its appearance of grandeur, was a society in a state of advanced decay. So, as frequently happened in the history of civilisation, the new movement (like the chicken inside an egg) developed all the necessary characteristics of thought and philosophy inside the old form, but reached the point where no further progress could take place without completely changing the social form of the community. Not until late in the eighteenth century was this change to happen in France; but in England Cromwell and his Ironsides had already toppled the old feudal monarchy, and though the Republic was short-lived, so was the Restoration. Directly James II endeavoured to present a real challenge to the new Parliamentary democracy, he was deposed and replaced by William of Orange – no longer an autocratic sovereign, but a willing leader of the new capitalist ruling class with whom he was very much in sympathy.

By the Revolution, England had carried the seed sown in Florence a stage further and had established the first capitalist democracy in the world. The new 'Natural' philosophy which had developed in France, including the Confucian concept of an enlightened and educated ruling class, exactly suited the social and administrative climate of the time in England.

The new landed gentry consisted of members of the old aristocracy whose attitude and outlook changed with the times. Quite as often, it also consisted of wealthy citizens who had bought or married their way into the body of English country gentlemen, some in the formative period during the reigns of Henry VIII and Elizabeth I (vast new wealth and the dissolution of the monasteries giving them their opportunity); others during Cromwell's brief span of power. This process, though slowed up, continued during the Restoration, receiving a great stimulus by the expansion of the wool trade and the enclosures of common land which followed in its wake.

A classic character in English literature who illustrates this trend, is in Scott's *Rob Roy.* Frank Osbaldistone, son of a merchant, inherited Osbaldistone Hall after his uncle and cousins had all been killed off in the abortive revolt of 1715. Frank even married his Royalist cousin, Diana Vernon. By the time Scott wrote *Rob Roy,* this seemed a perfectly logical and understandable metamorphosis. Scott rendered it even more plausible by making the merchant and the landowner brothers.

Such rural-based intellectuals were looking for new forms to express the new way of life which had come into being. The old feudal, regimented, formal landscape was quite unsuitable. Intellectuals as early as Francis Bacon had

212

A most interesting hand-painted 'Chinese' wallpaper on the walls of a drawing-room at Ightham Mote in Kent. Dated *c.*1672, it shows a surprising knowledge of Chinese garden idiom. It is interesting to compare this detail of the hand-painted wallpaper at Ightham Mote with *Partridge and Sparrows,* Plate 25.

Temple, had the temerity to take up the challenge of the new landscape concepts, was Anthony Ashley Cooper, later Lord Shaftesbury. Writing in *The Moralist* in 1709, he says:

> I shall no longer resist the passion growing in me for things of a natural kind, where neither art nor the caprice of man has spoilt the genuine order by breaking in upon that primitive state. Even the rude rocks, the mossy caverns, the irregular unwrought grottoes and broken falls of water, with all the horrid graces of the wilderness itself, in representing nature more, will be the more engaging, and appear with a magnificence beyond the mockery of princely gardens.[5]

Ashley Cooper's phraseology is particularly interesting in that it expresses his changing way of thinking, for he still clings to the old vocabulary of 'rude' rocks and 'horrid' graces of the wilderness, which belong to the previous attitude of abhorrence of nature and natural things.

Later in the same paper he refers to nature as 'all loving, all lovely, all divine'.

Ashley Cooper's essay demonstrates clearly that the philosophical movement begun in France was now being accepted and developed in England, where the objective conditions were so much more favourable for it to blossom in landscape architectural form. By 1712 Joseph Addison was writing his now-famous essay in *The Spectator:*

> The Chinese laugh at the plantations of our Europeans which are laid out by the rule and line, because they say anyone can place trees in equal rows and uniform figures. They choose rather to discover the genius in trees and in nature, and therefore always conceal their art.
>
> . . . Our trees rise in cones and pyramids, we see the mark of the scissors upon every plant and bush. I do not know if I am singular in my opinion, but for my own part I would rather look upon a tree in all its luxuriance and diffusion of boughs and branches, than when it is cut and trimmed into a mathematical figure; and cannot but fancy that an orchard in flower looks infinitely more delightful than all the little labyrinths of the most finished parterre.
>
> Why may not a whole estate be turned into a kind of garden by frequent plantations, and man might make a pretty landscip of his own possessions?[6]

Alexander Pope, fifteen years Addison's junior, then took up the aesthetic fight. Not only in his writings and poems did he express his support for the new theory, he also actually built a transitional informal garden of his own at

213

Two details from a twelve-fold screen (now a wall hanging in the National Gallery of Victoria). Screens like these were common in Europe in the late seventeenth century. By the turn of the century potters in Delft and Frankfurt were already producing porcelain products decorated with informal Chinese landscape garden themes.

210

Return from a stroll in Spring. Tai Chin, early Ming.

211

Listening to the Wind in the Pines. Ma Lin. Southern Sung hanging scroll. This painting illustrates what became known as the picturesque in the English School of Landscape Gardening that followed in the eighteenth century.

> their best screens or porcelains, will find their beauty is all of this kind, that, without order.
>
> . . . But I should hardly advise any of these attempts in the figure of gardens amongst us; they are adventures of too hard achievement for any common hands, and though there may be the more honour if they succeed well, yet there is more dishonour if they fail, and it is twenty to one they will, whereas in regular figures it is hard to make any great and remarkable faults.[4]

An Englishman who, despite the warnings of William

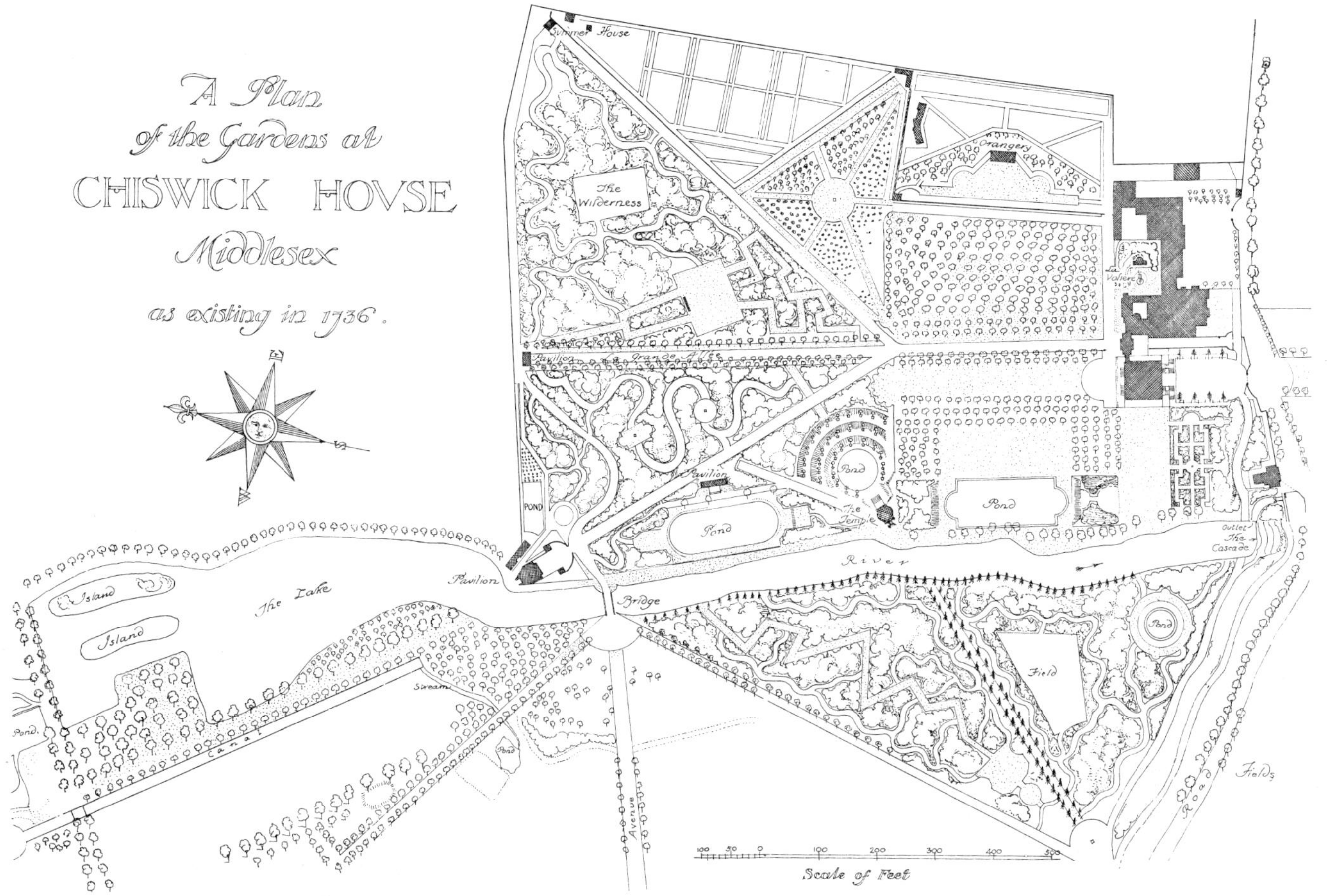

A Plan of the Gardens at CHISWICK HOVSE Middlesex as existing in 1736.

seen and complained of this. Though it grew out of the Commonwealth, this movement had many anti-democratic characteristics, such as the enclosures of the common land. These enclosures were later to give rise to the 'Park Movement'; and it is interesting to notice that it was the Commonwealth which took the first steps towards the establishment of public parks when in 1649 Parliament passed an Act presenting Richmond Great Park to the City of London. Though returned to the former Royal owners at the Restoration, it was ultimately opened to public use.

Of course none of these movements was recognised at the time in this historical way, and much or most of the argument took place in the field of aesthetics. It was not until the park movement was transported to the Colonies in the mid-nineteenth century that Andrew Jackson Downing and Frederick Law Olmsted recognised clearly, and with enthusiasm, its democratic character.

Besides these objective historical conditions, there was another reason that England provided such fertile ground for developing the new 'natural' school of landscape gardening. Though the prevailing intellectual climate in seventeenth-century England was antagonistic, if not actively hostile, to the 'horrid rocks and blasted heaths of wild nature' (Fitzgerald), a new romantic approach to the countryside was emerging. Centuries earlier the troubadours of Moorish Spain had expressed a romantic 'literary movement'; in the eleventh and twelfth centuries this had crossed the Pyrenees to France, and from thence to England, creating a strong literary undercurrent, which

215

A plan of the gardens at Chiswick, a seat of the Earl of Burlington. He was enthusiastic about the new, naturalistic ideas coming from France, and tried to introduce a number of them at Chiswick. It is essentially a traditional garden: many of the curving lines look extremely forced. The cascade, lake and islands are the finest part of the composition.

216

An early view (1736) of Chiswick. William Kent, the first great English landscape designer, worked with Pope on this garden. Chiswick, like Pope's garden at Twickenham, was transitional – a mixture of formal and informal elements.

217

Castle Howard. A painting by Hendrik de Cort (1742–1816). Here the new informal landscape ideas are beginning to replace the formal ones.

showed a growing love of the countryside, especially when it had been tamed by man.

Christopher Marlowe wrote his charming pastoral ballad 'Come Live With Me and Be My Love'; Spencer and Shakespeare frequently convey the true spirit, as well as accurate portraits of country life; and it has been said of Milton's young friend and secretarial assistant, the poet Andrew Marvell, 'No English poet, indeed, has loved nature more than he.'[8]

Izaak Walton escaped in late middle age from the worries and frustrations of city life into the countryside he loved. At the age of forty-seven, in 1644, he wrote his *Compleat Angler* and his *Lives*. The *Compleat Angler* was the finest tribute to the English countryside up to that time: and Wordsworth, the supreme nature poet of English literature, said of his *Lives*:

The feather whence the pen was shaped,
That traced the lives of these good men,
Dropped from an Angel's wing.[8]

During the sixteenth and seventeenth centuries English literary men had also reaped the benefit of the historic changes brought about in navigation, science and literature by the Renaissance – though like Francis Bacon in his *Novum Organum* they were either unaware of some of their sources, or considered them too 'obscure and inglorious' for their consideration.

Bacon himself was one of the forerunners in the 'natural' undercurrent. Though still enamoured of many of the characteristics of the formal gardens, he was uneasy about parterres and knots. 'I for my part do not like images cut out in juniper or other garden stuff, they be for children', and 'as for the making of knots or figures . . . they be but toys; you may see as good sights many times in tarts.' And he favoured 'wilderness' as part of the garden. It is no wonder that the seed of the 'natural' movement flourished in the soil of England . . .

Another aspect of the French natural movement was the enthusiasm that developed there for painting the virgin landscape as a subject in itself. Until this time in France and England, landscapes were largely regarded as backgrounds to a paintings' main theme, usually a religious subject, classical drama, human passion, or portraiture. Now painters such as Poussin and Claude Lorraine became enthusiastic about the beauty of the landscape itself – of trees, rivers and lakes, of mountains and rocks. Following the Dutch and Italian masters they made these the subjects of paintings in which the human element became quite secondary; in the paintings of Claude it was eventually to disappear.

Without being aware of it, these artists were also helping to provide the basis for the landscape garden design movement that lay ahead.

218

***St. John on Patmos* by Nicholas Poussin, one of the best-known painters who influenced the English School of Landscape Design in the eighteenth century.**

219

***Aeneas on the Coast of Delos* by Claude Lorraine, perhaps the most influential of the French landscape painters in the development of informal landscape garden design.**

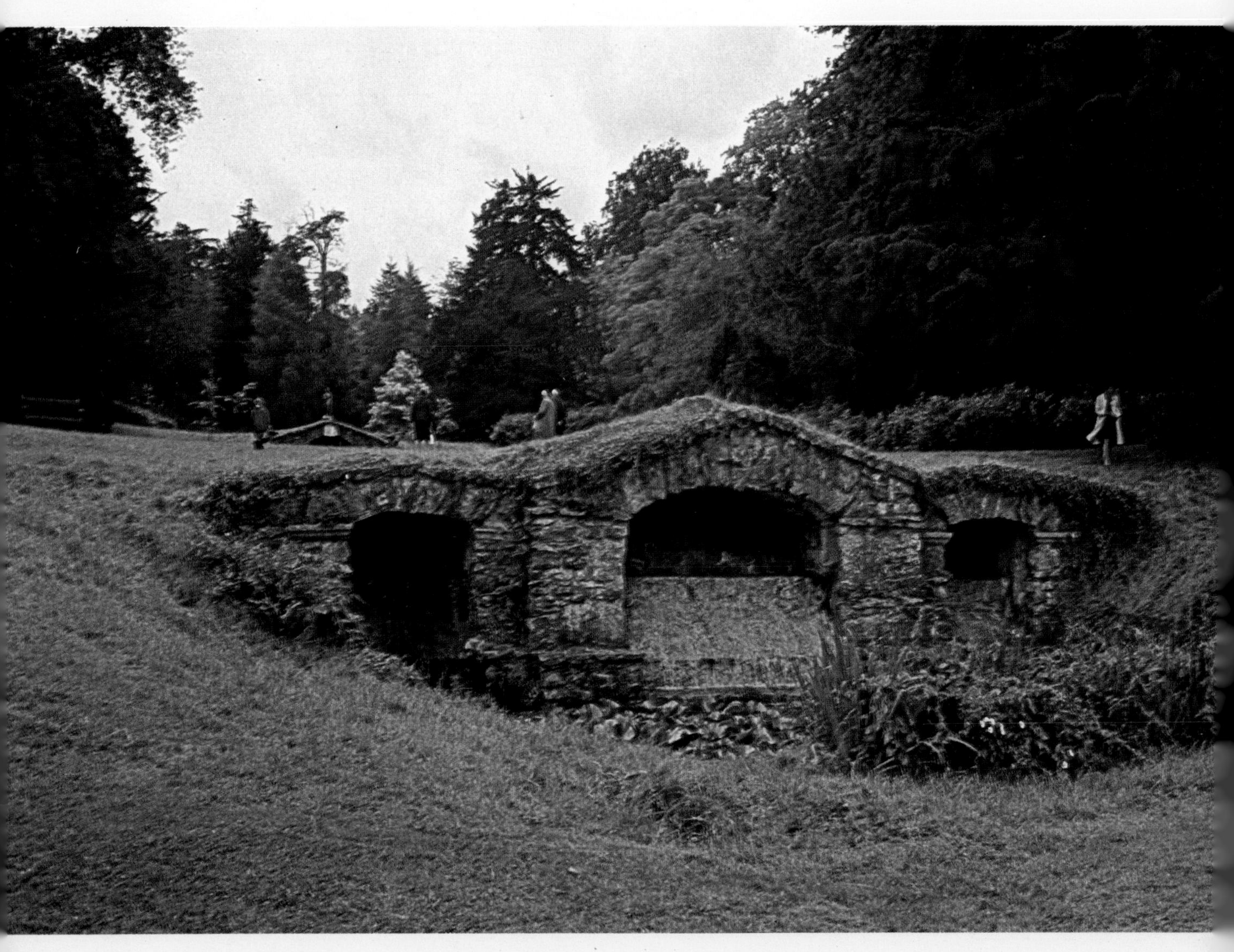

CHAPTER 9

THE ENGLISH SCHOOL OF LANDSCAPE GARDENS

Up to the 1720s the 'natural' school of landscape design had been fostered by the 'propagandist' writers, Ashley Cooper, Addison and Pope, and by talented amateurs such as the Lords Burlington, Cobham, Bathurst and Carlisle.

Bridgeman, the Royal gardener, who worked at Stowe, had been trained in the formal school by his predecessor Henry Wise; and though encouraged to design informally, he never overcame his early training.

Pope's garden at Twickenham was a 'transitional' one, for as always happens with new developments, however clear one may be in theory, one cannot immediately shake off the earlier forms. There are many other transitional gardens, both in France and England. It has even been suggested that Sir William Temple, despite his reservations, made an early attempt at an informal garden at his manor at Moor Park, Surrey.

The first professional English landscape gardener, William Kent, though he started as a coach painter, was fortunate to obtain early patronage and was sent to Rome to study. There he met the Earl of Burlington, perhaps the best informed of the amateurs of the new informal movement. Among the coterie which developed around the Earl of Burlington, Kent was young, enthusiastic and of a new generation. He burst the bonds of formalism and became the first great professional landscape designer of the English School.

220

The Lower Cascade at Rousham. There are ponds and another cascade in the grassed area above.

Though Alexander Pope was unable to carry his landscape ideas very successfully into practice, he was of great assistance to Kent, collaborating with him on work for Lord Burlington at Chiswick; Lord Bathurst's Oakley Woods; Viscount Cobham's Stowe; and Rousham for General Dormer. Rousham is still beautifully preserved and illustrates wonderfully well, the combination of 'informal' landscape treatment with classical 'incidents' which is so characteristic of the early gardens of the 'Natural' school.

Italy was still a Mecca for artists and garden makers so the introduction of classical incidents became a fashionable trend and they played a prominent part in these early English gardens. This classical taste is understandable when one remembers the earlier architectural preoccupation of intellectuals with everything from classic Greece and Rome. So miniature Greek or Roman temples were introduced as resting places on the main walks, or as focal points in the main vistas. But these were merely incidental to the basic garden form and did not seriously affect the overall unity of design. They played the same role in the English gardens as the tea houses, sculptured rocks, waterfalls and lanterns of

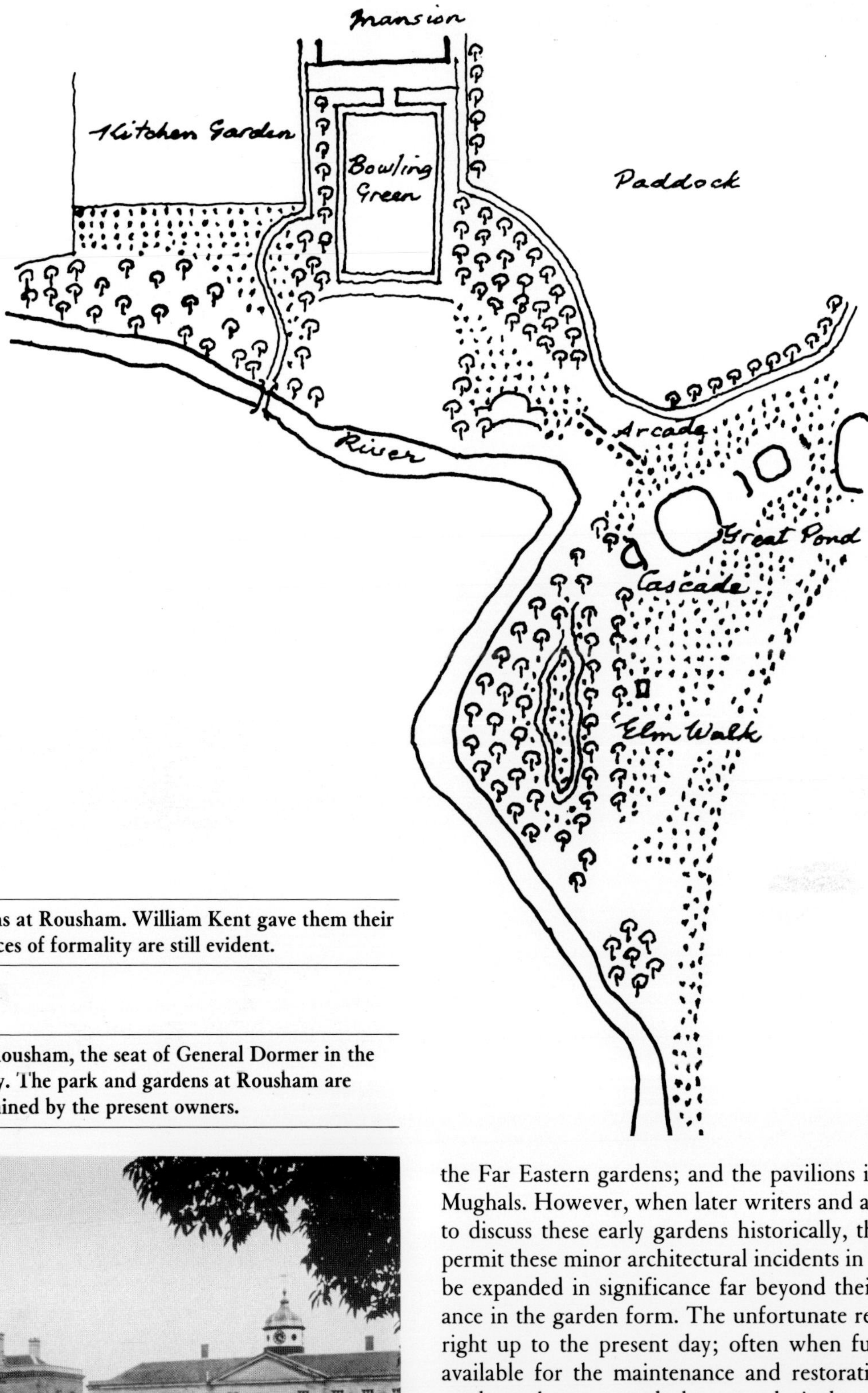

221

Plan of the gardens at Rousham. William Kent gave them their present form. Traces of formality are still evident.

222

The entrance to Rousham, the seat of General Dormer in the eighteenth century. The park and gardens at Rousham are beautifully maintained by the present owners.

the Far Eastern gardens; and the pavilions in those of the Mughals. However, when later writers and architects came to discuss these early gardens historically, they frequently permit these minor architectural incidents in the gardens to be expanded in significance far beyond their real importance in the garden form. The unfortunate results continue right up to the present day; often when funds are made available for the maintenance and restoration of historic gardens, they are used almost exclusively to restore these often trivial constructions, rather than to maintain and preserve the garden itself.

The first professional English landscape gardener, William Kent, like Pope, approached informal garden-making as a kind of projection of picture-making. They both sought inspiration from the landscape painters, especially from Claude and Poussin. But this was only a point of departure, and Kent soon became involved with landscape design in three dimensions. Horace Walpole summarised Kent's contribution in this way:

223

Rousham. A walk beside the river. Classical incidents combine with open prospects in a delightful way.

224

Rousham. Looking along the Elm Walk.

Painter enough to taste the charms of landscape, bold and opinionate enough to dare to dictate, and born with the genius to strike out a great system from the twilight of imperfect essays. He felt the delicious contrast of hill and valley changing imperceptibly into each other – remarked how loose groves crowned an easy eminence with happy ornament, and while they called in the distant view between their graceful stems, removed and extended the perspective of delusive comparison. But of all the beauties he added to this beautiful country none surpassed his management of water. Adieu to canals, circular basins, and cascades tumbling down marble steps, that last absurd magnificence of Italian and French villas. The gentle stream was taught to serpentine seemingly at its pleasure, and where discontinued by different levels its course appeared to be concealed by thickets properly interspersed, and glittered away at a distance where it might be supposed naturally to arrive.[1]

Walpole's sketch is probably a faithful one of Kent. But it does less than justice to the contributions of the talented amateurs who played an important role in the development of the English School during the 1730s and 40s. The best known of the surviving pleasure grounds designed in this way is Stourhead at Stourton, laid out by Henry Hoare between 1741–1750. Now owned by The National Trust, this is a closed circuit 'stroll garden' designed around a beautifully formed lake. The handling of open and enclosed space is particularly fine, and the whole has a unity not always achieved at this time. The very considerable planting additions to the park in the ensuing years have been done with judgement and taste, and the unity of the whole has been happily preserved. The new plantings include conifers, maples, rhododendrons and azaleas, which were unknown in Europe until the nineteenth century.

Beginning with Woburn Farm by Philip Southcote in the 30s, and carrying through to Leasowes designed by the poet Shenstone, Painshill by Charles Hamilton, Envil by Lord Stamford (still in an excellent state of preservation), and Walpole's own Strawberry Hill, all designed in the 1740s, these individual private parks had a considerable impact on the new school. The direct influence was important, but they also encouraged amongst the English landed gentry a confidence in their own powers of perception. The movement thus acquired a very broad base by the end of the eighteenth century, and provided an expanding field of work for the professionals.

William Kent died in 1748. He was succeeded by the best known of the professionals of the English School, Lancelot (Capability) Brown. Brown was born in 1715 of a lower-middle class Northumberland family. His first post was gardener to Sir William Lorraine. In 1739 he moved to Wotan to work for Sir Richard Grenville. A year later, under Kent at Stowe he absorbed the principles of architecture and landscape design which the other had developed, and when Kent died he succeeded him.

Lord Cobham died in 1749, one year later; but by then Brown had become expert in his new profession. In 1751 he moved to London and built up a remarkable practice as an architect and landscape designer. He must have had a magnetic persuasive personality. His nick-name is supposed

225

A view over the lake at Stourhead, one of the finest of the landscape gardens of the English School. It was created by Henry Hoare, a member of a family of bankers, between 1740 and 1750. It is a stroll-garden punctuated by a number of classical incidents.

226

One of the superb beech trees which form a framework to the stroll garden at Stourhead.

to have arisen from his invariable enthusiasm on the 'capabilities' of a potential site. George III became his patron and William Pitt his friend. He was a man of consequence in circles of people who were shaping the times in which they lived.

Unlike Kent, he had a thorough knowledge of the craft of gardening, which gave him even greater confidence than his mentor. Under Brown's guidance and direction over 150 important parks and pleasure grounds, through the length and breadth of England, were developed or modified in the new English style.

These included Stowe, Blenheim Palace, Audley End, Ingestre in Staffordshire, Blickling Hall in Norfolk, Chroome for Lord Coventry in Worcestershire (one of his most lavish undertakings), Ragely Hall in Warwickshire, and Berrington in Herefordshire. Now vested in The National Trust are Stowe, Blickling Hall and Berrington.

As a result of these activities Brown created countless lakes and water gardens, thousands of acres of rolling pasture and woodland, going far to achieve his boast that he was 'finishing England'. The Ha ha, or sunken barrier, first used in England by Beaumont, the pupil of Le Nôtre, at Levens Hall in the late seventeenth century; and by Bridgeman at Stowe in the early eighteenth century, was widely employed by Brown to preserve the uninterrupted visual link between Manor House and pasture land.

227

The Pantheon, Stourhead. The most successful of the classical incidents in the garden. Stourhead's garden was designed as an entity quite independent of the manor house.

228

Stourhead. One of the many delightful views over the lake.

229

Stourhead. Another vista to the lake, looking back towards the entrance from the other side of the valley.

230

Sketch showing a Chinese sunshade that once adorned the upper area of the Stourhead garden.

231

Plan of Stourhead. Key: 1. Temple of Flora. 2. Grotto. 3. Pantheon. 4. Temple of Apollo.

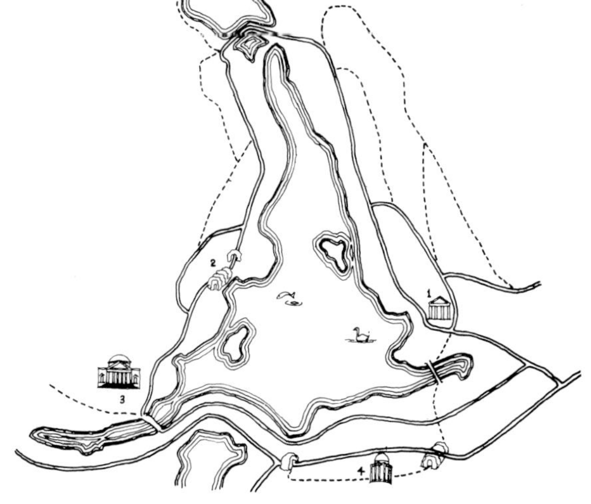

232

Leasows. William Shenstone, the poet, designed this *ferme ornée* (ornamental farm) in 1743. His estate was a working farm, and his ideas had considerable influence. The name *ferme ornée* seems to indicate that the first of these farms were most probably built in France.

Brown's parks, though informal in character, had a strong, bold, almost classical structure. They lacked the variety and sensitive detail of some of those created by contemporary amateurs and later professionals, probably because he could not devote the loving care and patient attention which can be bestowed only by someone living and working on the site over an extended period.

Kent had pioneered the new landscape style, but Brown firmly established informal parks as the accepted English model, which was to influence the whole future of man's relationship with his environment.

Sir William Chambers was another professional architect and landscape designer who exerted considerable influence during the 1760s and 1770s, both in England and abroad. Swedish-born, and son of a Scottish merchant, he received early patronage from Count Carl Frederick Schaffer, a Minister to Gustaf III of Sweden. Chambers visited China three times in the 1740s and was an enthusiastic propagandist of Chinese form in both gardens and architecture. He was employed by Augusta of Sax-Gotha at Kew Gardens from 1760–1763, and there built the still-surviving Pagoda. He published *Views of the Gardens and Buildings of Kew* in 1763, and a dissertation on Oriental gardening in 1772. His influence on garden design was considerable and extended to the land of his birth, Sweden.

Something of a vacuum was left in the professional field when 'Capability' Brown died in 1783. This was quickly filled by Humphrey Repton. Born in 1752, son of an officer in the Excise Department, Repton received a good education. At twelve years of age, he went into the home of a merchant banker in Holland, where he fostered a taste for poetry, music and drawing. His father gave him a start as a merchant after his marriage at twenty-one to Mary Clarke, with whom he had been in love for three years. They had sixteen children, seven of whom survived.

Repton was unsuccessful as a merchant, and on the death of his parents, who left him a small fortune, he bought a modest estate in Sustead, Norwich. It was here he first gave reign to his interest in landscape design.

Repton became one of the most important designers of the English Landscape School for a number of reasons. First, his work had a direct influence, for his projects included schemes for over two hundred English estates. Secondly, he wrote down the theories and principles of landscape design which evolved through his work, and these publications became a guide and inspiration both to his countrymen in Great Britain, and to the whole of the English-speaking world. Thirdly, his theories gave rise to those of others, notably Uvedale-Price and Richard Payne-Knight.

233

Plan of Painshill. The seat of Charles Hamilton.

234

The lake at Painshill, a landscape estate designed by Charles Hamilton, another talented amateur of the English School.

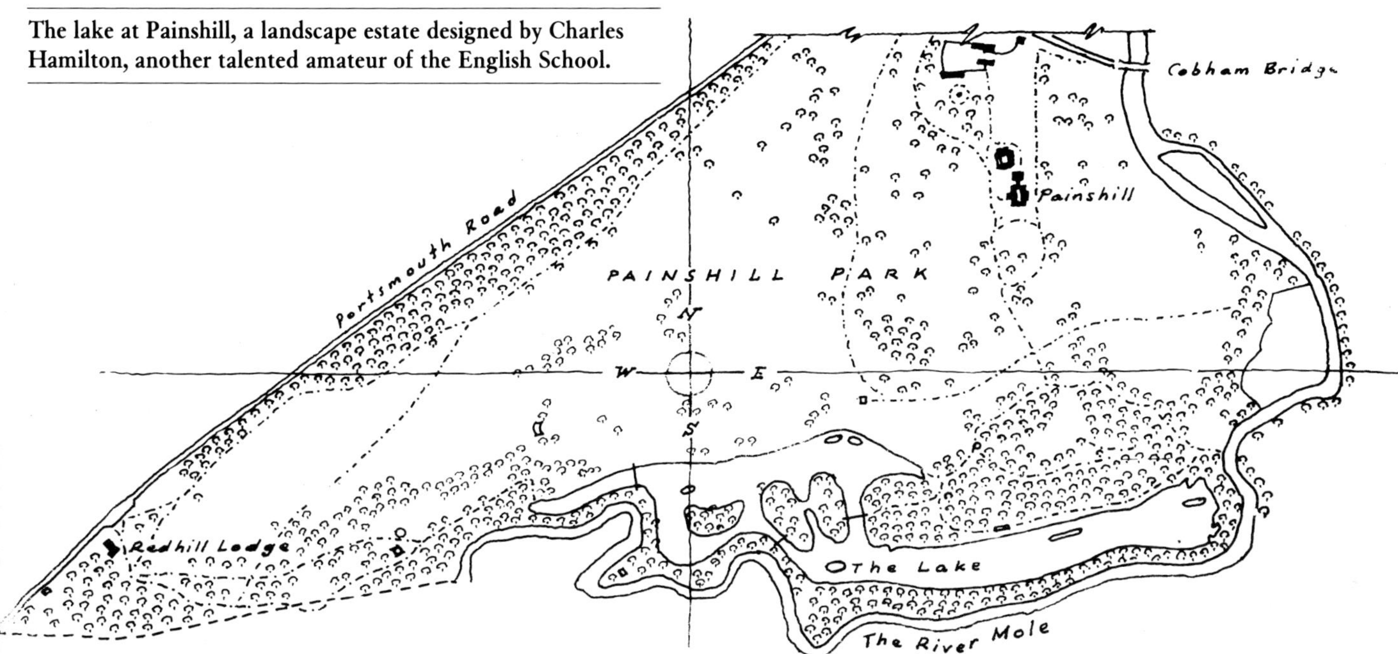

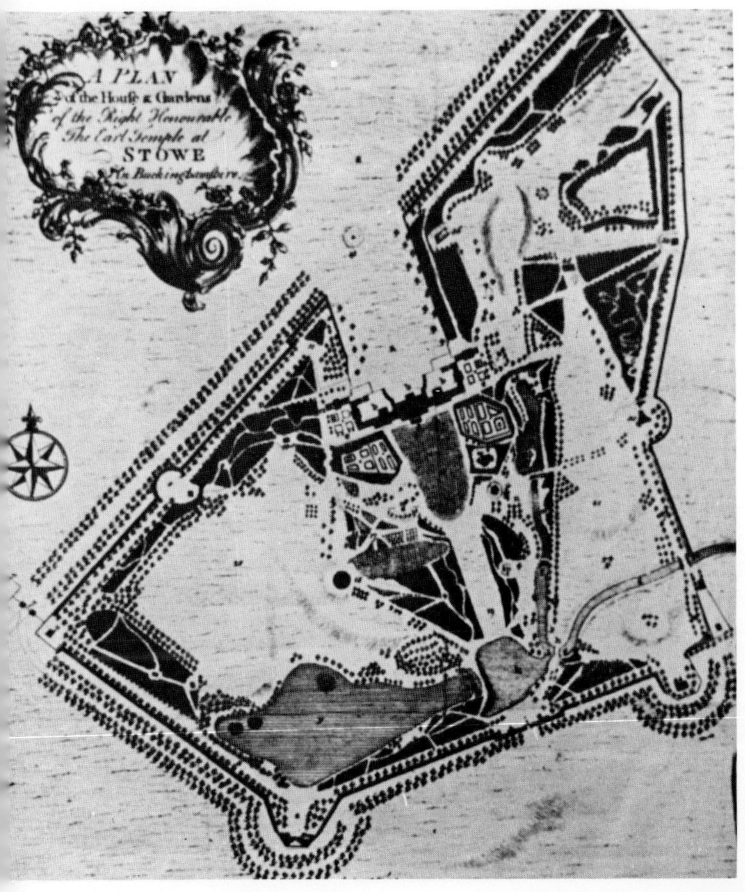

235

Plan of Stowe. By William Kent. Kent succeeded Charles Bridgeman as landscape garden designer at Stowe. Bridgeman's original plan was much more formal and Kent's still shows traces of this formality; as did most of his plans, including that at Rousham. During Kent's later years at Stowe, Lancelot (Capability) Brown worked closely with him.

236

This aerial sketch shows Stowe as it was finally planned by Capability Brown. Very much as it is today.

237

The mansion, Stowe. A football field is in the foreground. The estate is now a boys' school.

238

The High Valley, Stowe, as left by Brown. It appears on Kent's plans with a more formal character.

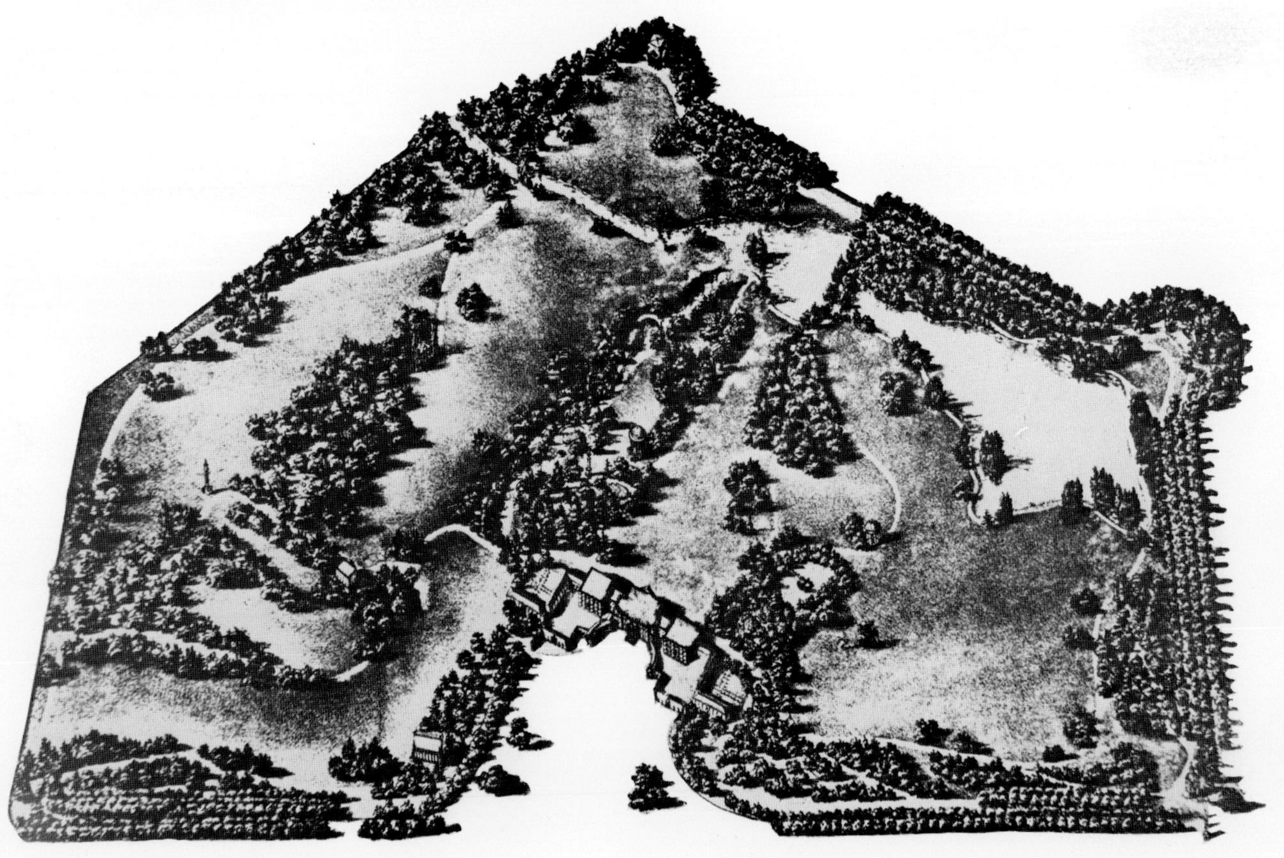

239

Morning glimpse of The Temple of Ancient Virtue at Stowe. One of the many charming incidents which enliven the walk around the grounds.

240

Downstream from The Shell Bridge, Stowe. These glorious man-made English landscapes helped to create a world-wide passion for natural beauty.

241

A view up to the Shell Bridge at Stowe. It is interesting to compare this with the cascade at Rousham. Complete naturalness has now been used with great success.

242

Morning on the Eleven Acre Lake, Stowe.

243

A swan and cygnets on the Eleven Acre Lake, Stowe.

244

Lily pads on the Eleven Acre Lake. The contribution of the English School to landscape aesthetics and conservation of the environment can hardly be exaggerated.

245

Richmond Park. Another of Capability Brown's projects.

246

The Backs, Cambridge. A plan was prepared for The Backs by Capability Brown.

247

The Lake, Blenheim. When asked to go to Ireland to plan an estate, Capability Brown is reputed to have replied: 'I must finish England first.'

248

Chinese Pagoda, Kew Gardens. Designed by Sir William Chambers, an enthusiast for things Chinese.

249

Cobham Park, Kent. The park was originally designed by Humphrey Repton, who consolidated the work of the professional designers of the English School. He wrote extensively about his design theories.

250

The woods at Cobham Park. Much of the beauty of the English landscape so admired today, was created by man.

251

Part of the park of Cobham, as at Stowe, is used as a golf course. The Manor is used as a school.

252

The golf course at Cobham is still quite beautiful.

William Gilpin, a clergyman of the Church of England, Sir Uvedale-Price, and Richard Payne-Knight engaged in considerable controversy over different aspects in informal landscape design, using such terms as The Sublime, the Beautiful and the Picturesque; most of these concepts are almost meaningless to us today. Time has tended to eliminate the shades of difference detected by the exponents of informal landscape design. The major effect of the controversies was to consolidate the achievements of the English School.

Repton consolidated the achievements of both the professionals and the amateurs. He realised that formality was appropriate in certain situations, especially where buildings were dominant in a landscape. 'I do not profess to follow either Le Nôtre or Brown,' he wrote, 'but select beauties from the style of each to adopt so much of the grandeur of the former as may accord with a palace, and so much of the grace of the latter as may call forth the charms of natural landscape.'[2]

This of course, like all quotations, does not give more than a hint of the design qualities of Repton. Repton was a consolidator; the aesthetic revolution was over, and the philosophy and practice of the Natural School was firmly established. He could safely seek the valuable material and techniques of the supplanted formal style, thus enriching the new movement without endangering it.

His theoretical writings are based upon his 'Red Books'. He produced one for every project with which he was involved, the contents consisting of a report, maps, plans and sketches to explain and illustrate the work, or alterations, proposed. Repton disliked 'fashion' and the inordinate search after novelty which he considered as characteristic of uncultivated minds. A 'functionalist' who appreciated the principle of utility, he had no sympathy with a design that did not provide adequately and frankly for the plain necessities of human living.

An immortal in his own right, he is also immortalised in the novels of Jane Austen, who was obviously a great admirer of his work. D'Arcy's estate at Pemberley, which is so excellently described in *Pride and Prejudice*, and which so bewitched Elizabeth Bennett, is clearly designed in the best 'English' manner. And in *Mansfield Park*, Jane Austen's plot sees that the somewhat dull Rushworth is urged by his betrothed, Miss Bertram, to consult Repton about plans to improve his estate at Sotherton.

Up to the end of the eighteenth century the main creative activity associated with the English School took place in the countryside, and the work of the professional designers and the talented improvers was largely confined to private estates.

The industrial revolution, with the consequent deterioration of the urban environment, created new objective conditions, which in turn caused a change of emphasis from rural to urban environment.

253-54

In his little 'Red Books' which he produced for each job undertaken, Humphrey Repton frequently used an illustration with an ingenious overlay, so that he could show his client how the landscape would appear before and after the alterations. 253 is Lanley Park, Kent, before his alterations, and 254 includes an overlay which shows how the removal of an avenue would transform the park.

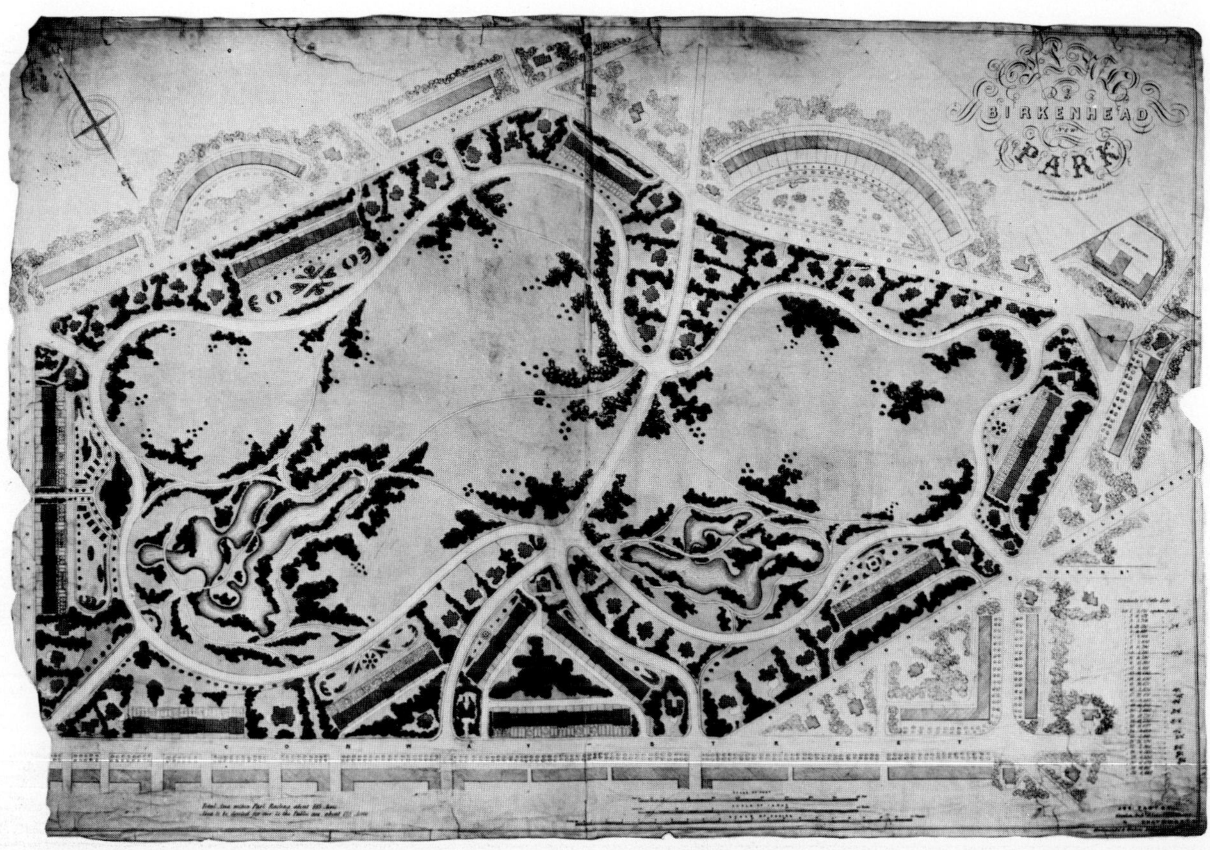

255

A plan of Birkenhead Park, Liverpool, designed by Joseph Paxton. This park had a profound influence on Frederick Law Olmsted when he visited Europe. Olmsted later became America's most notable landscape architect.

The poet and artist, William Blake (1757–1827) drew attention to the plight of city-dwelling working people, in passionate and stirring terms. William Wordsworth (1770–1850) consolidated the new ethos of the beauty of nature and natural things. Renowned for writing the finest nature poetry of English literature, he said of gardens: 'The poet of the garden should weave into one sympathetic whole the joy of every living being, of men and children, birds and beasts, hills, rivers, trees and flowers.'[3]

A strong movement grew, to campaign for an improved city environment. By the end of the eighteenth century the Royal Parks of London were made available to the people – a privilege which had become practically a public right. Even land speculators found it was rewarding to include public parks and gardens in their sub-divisions. A Select Committee was appointed by parliament in February 1833 'to consider the best means of securing open spaces in the vicinity of populous towns, and public walks and places of exercise, calculated to promote the health and comfort of the inhabitants.'[4]

Repton died in 1818, too early to participate fully in this new development, though he collaborated successfully with John Nash in his plan for West London extending from St James's Park to Regent's Park. His successor in the field of professional landscape gardening, Joseph Paxton, played the major role in the development of the English urban parks movement.

Joseph Paxton was born in 1801, of working-class origin. He had an unhappy childhood and received no formal education. As a first step towards migrating to the United States he obtained work at Chiswick, the experimental garden of the Horticultural Society. He was put in charge of the arboretum, and met the Duke of Devonshire, an active member of the Society. In 1826 the Duke offered him the head gardnership of his estate at Chatsworth at £6 a month and a cottage. By the age of thirty-seven Paxton had made Chatsworth one of the most famous gardens in the world. At this time he refused an offer of £1,000 a year to go to Windsor Castle. Like his predecessors, Paxton broadened his design skills to include architecture, engineering and even elementary town planning.

Though his name will always be associated with Chatsworth his most important contribution was that he made the fruits of English landscape design available to the common people of Great Britain in a series of urban parks. These include Prince's Park, Liverpool 1842; Birkenhead Park and Sub-division; Kelvingrove and Queen's Park, Glasgow, 1852–53; People's Park, Halifax (assisted by Ed-

256

St. James's Park, London. The lake was transformed by John Nash in the nineteenth century. Joseph Paxton also worked on this delightful park.

257

Child feeding geese on the lake-edge in St. James's Park.

ward Milner) 1857; Baxter Park, Dundee 1863; Public Park, Dumferline (shortly afterwards). His advice was sought on St. James's Park and the Serpentine in Hyde Park; and, as is well known, he designed The Crystal Palace. The lake in St. James's Park was designed by John Nash, another designer of the nineteenth century.

An insight into Paxton's attitude to design is given by his own comment on the writings of Repton and Uvedale-Price. He felt that Uvedale-Price's chief error was . . . that of sacrificing convenience and comfort on some occasions for the sake of picturesque effect; and the overlooking or under-valuing on that account, of the beauties of the wild scenery . . . Repton and Price may be regarded as the two best writers we have on landscape gardening,' he wrote 'both different, both excellent. The mean of the two will be found the surest path to success.'[5]

258

Bodnant, Denbighshire, the seat of the first Lord Aberconway. A great garden of the English School which we discuss in detail towards the conclusion of Chapter 10.

259

Looking across the canal at Bodnant to one of the giant *Cedrus atlantica glauca* trees planted in the park.

260

Colourful plantings emphasise the late-Victorian character of the Bodnant gardens.

261

A lake view in the valley garden at Bodnant.

The authors consider the quality of Paxton's work is best illustrated by a quotation from *Walks and Talks of an American Farmer in England* by Frederick Law Olmsted. While in England, Olmsted – who was later to become America's most notable landscape architect – visited Birkenhead Park, and was entranced. He wrote:

> I cannot undertake to describe the effects of so much taste and skill as have evidently been employed. I can only tell you that we passed by winding paths over acres and acres of a constant varying surface, where on all sides were growing every variety of shrubs and flowers, in more than natural growth, all set in borders of the closest turf; all kept with the most consummate neatness. At a distance of a quarter of a mile from the gate we came to an open field of clean bright green sward, closely mown, on which a large tent was pitched, and a party of boys on one part, and a party of gentlemen in another, were playing cricket. Beyond this was a large meadow with rich groups of trees under which a flock of sheep were reposing, and girls and women with children were playing. While watching the cricketers we were threatened with a shower, and hastened back to look for shelter, which we found in a pagoda on an island approached by a Chinese bridge. It was soon filled, as were the other ornamental buildings, by a crowd of those, who, like ourselves, had been overtaken in the grounds by the rain, and I was glad to observe that the privileges of the garden were enjoyed equally by all classes. The site of the garden was, ten years ago, a flat sterile clay farm. It was placed in the hands of Mr Paxton in June 1844, by whom it was laid out in its present form by June the following year.[6]

With Paxton we conclude our review of the English or Natural School. Many important landscape designers and gardeners came after him, but they do not belong to the main stream of design which we are here committed to follow. William Robinson and Miss Gertrude Jekyll, both of whom made very significant contributions to garden design, belong more correctly to our concluding chapter, where we shall pick up again the thread of English landscape design and link it with the twentieth century.

We now move briefly to Europe, in particular to Germany and Scandinavia; thence to the United States of America, where the main stream of landscaping was located from the second half of the nineteenth century.

CHAPTER 10
A 'NEW WORLD' OF LANDSCAPE ARCHITECTURE

The English school was destined to influence landscape design far beyond Great Britain. From the 1760s onwards, Europe became enamoured of the new English or Natural School, to which they gave the name of 'Anglo Chinoise'. Gardeners from England, or more often from Scotland, were brought to France and Russia to design parks in the 'English' manner. These included the Petit Trianon at Versailles, laid out for Marie Antoinette; the garden at Ermenonville by Geradin, which contained Rousseau's cottage and tomb; and Bagatelle, built by Count d'Artois in seven weeks to win a bet with his sister-in-law, the Queen Marie Antoinette.

A Scot, Thomas Blackie, laid out the English parks at Bagatelle. In Russia, Field Marshall Prince Potempkin employed a gardener named Gould (who had worked under 'Capability' Brown) to lay out his estate. But the most important influence exerted by the English School in Europe took place in Germany and Sweden.

262

The South Pond, Central Park, New York. The Park replaced a degenerate area of waste land and rubbish dumps, two miles by half a mile, in the central city. The Park that Frederick Law Olmsted created from 1858 would have gladdened the heart of Andrew Jackson Downing who earlier had a concept in his imagination. Olmsted's park met the needs of every kind of citizen, and the sylvan setting still provides refreshment from the turmoils of the city.

The German development of the Natural School grew out of a literary circle in a manner somewhat similar to that of England. A group of Swiss poets around Bodmer adopted Shaftesbury's and Thompson's ideas of 'the greatness and ennobling effect of untouched nature.' Kliest and Gesner both supported the movement, the former writing: 'Why strive to adorn Nature by using imitative arts? What I love is the country meadow and the wild hedge.'

Christian Hirschfeld wrote his *Observations on Garden Art* and *History and Theory of Horticulture.* Hirschfeld steeped himself in the new landscape ideas from England and considered he was their representative and champion in the Fatherland.

Goethe (1749–1832), designed the great parks of Weimar. He was influenced by Hirschfeld's work and also by the earlier park at Worlitz (1769–1773) by Duke Francis at Dessau. Schiller, ten years younger than Goethe, first met him in 1794 and they became firm friends. Schiller wrote an appreciative analysis of the English landscape movement: 'Nature which we find in the English gardens is no longer the same nature as the one we had left outside. It is a nature enlivened by a soul, a nature exalted by art, which delights not only the simple man, but the man of education and culture; the one she teaches to think, the other to feel.'[1]

Some of the early 'natural' parks in Germany were somewhat grotesque affairs, incorporating ruins and romantic structures of extravagant dimensions, imitating and exaggerating a detail, but failing to comprehend fully

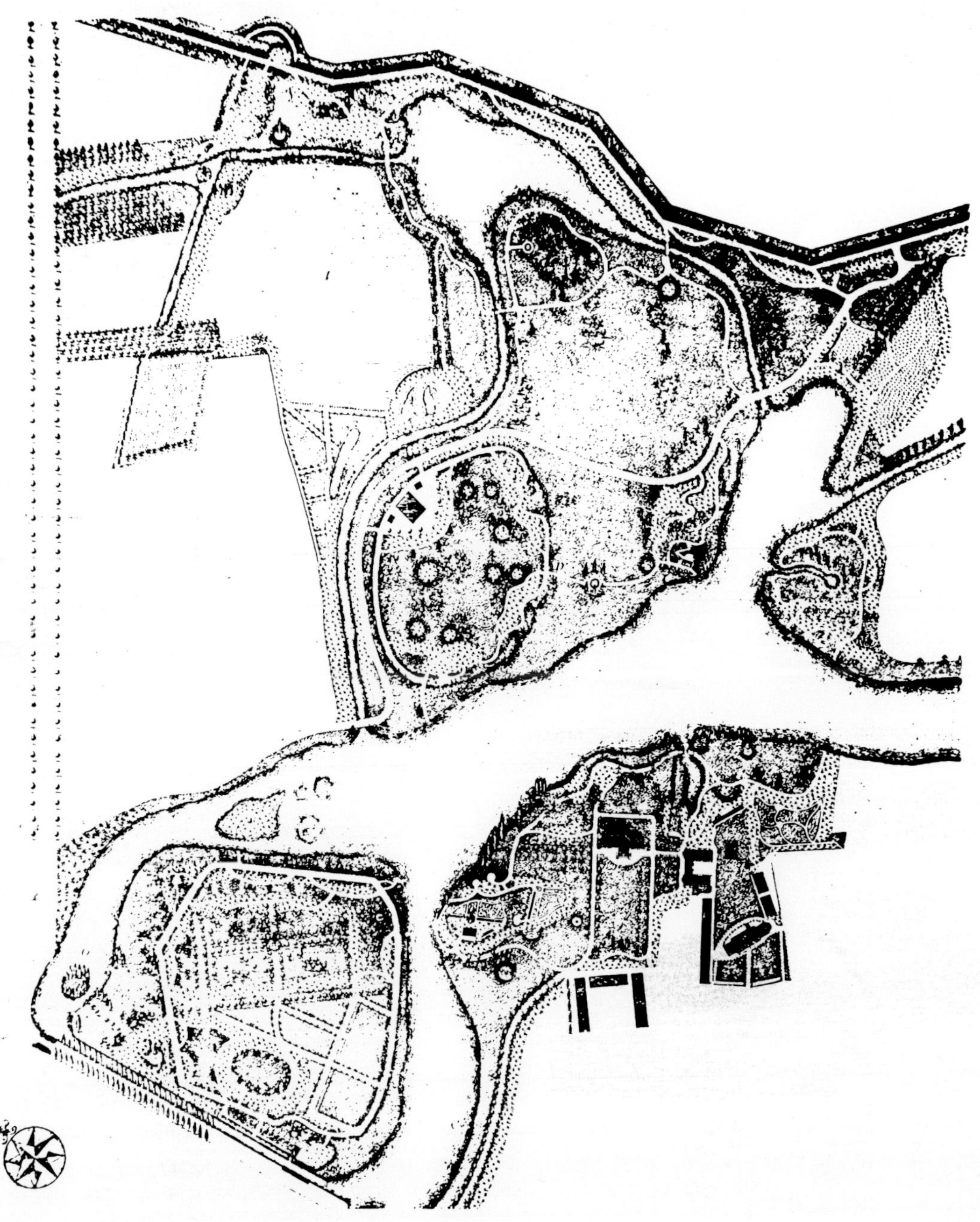

263

Worlitz Park, the summer home of Duke Francis of Dessau, was one of the first English-type parks built in Germany. This is the plan, the basis of which was a large informal park.

the underlying principles on which the design was based. One of the most successful, known as Puckler Park, was built by Prince Von Puckler Muschau. In 1834 he published *Hints on Landscape Gardening* which was a considerable contribution to the theory of informal landscape design. Puckler Park had a strong impact in Europe. When Louis Napoleon decided to re-design the Bois de Boulogne in the English manner, he sought the advice of Von Puckler.

In Germany the movement also gave rise to public parks: a notable one at Munich, designed by Count Rumford; and another at Frankfurt, comprising a broad belt two miles long surrounding the city. These parks not only established the 'natural' movement, which was to continue up to the present day; but considerably affected the New World, through visiting theorists such as Andrew Jackson Downing and F. L. Olmsted. F. L. Olmsted was also impressed by the re-designed Bois de Boulogne. The new design, by Georges E. Haussman and Jean C. A. Alphand, was part of a huge programme for Paris carried out by Haussman between 1853 and 1870.

In Sweden, interest in Chinese philosophy and landscaping had developed at the end of the seventeenth century, but did not become widespread and of practical importance until the middle of the nineteenth century. The famous East India Company was formed in the year 1731 and from that time, valuable information and descriptive material flowed into Sweden. Carl Gustaf Ekeberg wrote an account of Chinese husbandry in 1753-54, and King Gustaf III introduced many political reforms based upon

264

The Hermitage in Weimar Park, Germany, starting point of a 'natural' scheme for the park, developed by the poet Goethe.

265

The Park at Ermenonville, France. Designed by the Marquis de Girardin on the inspiration of Rousseau. Rousseau was buried on an island in the park.

English precedents. As a result Sweden became fertile ground for export of the English landscape ideas; and, encouraged by Sir William Chambers, Frederick Magnus Piper came to England to study between 1772–1780. He later designed Haga Park, Stockholm Park and Drottningholm Park and successfully introduced the 'natural' school to Scandinavia.

Unlike the situation in France, the competition of the formal landscape design in Germany and Scandinavia was not overwhelming, with the result that the informal aesthetic has persisted in both Germany and Sweden as a major continuing influence right into the twentieth century.

Although we have been unable to obtain detailed information about Switzerland, it had a democratic constitution, and Swiss poets were active in Germany; so we feel fairly confident that landscaping in Switzerland was also influenced at this time by the English Landscape School.

Despite the fact that they illustrate the considerable impact that the English School had upon surrounding countries, these movements in Europe did not become the main stream. Not for almost a century – in the 1840s – were the theories of the English School of Landscape Design destined to flow in a powerful stream out to the New World of

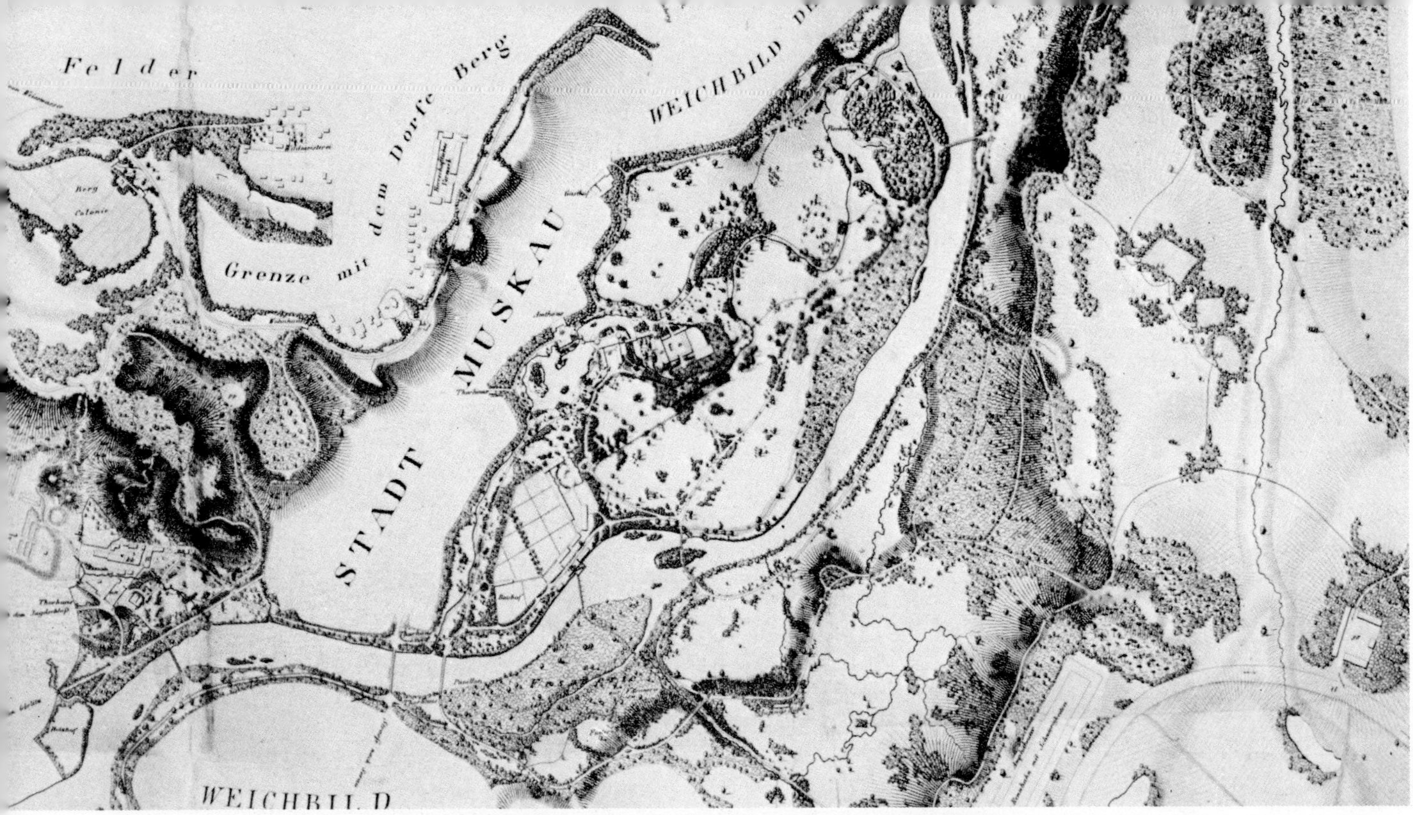

266

Plan of Puckler Park, Muskau. This was another famous German park designed in the English manner. It was created by Prince Puckler who went bankrupt in the process of building it.

267

A view of Puckler Park, Muskau, designed by Prince Puckler.

North America. This change was pioneered by Andrew Jackson Downing.

A foundation had been laid in America by earlier writers. Edgar Allen Poe (1809–1849) wrote:

> Ellison might have become a musician, poet, painter or sculptor. I have now mentioned all the provinces in which the common understanding of the poetic sentiment has declared it capable of expatiating, but Ellison maintained that the richest, truest, and most natural, if not altogether the most extensive province had been unaccountably neglected. No definition had spoken of the landscape gardener as of the poet, yet it seemed to my friend that the creation of the landscape garden offered to the proper muse the most magnificent of opportunities. Here, indeed, was the fairest field for the display of imagination in the endless combining of forms of novel beauty, the elements to enter into combination being, by a vast superiority, the most glorious which the earth could afford. In the multi-form and multi-colour of the flowers and trees he recognised the most direct and most energetic efforts of Nature at physical loveliness. And in the direction and concentration of this effort, or more properly in its adaptation to the eyes which were to behold it on earth, he perceived that he would be employing the best means, labouring to the greatest advantage, in the fulfilment, not only of his own destiny as a poet, but of the august purpose for which the Diety had employed the poetic sentiment in man.
>
> Mr Ellison did much towards solving what has always seemed to me to be an enigma; I mean the fact, which none but the ignorant dispute, that no such combination of scenery exists in Nature as the painter of genius may produce; no such paradises have been found in reality as have glowed on the canvas of Claude.[2]

Andrew Jackson Downing, writer, landscape gardener and horticulturalist, was born in Newburgh, New York State, in 1815, where his father, originally a wheelwright, then ran a plant nursery. A delicate, reserved boy, he completed an education interrupted by ill health at the age of sixteen. When his father died, he joined his brother Charles in operating the nursery.

From his youth he had a strong affinity with nature; and, encouraged by wealthy neighbours Baron de Lidderer and Edward Armstrong, he developed an enthusiastic interest in landscape design and made contact with 'refined and polished society'. He began writing in his teens and was published early in the *New York Mirror,* but decided afterwards to improve his authority by further study and to refrain from publishing in the meantime. He married in 1838 Caroline Elizabeth De Wint, a young woman of spirit, refinement and intelligence, and established himself on a 6-acre tract, applying the principles of landscape design and architecture which he had acquired since leaving school.

In 1841 he completed and published his most important work, *A Treatise on the Theory and Practice of Landscape Gardening, adapted to North America.* The book made an instant impression on his contemporaries and went through numerous editions; and from its publication until his death, he was recognised in both Europe and the United States as the chief American authority on Rural Art. English writers Louden and Linley eagerly sought his opinion. His theory was based upon that of Humphrey Repton, but in the process of applying Repton's writings to the American scene, he introduced a great deal of original thought. In 1846 he became editor of *The Horticulturalist,* a new periodical, through which, by editorials, he reached a very wide public. He continued as editor for the remainder of his life.

It is unlikely that Andrew Jackson Downing was aware that it was the thousands of years of development of an informal landscape aesthetic in China that was the true origin of the English Landscape School.

In 1850 he visited Europe; a long awaited trip where he met Calvert Vaux, a young English architect, who became his partner. With Vaux, he designed and constructed houses and grounds for a number of estates on Long Island, along the Hudson, and in other parts of the eastern United States. In 1851 Downing was engaged, with Vaux, to lay out the grounds of The Capitol, The White House, and the Smithsonian Institution in Washington.

Downing was the first great American landscape designer. Though influenced strongly by the English School, he succeeded in pioneering a distinctly American movement. The most important contribution of his later years was his leading role in establishing Central Park in New York. He began campaigning through *The Horticulturalist* in the late 1840s, continuing with *Letters from Europe* in 1850. His campaign fell on fertile ground. William Cullen Bryant had sown the first seeds in the *Evening Post* as early as 1844, but Downing's editorials gave authority and definition to these pleas.

In the 1850 Mayoral elections in New York, both candidates favoured the establishment of the Park; and upon his election Mayor Kingsland sent a message to the Common Council requesting the setting aside of land for the Park as a matter of urgency. The Committee reported favourably on the idea, and selected Jones Wood, an area of 160 acres, as a suitable site. Downing felt that this was not central enough, and much too small, and advocated the present site in these terms:

> Five hundred acres may be selected between 39th Street and Harlem River, including a varied surface of land, a good deal of which is yet waste area, so that the whole may be purchased at something like a million dollars. In that area there will be space enough to have broad reaches of park and pleasure grounds, with the real feeling of breadth and beauty of green fields, the perfume and freshness of nature. In its midst would be located the great distributing reservoirs of the Croton aquaduct, formed into lovely lakes of limpid water, covering many acres, and heightening the charm of the sylvan accessories by the finest natural contrast. In such a park, the citizens who would take excursion in carriages, or on horse back, could have the substantial delights of country roads and country scenery, and forget for a time the rattle of the pavements and the flare of brick walls. Pedestrians would find quiet and secluded walks when they wished to be solitary, and broad alleys filled with thousands of happy faces when they would be gay. The thoughtful denizens of the town would go out there in the morning to hold converse with the whispering trees, and the varied tradesmen in the evening, to enjoy an hour of happiness by mingling in the open spaces with 'all the world'. Where would be found so fitting a position for noble works of art, the statues, monuments and buildings commemorative at once of the great men of the nation, of the history of the age and country, and the genius of our highest artists? In the broad area such a verdant zone would gradually grow up, as the wealth of the city increases, winter gardens of glass, like the great Crystal Palace, where the whole people could luxuriate in groves of the palms and spice trees of the tropics, at the same moment that sleighing parties glided swiftly and noiselessly over the snow covered surface of the country-like avenues of the wintry park without.[3]

In this quotation and in that of Olmsted about Birkenhead Park quoted previously, the enthusiastically democratic character of the landscape movement of the United States was clearly evident. It is also apparent that the principles

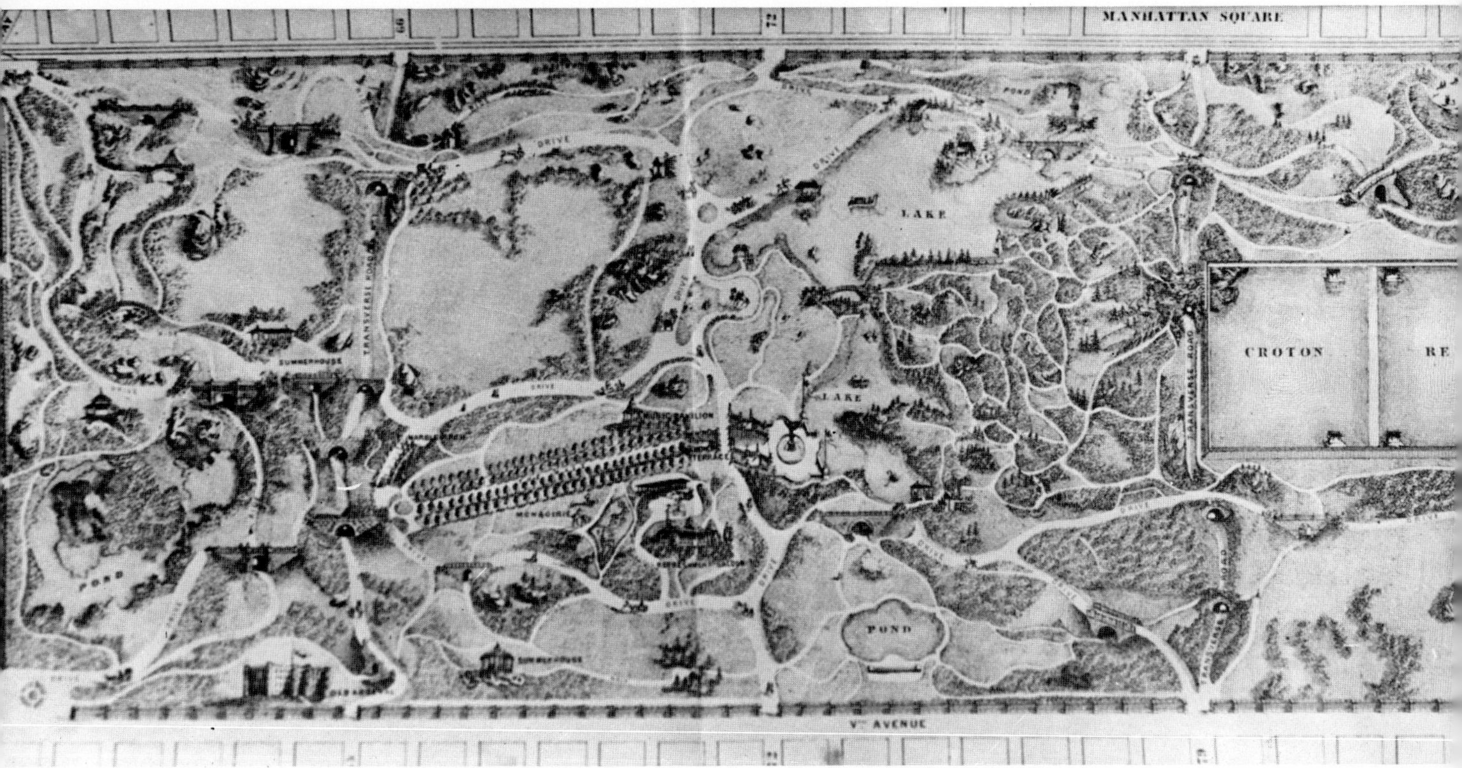

268

An early isometric drawing of 'Greensward', the landscape scheme that Olmsted and Vaux prepared and carried out for Central Park, New York.

adopted by Olmsted and Vaux in their successful scheme for Central Park had already been clearly enunciated by Andrew Jackson Downing.

Downing was not destined to see his ideas for Central Park put into operation, nor to carry out any work on his Park commissions in Washington. In July 1852, less than a year after he wrote the editorial quoted, Downing was drowned in a ferry accident. He and his friends were bound for New York from Newburgh on the steamer Henry Clay. The Captain engaged in a race with another boat, and the *Henry Clay* caught fire. Downing helped organise the evacuation, which reached a panic stage; though a strong swimmer himself he was drowned while endeavouring to save his friends. His body was not discovered until the following day.

It was no accident that the initiative in the development of landscape gardening in the nineteenth century had moved to North America. The urban park movement in Europe grew out of the new democratic forces released by the Industrial Revolution.

Joseph Paxton, England's most prolific park designer came from an English working class background, and the demand for public open space had the deliberate objective of alleviating the lot of the working man.

Voltaire in the 1760s advocated tolerance and sympathy as an alternative to revealed religions, blind belief and submission. Rousseau's *Social Contract* at about the same time stated: 'Man is born free, and everywhere he is in chains,' and claimed that the people should be sovereign, and their will carried out by an executive chosen by them.

Beethoven composed his symphonies, Schiller wrote the epic William Tell, originally planned by Goethe. William Tell was a tremendous success, 'rapturously received throughout Germany, crystallising as it did the national aspirations towards freedom.' The poet Heinrich Heine, and the social philosophers Karl Marx and Frederick Engles were the final products of this European movement.

The social development which had produced the English School of Landscape Design continued in Europe, influenced by important personalities. Rousseau and Goethe played a conscious and active role in the European Park movement, Rousseau's cottage and tomb being located at Ermenonville on one of the finest French 'Natural' parks.

But just as happened in the development of the 'Natural' movement in France over a century earlier, the objective conditions no longer existed for the expansion of the park movement as a democratic form in Europe – even in England. In North America the position was totally different. The mood of the whole country was actively, even aggressively, republican. The scale and tempo of development, and the open space available in the vast new continent were quite unprecedented. It was inevitable that a new, modern, profession of landscape architecture should first develop in the United States of America, carrying on the traditions of the landscape designers of England.

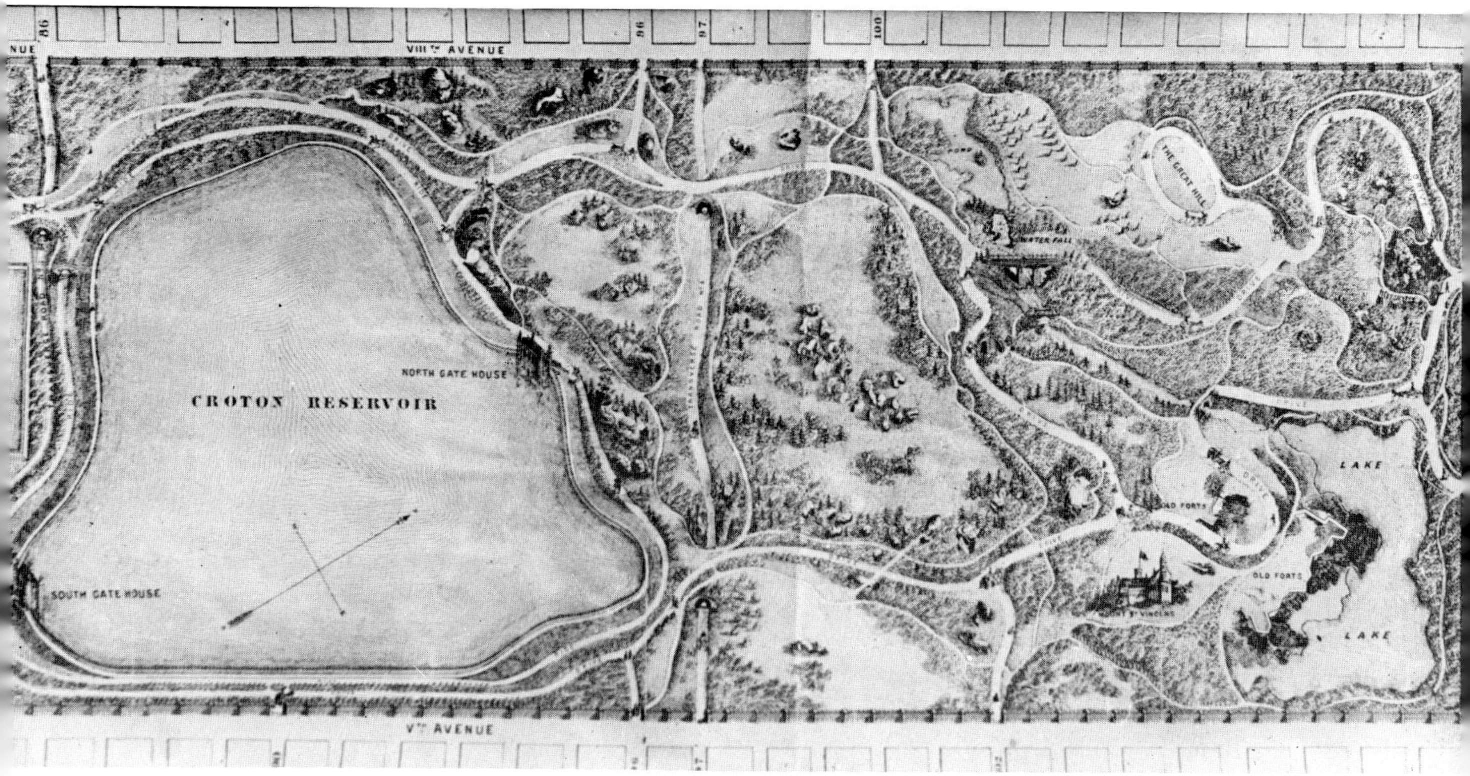

269

Frederick Law Olmsted. His place in landscape architecture is similar to that of Beethoven in music.

One of Andrew Jackson Downing's friends at the time of his death was an enthusiastic farmer, traveller and writer, Frederick Law Olmsted. Olmsted, born in 1822, was seven years Downing's junior. He was the son of a well-to-do merchant at Hartford, Connecticut.

Olmsted's paternal forebears had been numbered amongst the intelligent townsmen and farmers of this region since its settlement in 1635. Both his father and step-mother were enthusiastic nature lovers, and were interested in people and places. By the age of sixteen Frederick and his younger brother John, had made four journeys, each over 1,000 miles, in New England, New York State and Canada.

Olmsted's early formal education was a desultory one, broken by solitary rambles around the countryside, in which he was welcome at the homesteads of a number of congenial friends and acquaintances. It is amusing to read that one of these was a shy, kindly man, with a moderate competence, a fine house and an old garden, and a keen interest in the natural sciences. Said Olmsted: 'He introduced me to Isaac Walton.' Olmsted's words show that he, like Wordsworth, admired and loved Walton's writings. During these early years Olmsted came to know the countryside intimately; to love nature and natural things intensely. This was to inform and guide him in his later great projects.

Olmsted was prevented from entering Yale University by his ill-health; he studied engineering for two years, and

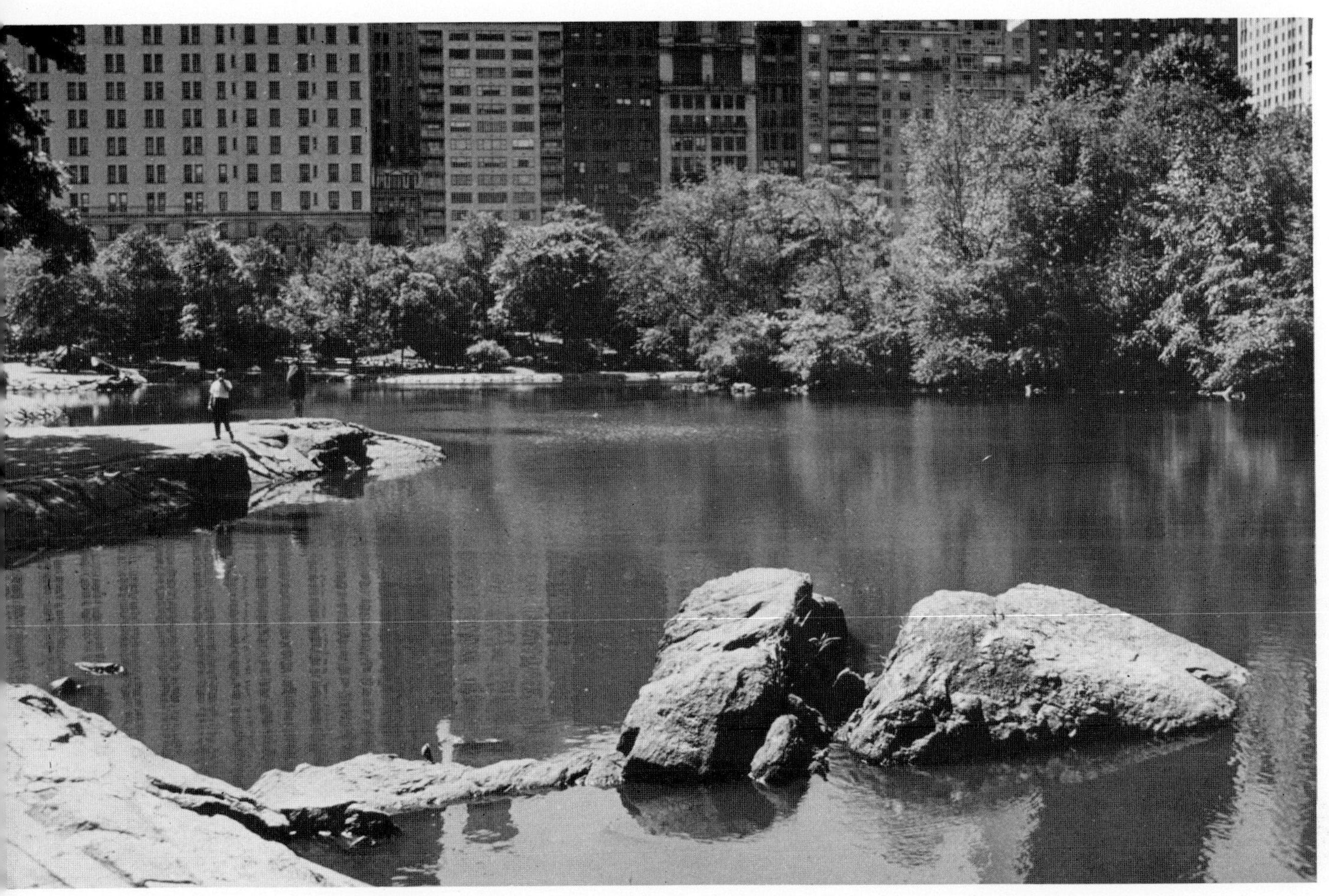

270

Another view of the South Pond in Central Park. Here the relationship to the busy city is quite apparent, but often careful screening creates an air of sylvan seclusion.

then in 1840 he worked for a couple of years in a dry-goods importer's office in New York. To escape from this uncongenial confinement, he travelled 'before the mast' to China and on his return a year later, decided to become a farmer. Through his brother John, who was attending Yale University, he met many intellectuals including Charles Loring Brace, and became interested in sociological problems. He farmed enthusiastically until 1850, when his literary activities began to overshadow farming. It was during this period that he met Andrew Jackson Downing, having contributed articles to *The Horticulturalist.*

In 1850, armed with introductions from Downing, he went to England, accompanied by his brother and Charles Brace. One of the results was his *Walks and Talks of an American Farmer in England,* 1852, a book in which we catch the first glimpse of the genius which was to come: 'What artist so noble, has often been my thought, as he who, with far-reaching conception of beauty and designing power, sketches the outline, writes the colours, and directs the shadows of a picture so great that Nature shall be employed upon it for generations, before the work he has arranged for her shall realise his intentions.'[5]

In the same book, Olmsted discourses on the subtle and elusive beauty and wonder of Nature:

> Dame Nature is a gentle woman. No guide's fee will obtain her favour, no abrupt demand; hardly will she bear questioning, or direct curious gazing at her beauty; least of all will she reveal it truly to the hurried glance of a passing traveller, while he waits for his dinner or fresh horses, or fuel or water; always we must quietly and unimpatiently wait upon her. Gradually and silently the charm comes over us, the beauty has entered out souls. We know not exactly when nor how, but going away we remember it with a tender, subdued, filial-like joy.
>
> Does this seem nonsense to you? Very likely, for I am talking of what I don't understand. Nature treats me so strangely; it is past my speaking sensibly of it, and yet, as part of my travelling experience, I should speak of it. At times I seem myself to be her favourite, and she brings me to my knees in deep feeling, such as she blesses no other with; oftener I see others in

> ecstacies, while I am left to sentimentalise and mourn, or to be critical and sneering, and infidel. Nonsense still – but tell me, do you think it is only for greed of trout that your great sensitive man lingers long, intently stooping over dark pools in the spray of the mountain torrents, or stealing softly away through the bended rushes, or kneeling lowly on the darkest verdure of the wooded meadow. What else? I know not what he thinks, but of this I am assured – while his mind is not intent upon his trivial sport his heart and soul will be far more absorbed of the rugged strength, the diffuse impetuous brilliance and the indefinite gliding grace or the beautiful twilight loveliness of the scene around him, than if he went out searching, labouring directly for it as for bread or fame.[6]

Two years after Olmsted's return from abroad, Downing met his tragic death. Olmsted, who became associated with a publishing business over the next few years, was in financial difficulties, and he travelled in Europe in 1856, probably to get away from the worry. He visited many countries and upon his return in 1857, by a happy accident he met a friend in New York who was influential on the Council of Central Park. The friend suggested he apply for the superintendent's job. Olmsted did so, and was appointed. Despite discouragement from the Chief Engineer, Viele, he entered upon his duties with enthusiasm. A year later a competition was held for a design for the Park. Calvert Vaux, architect, and previous partner of A. J. Downing, asked Olmsted to join him in submitting a scheme. Olmsted at first refused, out of respect for his senior, Viele. But when Viele treated this action with contempt, Olmsted changed his mind and he and Vaux submitted a scheme under the title of Greensward. It was successful, receiving almost universal acclaim.

The scheme, covering an area of two and a half miles by half a mile in the centre of a teeming metropolis, was not only a work of genius, but it was a forerunner, meeting and solving many problems of twentieth-century urban landscape. High-speed and recreational traffic were segregated within a park system for the first time. Four major traffic roads bisected the Park: they were visually concealed by sinking, and the landscape form flowed over them without apparent interruption, each transverse road having a similar effect to the early ha-ha's of Europe. Pedestrian walks and bicycle tracks were separated from vehicle drives by underpass and foot bridge, and yet, as Olmsted himself proclaimed: 'The Park throughout is a single work of art, and as such, subject to the primary law of every work of art, namely that it shall be framed upon a single noble motive, to which the design of all its parts, in some more or less subtle way, shall be confluent and helpful.'[7]

Olmsted also quite deliberately designed Central Park to serve the people, especially the working people who could not afford to travel. 'It is one great purpose of the Park', he wrote, 'to supply to the hundreds of thousands of tired workers, who have no opportunity to spend their summers in the country, a specimen of God's handiwork that shall be to them inexpensively, what a month or two in The White Mountains or the Adirondacks is, at great cost, to those in easier circumstances'.[8]

Olmsted now made a most important decision, with the realisation that he was embarking on a new field of activity which went far beyond the usual concept of landscape gardening. He considered it was essential to differentiate between the horticulturalist and the park and garden designer. He decided to call himself a 'landscape architect', terms which had a logical derivation. Kent and Capability Brown were architects as well as landscape gardeners: Andrew Jackson Downing had found he needed architect Vaux to assist him in his work. A new profession of Landscape Architecture was the next step.

It was one thing to produce a scheme for Central Park, but it was quite another to put it into effect. Olmsted's training as an engineer and his farming experience, now stood him in good stead. From 1858 until 1861 he worked and lived on the site, having been appointed Architect-in-Chief and Chief Executive Officer of the Board.

271

A miniature gorge in the forest of Central Park looks over a foot path to the main lake. Central Park became the inspiration and model for hundreds of city parks throughout the United States.

272

Weekend boating is popular in summer on the main lake of Central Park. The lake has many little backwaters, half hidden, which visitors enjoy exploring.

273

A long view of the sweeping, contoured area called The Long Meadow, which helps to unify Prospect Park, Brooklyn, U.S.A. Designed by Olmsted and Vaux in 1865.

274

Waterlilies in the Botanic Garden section of Prospect Park.

275

Prospect Park, Brooklyn. A dry stream bed with rock arrangement very reminiscent of Japan.

276

This early photograph of work on the construction of Prospect Park, Brooklyn, gives some idea of the vast scale of the undertaking when modern machinery was unavailable.

277

Another field in which Olmsted made an important contribution was in the design of grounds of universities. This is Olmsted Lawn in the campus of Michigan State University.

Some idea of the scope of his construction activities may be gained from the following: he re-arranged five million cubic yards of earth and rock to achieve the new landscape forms, and laid 114 miles of drainage pipe to create the 'natural' ponds, hills, valleys and open fields which finally took shape.

In June 1861 during the American Civil War he was appointed Executive Officer of the Sanitary Commission in Washington (the American equivalent of the Red Cross), entailing considerable absence from New York. He still found time to continue design supervision of the work in Central Park.

Olmsted felt a compelling need to participate fully in the creative process of building the Park, but in this his enthusiasm was not shared by his partner, Vaux. This is revealed in a letter to Vaux written in 1863, when their position in the Park was prejudiced by a conflict of personalities. This was between the team of Olmsted and Vaux on the one hand, and Andrew H. Green, the Comptroller of the Park, on the other.

From the beginning of the work Olmsted had been plagued by constant interference from patronage-minded members of the city administration – a condition which was to exist throughout the whole of his association with the Park. But the situation deteriorated when Andrew H.

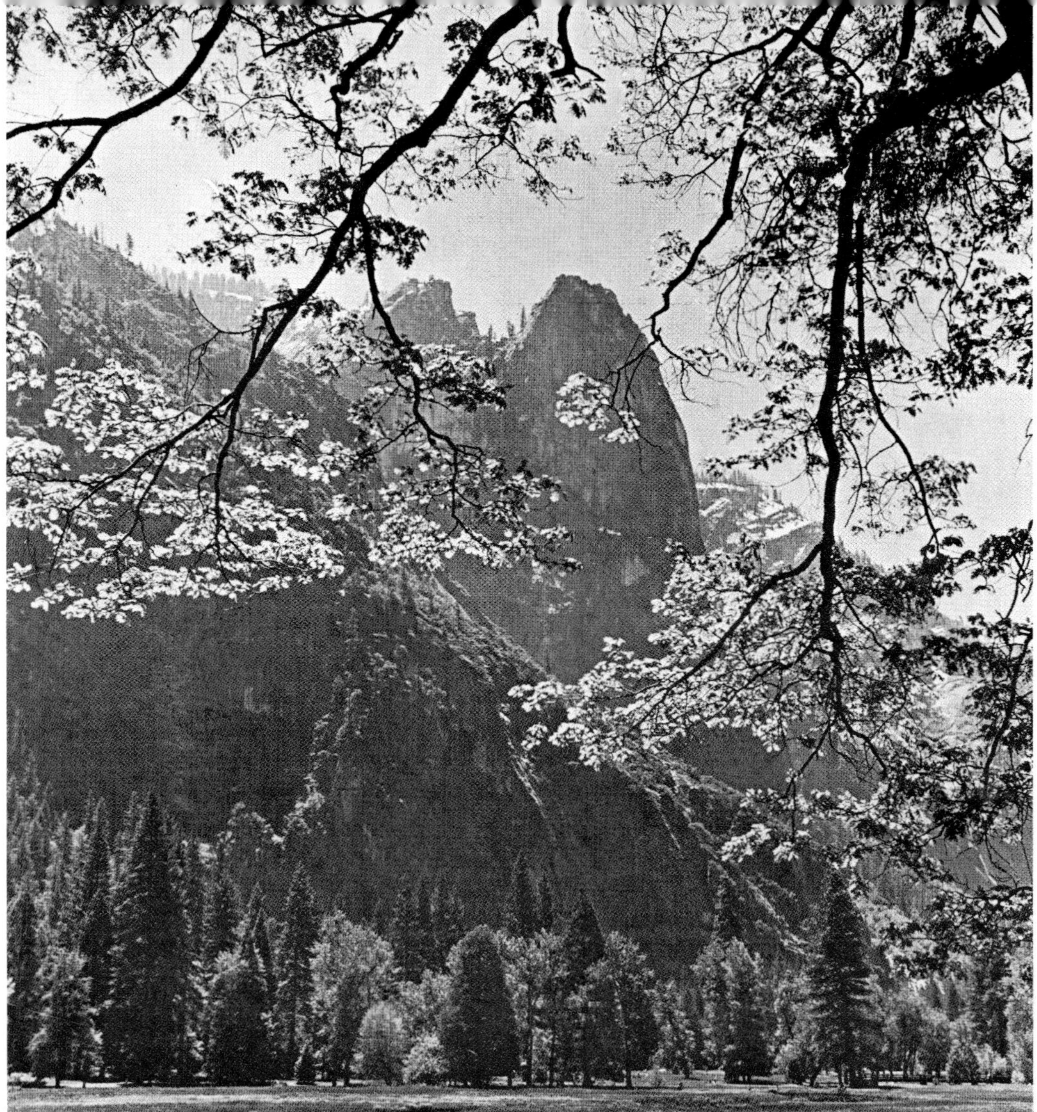

278

Yosemite Valley, U.S.A. Olmsted played a decisive role in the establishment of the National Parks Movement in the United States. He helped to frame the National Bill making Yosemite Valley into a State Reservation in 1864. Olmsted considered that natural beauty was even more restful than man-made imitations of nature.

Green was appointed Comptroller of the Park in 1859. With the best of motives Green interfered with the creative work of Olmsted and Vaux until by 1863 they felt that their position was intolerable. It was at this time that Olmsted wrote Vaux the following letter:

> But you know the advantages offered in the office of Superintendent for spending a good deal of my life in the Park, being with the people in it, watching over it and cherishing it in every way – living in it and being a part of it (whatever else there was) – were valued by me at a valuation which you thought nonsensical, childish and unworthy of me, but it was my valuation of them, and not yours, that was concerned, and that this was something that was deeper than a whim you know, for you know that it existed essentially years before it attached itself to the Central Park, as was shown by the fact that while others gravitated to pictures, architecture, Alps, libraries, high life and low life when travelling, I had gravitated to parks – spent all my spare time in them when living in London for instance, and this with no purpose whatever except the gratification which came from sources which the superintendance of the Park would have made easy and cheap to me to say the least, every day of my life. What I wanted in London, and in Paris, and in Brussels, and everywhere I went in Europe – what I wanted in New York in 1857, I want now, and this for no regard for Art or Fame or Money.[9]

Olmsted's passionate devotion to the Park enabled him to overcome all obstacles, and despite constant harassment, to create the masterpiece which was to lead and inform landscape design in the United States of America.

The conflict with Green led to the resignation of Olmsted and Vaux in 1863, but they were re-appointed as landscape architects in 1865, continuing to advise until 1870, when Mayor Tweed's administration engaged in such blatant jobbery and 'patronage' that Olmsted and Vaux again resigned. Re-instated in 1871 due to public pressure, they were finally discharged in 1878 on the grounds of economy.

Though the problems of staff on the site, clash of personality with Green and interference by patronage-minded

politicians placed a great strain on Olmsted and made his work considerably more difficult, many positive results grew out of these conflicts. As he probably would not otherwise have done, Olmsted was forced to express his ideas in writing, resulting in a volume of landscape architectural theory which has constituted a major contribution to the profession.

In this period he also learned to work with all kinds of people and this experience stood him in good stead during his long and productive professional career. Perhaps most importantly, he was obliged to proliferate, to carry his landscape architectural talent and experience through the length and breadth of the United States. His practice with Vaux developed from a two-man office in 1857-8 to a forty-man office in Boston in the 1880s. In this office 'Olmsted trained the majority of designers and planners who were to shape the country's physical growth throughout the late nineteenth and early twentieth century.'[10]

During this period in California immediately following his resignation from the United States Sanitary Commission, Olmsted played a decisive role in the establishment of the National Park Movement in the United States. He helped frame a national Bill making Yosemite Valley and Mariposa Big Tree Groves into State Reservations, being appointed Commissioner for both Reservations in 1864. A policy report framed under his supervision stated: 'The establishment by Government of great public grounds for the free enjoyment of the people is justified and enforced as a political duty.'[11]

Olmsted in fact felt that natural beauty was even more restful than man-made imitations of nature.[12]

Olmsted and Vaux in 1883 prepared a master plan for the preservation of Niagara Falls. This required the removal of buildings at the edge of the Falls, and provision of forest planting, walks and park areas for public use.

In addition to giving landscape architecture a new dimension during the years of private practice from the 1870s onwards, Olmsted and Vaux helped to pioneer town and regional planning in the United States. Their most notable contributions in this field were Riverside Residential Development, Chicago; Stanford University Campus and Environs, California; circulation and site plannings of the Columbian Exhibitions at Lake Michigan, Chicago; and also the master plan and detailed planning of the Boston Park System.

A leading colleague and ally of Olmsted in the 1880s and 90s was Charles Eliot. Eliot came into Olmsted's office in Brooklyn, Mass. in 1883-4 and played an important role in the development of plans for the Boston Park System.

Eliot, son of one of the most notable Presidents of Harvard University, Charles William Eliot, had every advantage that ancestry, education, wealth and position could give. Early in his life he acquired an appreciation of nature, a talent for drawing and sketching and a sense of locality. He took his B.A. at Harvard in 1882, did a special course at Bussey Institute for a year, and then joined Olmsted's office. In 1885 Eliot visited Europe, including in his itinerary England, France, Italy, Germany, Holland, Denmark, Sweden and Russia. On his return he commenced private practice in Boston, entering enthusiastically into the movement for a unified park system for Greater Boston, and promoting the acquisition of scenic regions as State Parks in Massachusetts. After becoming professional adviser to the new Metropolitan Park Commission of Boston in 1892, in 1893 he re-joined the Olmsted firm at Olmsted Senior's urgent invitation. The firm was re-named Olmsted, Olmsted and Eliot, and from that time till his death in 1897 Eliot was associated with a series of large public and private projects in many parts of the United States.

Considering his short life, Eliot made a most valuable contribution: 'his kindly, earnest uprightness, his family and social connections, his persuasiveness as a public speaker, and his literary and artistic abilities had placed him in the forefront of a young profession, which he joined with his master, Olmsted, in defining and establishing.'[13]

By the time Eliot joined the Olmsted firm the partnership between Frederick Law Olmsted and Calvert Vaux had been dissolved. Olmsted had also severed all connection with Central Park. Calvert Vaux had been appointed Landscape Architect to the Department of Public Parks, New York in January 1888, a position he held until his death in 1895.

There is no doubt that Calvert Vaux made significant contributions in many, if not most, of the projects designed by the Olmsted firm in the 1880s. Due to Olmsted's outstanding genius, his unusual literary ability, and brilliant organising capacity, Vaux's contribution is often partially obscured. He was a vital early link between Olmsted and the pioneering, though short-lived, Andrew Jackson Downing. Calvert Vaux's architectural training would have been invaluable in the more formal sections of the design programmes.

Frederick Law Olmsted's contribution to environmental design in America has been summarised thus:

279

Down from a pass in the Rocky Mountains to the Shadow Mountain water conservation area. National Parks, water conservation and forestry practices, begun in the Olmsted era, have spread throughout the world; and due to this leadership from America, most countries in the world now have policies for the preservation of large areas in their natural state.

280

Boston Common, part of the integrated park system of the city. Four of the popular 'Swan' paddle boats can be seen across the lake. They add a touch of fantasy to the park.

By the end of his lifetime (1903) Olmsted's projects covered the continent from New York to San Francisco, and from Montreal to New Orleans. The success of Central Park showed that for the first time America had found a planning talent sufficient to the task of anticipating national needs. Later years proved Olmsted able to train others in his skills.

At a time when schools of architecture were almost non-existent in America, Olmsted's office educated most of the later leaders in landscape architecture – among them Henry Codman, Charles Eliot Jr., Sidney Shurcliff, and Frederick Law Olmsted Jr. These men later trained their own office staff using Olmsted's techniques. Today there are over 40 schools of Landscape Architecture in America. City planning, developed in part as an adjunct of Landscape Architecture in the 1920s, as were later courses in urban design, now boasts thirty-seven schools. Such schools are a direct result of the efforts of men trained by Olmsted.

We could say that planning for American physical development alternates in its concern between long range and short range needs. Faced with a birth rate that will increase population more rapidly than all past immigration, we are again beginning to focus on the needs of future generations. Among present efforts are the promotion of new towns, a renewed interest in public preserves, and public action in some cities, such as San Francisco, to ensure design focus on natural assets. In such projects, it is perhaps Olmsted's example that is most relevant.[14]

This quotation from a recent publication on Olmsted's work, published in the United States, takes too insular a view of his contributions toward solving environmental problems of world population growth and modern technological invention.

As a citizen of the New World Olmsted thought as an American, and he did not realise, so soon after the apparently unlimited expansion of the nineteenth and early twentieth centuries, such situations would arise. He was, however, well aware of the 'civilising effect' of his contribution to both nineteenth and twentieth-century America, as the following extract from a letter to an old friend, written in the 1890s, clearly indicates:

> I need not conceal from you that I am sure that the results of what I have done will be of much more consequence than anyone else but myself supposes. As I travel I see traces of influences spreading from it that no one else would detect, which, if given any attention by others, would be attributed to fashion. There are, scattered through the country, seventeen large public parks, many more smaller ones, many more public or semi-public works, upon which, with sympathetic partners and pupils I have engaged. After we have left them they have, in the majority of cases, been more or less barbarously treated, yet, as they stand, with perhaps a single exception, they are a hundred years ahead of any spontaneous public demand, or of the demand of any notable cultivated part of the people. And they have had an educative effect perfectly manifest to me, a manifest civilising effect. I see much indirect and unconscious following of them. It is strange how often I am asked 'Where did you get that idea?' as if an original idea on the subject had not been expected. But I see in the new works of late much evidence of effects of invention, comprehensive design, not always happy, but symptomatically pleasing. Then I know that I shall have helped to educate in a good American school a capable body of young men for my profession, all men of liberal education and cultivated minds. I know that in the minds of a large body of men of influence I have raised my calling from the rank of trade, even a handicraft, to that of a liberal profession, an art, an art of design. I have been resolute in insisting that I am not to be dealt with as a mere agent of my clients, but as a councillor, a trustee on honour. I have always refused to take employment on other terms.[15]

Frederick Law Olmsted was a man of genius. He can be compared in stature only with those other men and women in the arts and sciences who tower above their fellows – William Shakespeare in drama, Leonardo da Vinci in painting, Anna Pavlova in the dance, Albert Einstein in science, to name a few.

But Olmsted was not alone in the practice of landscape architecture and garden art in the nineteenth century. In the United States as early as 1861 a Swiss-born architect and engineer, Jacob Weidenmann, became superintendent of parks in Hartford, Connecticut. He published a book setting out his theories in 1870, *Beautifying Country Homes, a Handbook of Landscape Gardening.* Weidenmann pioneered the conversion of cemeteries in U.S.A. to beautiful landscaped parks, and in 1888 published a book on this subject: *Modern Cemeteries*. He died in 1893.

Another important pioneer in landscape architecture was Horace William Cleveland who was active in landscape gardening in Salem, Massachusetts in the 1850s. With his partner Robert Morris Copeland, he assisted in the promotion for a Central Park in New York. He worked with Olmsted and Vaux in Prospect Park, Brooklyn. Olmsted valued him highly and they became firm friends. Cleveland moved to Chicago in 1869, setting up practice there, and was appointed landscape architect for the South Park and Connecting Boulevard in 1872. He collaborated again with Olmsted and Vaux on the Chicago South Park.

281

The Pond, Graceland Cemetery, Chicago. The designer O. C. Simonds became renowned as a designer of park cemeteries in America.

Weidenmann and Cleveland made their start as landscape gardeners designing individual gardens and estates; as Olmsted and Vaux had done, both finished with a much wider vision of landscape design.

Perhaps the most significant event for environmental design that happened at the end of the nineteenth century, was the formation of the American Society of Landscape Architects. The initiative came from Warren H. Manning, a landscape architect working in Boston. In 1897 he wrote to Charles Eliot seeking his support but Eliot was discouraging. Next Samuel Parsons, a previous partner of Calvert Vaux in New York, sent a circular letter to landscape architects suggesting the formation of a Society; but the younger Olmsted felt it was too soon. After Manning and Parsons got together in New York, the Olmsteds decided to co-operate. Although neither Eliot nor Olmsted at first supported the idea of a Society this was probably because they were very busy and did not feel the need of one.

In 1899 eleven people met in the New York office of Parsons and Pentecost and founded the American Society of Landscape Architects. They called themsleves Charter Members and consisted, besides W.H. Manning and S. Parsons, of the following: Nathan F. Barrett, Miss Beatrix Jones (later Mrs Max Farrand), Daniel W. Langton, Charles N. Lowrie, John Charles Olmsted, Frederick Law Olmsted Jr., Ossian C. Simonds of Chicago and Downing Vaux. The first President was John Olmsted, Vice-President S. Parsons, Treasurer C. N. Lowrie and Secretary D. W. Langton.

The background of the group is of interest: two were civil engineers, three were from landscape architectural families, several had trained in the Olmsted firm, others were talented amateurs who had been attracted to a study of landscape design and practice by aesthetic and environmental interests.

One year later, in 1900, the first professional training course was inaugurated at Harvard University.

The formation of the American Society was an epoch-making event for the new profession which has just been identified by Frederick Law Olmsted when he adopted the title Landscape Architect. It was of world consequence, since the title landscape architect has been universally adopted for professional people working in the field of Landscape Design and garden art. There are now four thousand members in the American Society of Landscape Architects and the profession is having a profound influence on the environment of the United States.

The landscape architects of Great Britain did not establish an Institute until thirty years later. But, although the profession had not been organised there, some important developments in landscape design and garden art were taking place in England.

ENGLAND IN THE NINETEENTH CENTURY

From the time of the Renaissance, we have seen that European navigators were given confidence by possession of the compass, and ventured far out into unknown seas in their search for a sea route to the fabled riches of the East. They had come upon many 'new' lands, including the southern portion of Africa, the Americas, the large island continent of Australia, the South Sea Islands and other islands; which they proceeded to annex for the benefit of their respective nations. Man's insatiable curiosity led him to investigate all the strange and wonderful products of these primitive lands, so that soon the exploratory expeditions included men of science – botanists and biologists – who avidly collected plants and animals to take back to Europe. Animals, dead, were identified, classifed, displayed in museums and books: live ones exhibited in zoos. Dried plants were identified, classified, stored in herbariums: living ones grown in private collections and in the botanical gardens which were soon established in most of the main European centres. Here the plants were acclimatised, naturalised, distributed and became widely available through the rise of commercial nurserymen.

The British Empire was then a cohesive world-wide 'international' organisation, with her sons and daughters stationed in many countries. Collectors in foreign lands sent their seeds and specimens to Kew Gardens, a former Royal Park which had been opened in the eighteenth century for the scientific study of trees. Botanical gardens in other centres carried out similar work.

It was a far cry from the days of Queen Hatchepsut who had proudly boasted that she had brought one species of tree from a distant land . . . now the suburban garden maker had readily available, hundreds of trees, shrubs and flowers from every country in the world. The prevailing scientific fervour for systematic botany had made

282

William Robinson, an ardent supporter of the English school, turned his attention to more intimate gardens in the last quarter of the nineteenth century. He advocated the wild garden. This drawing of Golders Green is from his book *The English Flower Garden.*

283

Gertrude Jekyll began her garden career as a talented amateur. Initially trained as a painter, she concerned herself with the question of a more restrained and tasteful use of colour in the garden. She drew much of her inspiration and ideas from the cottage gardens of the English countryside. This is the garden of her own home, Munstead Wood.

'botanising' all the rage among educated people of the nineteenth century.

But the patrons of private gardens had changed. Initiative had passed in the nineteenth century from the person of royal or aristocratic lineage, owner of vast private estates, into different hands – the new middle-class – and we shall first discuss the multitude of suburban owners of a few acres or considerably less.

Analysing these smaller gardens from the point of view of design, we find that the suburban garden, because of its limited extent, often derived its aesthetic inspiration – albeit unconsciously – from traditions of the country cottage garden. This was a pleasant place; its neat borders and beds of flowers, fruit and vegetables provided a gay display of annual flowers against a unifying background of green fields, trees and lanes. However, when transplanted to the suburbs, tidied up and bereft of the unifying background of green fields and trees, the cottage garden loses much of its unself-conscious charm.

Other influences were also at work. The great gardens of the Renaissance in France and Italy had become known through books and travel, and many people sought to emulate them. The small suburban garden-owner could not run to acres of elaborate parterres, but at least could he not have a few geometrically-shaped flower beds? In the ubiquitous hedge and the excessive pruning and shaping of trees and shrubs, can one not trace a longing for topiary, that ultimate expression of man's domination over Nature?

Some talented amateurs endeavoured to meet the challenge presented by the new, small garden. In England, William Robinson and Gertrude Jekyll are probably the best known and represent tendencies which arose in other places too. Their work extended from the late nineteenth century into the first part of the twentieth and they exerted considerable influence by their practical work and by their writings in horticultural journals, magazines and books.

William Robinson was an ardent admirer of the informal design of the large country estates which had transformed the English countryside during preceding centuries. He concentrated his attention on the garden rather than the park, and vigorously opposed the architectonic trend (represented by Sir Reginald Blomfield) which sought to project the structural form and formality of the house into the surrounding garden.

Of the exotic plant material, he advocated the use of those which could readily adapt to their new environment; and in place of the geometrical flower bed and regular borders, he was enthusiastic about the 'wild' garden, a permanent informal arrangement of trees, shrubs and flowers presented so beautifully that a painter would be inspired to depict it on canvas . . . a curious reversal of the period when gardens sought their inspiration from paintings! He stressed the need to organise this 'wild' garden so that every plant would be hardy and suitable for the micro-climate in which it was planted, could grow 'naturally' among its fellows and make a happy contribution to the whole garden composition.

Robinson abhorred the garish 'bedding out' then so prevalent in public and private gardens. Endeavouring to bring some unity of design into the super-abundance of new plant material flooding the market, he evolved the herbaceous border. A great variety of flowering plants, perennial and annual, of different heights and shapes and colours, were combined in the herbaceous border in an overall unity of harmonious form and colour.

284

Hydrangeas and iris in a shrubbery at Sissinghurst Castle.

Robinson's book *The English Flower Garden,* first published in 1883, had run to fourteen editions by the time he died in 1926 when he was eighty-seven years of age. William Robinson found a wide body of support for his ideas and succeeded in consolidating the English informal garden as we know it today, with its soft edges, verdant lawns, shrubberies, herbaceous borders, and loose framework of trees. His theory and practice were ideally suited to the smaller garden and were enthusastically applied to the new suburban garden.

And the number of educated people had appreciably increased. Increased efficiency in printing had led to a proliferation of books, magazines, newspapers. Literacy became widespread. As a result of the industrial revolution and the exploitation of the newly acquired colonies, the advanced countries now had a large organised labour force and a new middle class, so that very large numbers of people had more resources and more leisure than before.

Towns and cities had changed. They expanded upwards and sideways — vertically as well as horizontally. Science with its newly evolved materials, new modes of construction, was transforming buildings from small-scale structures of brick and stone, to towering sky-scrapers of steel, glass and concrete.

Cities were expanding into the countryside. Time and distance had been so reduced, first by the railroad, then by the motor vehicle, that people whose daily employment was in the city, could live further and further from their place of employment. The dwellings of the new middle-class spread out in suburbs.

All these changes had far-reaching effects on the environment and on people. In this study were are considering only one small facet of people's activity — how they manage the environment, and in particular, how they make gardens. So let us now look briefly at the effects on garden-making.

The patrons of garden-making had changed from the wealthy, powerful and aristocratic individual to a multitude of small property-owners. The new suburban landowner, educated, comparatively affluent and with leisure, often made the house and garden a major preoccupation. He — or quite often, it was she — learnt the science and the craft of garden-making from newspapers, magazines, and specialist horticultural and garden journals; they exchanged and enlarged their experience with others of similar interests, through horticultural societies and garden clubs. The Royal Horticultural Society was founded in 1804. The new plant material coming from all over the world could be obtained from commercial nurseries.

The *embarras de richesse* often bewildered, so that the

285

'The Dial', Kemsing, Kent. One of hundreds of thousands of private gardens with layout and shrubberies in the Robinson-Jekyll manner. Although most of the people who build these gardens today have never heard of either Gertrude Jekyll or William Robinson, their theory and practice have become an unconscious part of our tradition.

suburban garden-grower became rather a plant collector than a garden designer. Due to the emphasis placed by botanists on the rare plant, and by the horticulturists on the skill necessary to raise an exotic one, the small suburban garden often became a display place for new specimens, or for the owner's horticultural expertise. The development of these many new garden plants has been described by Walter P. Wright:

> The present writer can remember when the introduction to commerce of a new variety of zonal 'geranium' – one of the principal components of the old 'ribbon border' – still created a furore. But that memory of childhood was fleeting. Superimposed upon it, and growing yearly stronger and stronger, was the recollection of new roses, new gladioli, new peonies, new carnations, new phloxes, new sweet peas, new Michaelmas daisies, new delphiniums, new irises. Such names as Paul, Bennett, Kelway, Burrell, Martin-Smith, Douglas, Eckford and Michael Foster (raisers of plants) became increasingly prominent, as did those of Bart and Engleheart with daffodils.[16]

Added to this was the nurseryman's obsession with 'bedding out' of the new annual flowers – a profitable and constantly recurring part of his business – which resulted in an enthusiasm both in public parks and in private gardens, for the seasonal display of large flowerbeds and ribbon borders of flowers, in which an ephemeral blaze of gaudy colour was the only desideratum. The grounds of large houses were often used as a status symbol to exhibit the newly-acquired wealth of the middle class . . .

Of course, this is to look with a jaundiced eye on the worst excesses of the suburban garden which emerged during the nineteenth century. Respect must also be accorded to its positive qualities. The new amateur gardenmakers did include many sensitive and talented people who found a creative outlet in the growing and arrangement of plants; so that hundreds of thousands of fine gardens have been made in the different countries; in the towns, the suburbs, the semi-rural areas and in the countryside. The best of these are superb works of art.

Gardening has become, in fact, a folk art in many lands, combining the science and the craft of plant growing with more creative elements of design. For many men and women, the garden often provides the only outlet for their inherent love of nature and of beauty, which is stultified in the everyday life in modern cities. Among these talented garden-makers was Gertrude Jekyll.

Gertrude Jekyll began as a talented amateur but soon joined William Robinson as a leader in the field of small gardens. Initially trained as a painter, she was largely concerned with a more restrained and tasteful use of colour in the garden. She drew much of her inspiration and ideas from the cottage gardens whose simple and tender charm then still graced much of the English countryside. Here could be found many a charming flower which had been pushed out of the more ostentatious gardens to make room for some new introduction from abroad. 'Plants typical of the English village,' was how she described these old favourites; but she was aware that the cottage garden owed 'something perhaps to a hundred years of foreign influences, but having so absorbed them that their origin is lost and they have become our own.'

In her writings and in the gardens she created, particularly that at her own house, Munstead Wood, Gertrude Jekyll demonstrated that new plant material could be brought into a more harmonious relationship with its environment. She also showed that the small garden of a few acres or even less, could become a self-contained romantic retreat, a tranquil and lovely refuge distinct from the busy modern world.

She developed William Robinson's ideas a stage further and she was able to come to terms with the architects. Miss Jekyll did not reject the projection of formal architectural structures into the garden, but she softened them, gave them rusticity and combined them with informal plantings, creating the happiest of links between house and garden.

She found a brilliant and sympathetic collaborator in the architect Sir Edwin Lutyens. Among English architects there had been an aesthetic reaction against the grim industrial cities with their sprawling suburbs of uniform houses. Under the influence of Ruskin, William Morris, Rosetti and Madox Brown, architects had reached for inspiration to the regional styles and traditional materials of the English countryside in a Domestic Revival and had evolved 'the small house for artistic people of moderate means'. Some critics have hailed this as England's greatest contribution to the architecture of the Western world. The best remembered of these nineteenth-century architects today is Sir Edwin Lutyens, probably the most original and sensitive of them all. Lutyens elevated the romantic English country cottage into a residence suitable for the new affluent and cultured upper-middle class by enlarging it, adding the comforts and conveniences of modern technology, while still retaining much of the picturesque and nostalgic associations of the simple cottage.

'A Lutyens house and a Jekyll garden' became a widely-held ideal, representing the breakdown of the former separation between town and country. Lutyens' insistence on the use of local materials may even have led his collaborator, Gertrude Jekyll, to extend her plant vocabulary to include wild plants of the English countryside in her gardens. To do so was quite unusual in those days, when rare and choice plants were generally considered to be essential to a fine garden.

Some large private gardens continued to be constructed during this period. Sissinghurst Castle was strongly influenced by Gertrude Jekyll; as also was Wisley, now the Royal Horticultural Society's Garden, formerly owned by Mr G. F. Wilson. But most newly made gardens contributed nothing fresh to design, often reverting to the formal Italian Renaissance style. The architect Sir Reginald Blomfield was illustrative of this trend.

Gertrude Jekyll's contribution to the art of garden-making can be best understood by a quotation from her own innovative writing:

> Merely having plants or having them planted unassorted in garden spaces, is only like having a box of paints from the best colour man; or, to go one step farther, it is like having portions of these paints set out upon a palette. This does not constitute a picture; and it seems to me that the duty we owe to our gardens and to our own bettering of our gardens is so to use the plants that they shall form beautiful pictures; and that, while delighting our eyes, they should be always training those eyes to a more exalted criticism; to a state of mind and artistic conscience that will not tolerate bad or careless combination or any sort of mis-use of plants, but in which it becomes a point of honour to be always striving for the best.
>
> It is just in the way it is done that lies the whole difference between commonplace gardening and gardening that may rightly claim to rank as a fine art. Given the same space of ground and the same material, they may either be fashioned into a dream of beauty, a place of perfect rest and refreshment of mind and body – a series of soul-satisfying pictures – a treasure of well-set jewels; or they may be so mis-used that everything is jarring and unpleasing.[17]

The work of both William Robinson and Gertrude Jekyll

286

Gertrude Jekyll and William Robinson had a wide influence in England which gradually spread abroad. The garden at Sissinghurst Castle, designed by Virginia Sackville West (Lady Nicolson) and Sir Harold Nicolson, is one of the great gardens of England that was influenced by the work of Gertrude Jekyll.

287

Bodnant in Wales, which we have discussed earlier, is another great garden that clearly shows the Jekyll influence.

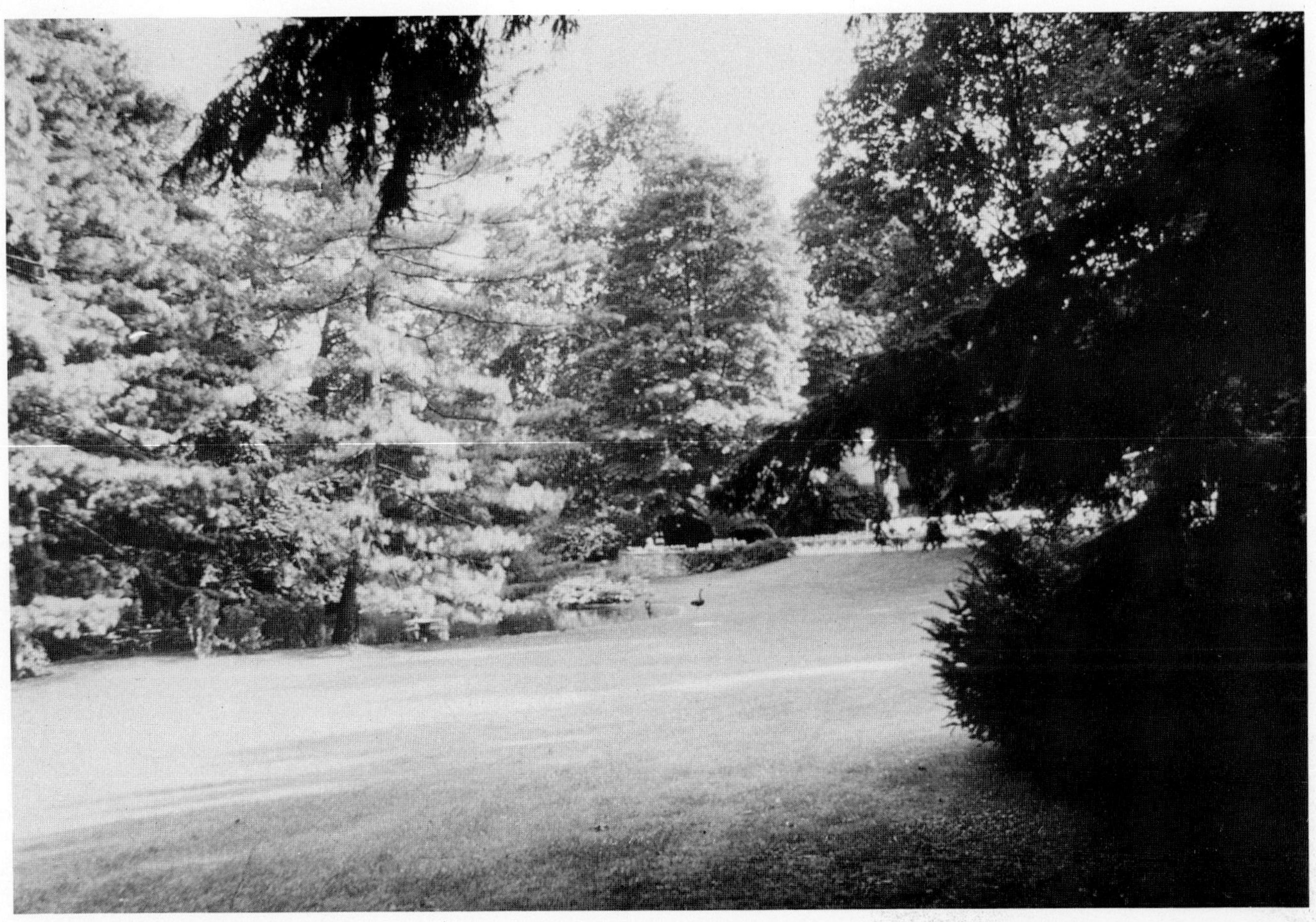

288

A park in Brussels, one of many beautiful informal landscaped open spaces that adorn the city.

(who became firm friends) brings us into our present era; just as the work of Olmsted and his colleagues, working in the broader fields of landscape design, had done in the United States of America.

And so we have come to the end of our excursion into 'Gardens in Time'. From their earliest beginnings we have traced man's efforts to come to terms with Nature: with land forms and water, with trees, shrubs and flowering plants ... How first he tended to dominate them; force them into his formal patterns, but later came to treat them more sympathetically; until an attitude of bringing out the natural qualities of plants and landscapes, of evoking their special beauties in man-made compositions, has become almost universal.

We have shown how formality in garden design commenced in the Western world and central Asia, and informality was characteristic of the garden art of China and Japan. We observed that the interchange between East and West has created the wonderful legacy of landscape design and garden art, to which we are heirs today. We have seen that a body of professional landscape designers and garden artists has been created in the last few centuries, equipped to help solve the environmental problems of the modern twentieth-century world.

The progress in landscape design and garden art in the first half of the twentieth century has been so remarkable that it would require a volume as long as this one to deal with it only in outline. When we first planned this book in the early 1950s we intended to write a sequel *New Horizons in Landscape Architecture* to cover developments in our field in the twentieth century. In the 25 years since then, so much has taken place in garden art and landscape architecture and such a fine volume of work and literature has been created, that the need for our second book is far less important than it appeared in the early 1950s.

Hundreds and thousands of superb gardens have been created in the twentieth century, ranging from park-like expanses such as Bodnant and Wisley to quite tiny city and suburban garden plots and squares. Created by both professional landscape architects and perhaps more often, by talented amateurs, these gardens have rendered our twentieth-century man-made environment more bearable than it otherwise would be. From our transparencies we have made a random selection of these as a finale.

THE CHALLENGE OF THE FUTURE

In the second half of the twentieth century, the promise of the Renaissance has been fulfilled . . . man can control his environment. We have the knowledge and the practical expertise to fashion the environment to man's needs, including the higher values of living. And yet . . . and yet . . .

The charming individual private house and garden, romantic retreat from the noise and congestion of the city, has often been engulfed by road extensions, by spread of suburbs, expansion of industry . . . well-planned and lovely large housing developments have been polluted by encroaching contamination. For example, at 'Riverside', designed by Olmsted in Chicago, the once-beautiful Des Plaines River no longer abounds with fish and fowl . . . the encroaching motor car slashes through whole regions bringing its fumes, noise and dust into the countryside, destroying all the natural beauty.

The City, high point of Western civilisation, has become unfit for human habitation, where every one of our senses is outraged – sight, sound, smell, taste and touch. The sun no longer shines in London, Paris, Los Angeles, Tokyo. Only smog. Our senses in self-defence become half-atrophied. The vast oceans, used as dumping grounds for industrial waste, have become contaminated and the whole balance of nature is fast becoming destroyed. The possible breakdown of our civilisation is now no longer the gloomy prophecy of cranks, but the reasoned warning of many of today's most eminent scientists. 'We have from twenty to fifty years to put our house in order.' So stated Sir Macfarlane Burnet, one of Australia's most distinguished scientists, and Nobel prize winner, speaking at a conference in Sydney in the early 1970s attended by more than 1,500 world leaders in medicine, industry and agriculture. He continued, 'Population increase, the evolution of weapons to the H-bomb and beyond, the irrestible momentum of industrial technology, the plunder and pollution of our planet, are all becoming intolerable . . . I believe the concept of a stable global ecological system is the most important objective of our age.'

And Sir Macfarlane Burnet is not a single voice: his views are shared by hundreds of thousands of serious-minded people in each country, by many millions throughout the world, who are concerned with the future of humanity and who project their thinking beyond the immediate present.

289

Colombus Park, Chicago by Jens Jensen. Jensen became famous for his advocacy of indigenous flora and developed what became known as the 'Prairie Style' in America. His work extended well into the twentieth century.

Man has harnessed physical and mechanical resources of undreamed-of magnitude but these have been applied too often to the creation of weapons of destruction ... destruction of the environment in the search for quick profits by 'the plunder and pollution of our planet' ... destruction of man himself by weapons of war 'to the H-bomb and beyond.' And as a result, education has followed this emphasis. Promotion and rewards are available in proportion to the individual who associates himself with this line of development. Increasingly national resources are channelled into the creation of sophisticated weapons of destruction or communication associated with weaponry.

Within the 'advanced' Western countries, an added destructive force has been uncontrolled industrial expansion with its concomitant monumental urban growth which has produced industrial and human wastes. These contaminate the natural waters and with the predominance of motor traffic, produce a continuous blanket of deadly smog over whole regions.

In the rural and primitive areas within these countries, the situation is ever more critical. Unplanned agriculture too often 'mines' rather than farms the existing resources, rendering sterile whole regions (the Dust Bowl in U.S.A., the salt-extension of millions of square miles in Australia, etc. etc.). The direct mining of minerals such as bauxite, ilmanite, iron and oil, make a web of trenches, tracks and denuded areas through previously untouched plains and forest areas and coasts. In *The Destruction of California* Raymond F. Desmann gives a powerful regional description of this process.

The 'developing' countries are in quite a different position, straining their resources to improve the standard of living of their peoples – who consist of over three-quarters of the population of the globe. There is so much to be done in these countries, so many immediate tasks to perform, that, to them, 'abstract' thoughts of the survival of the world would seem quite unreal.

Perhaps some garden lovers and landscape architects may consider these final thoughts savour too much of politics and should have no place in a book about landscape design and gardens?

290

The private garden of Walter Leder in Zurich, Switzerland. A delightful exercise in informal landscaping. Walter Leder is a distinguished Swiss landscape architect.

291

An informal lawn and herbaceous border in the Leder Garden which overlooks the city of Zurich.

It is not a case of politics, but, as Sir Macfarlane Burnet put it, one of survival of the human race. If we wish to pass on to posterity all the wonderful and beautiful things which man has created since he first emerged from pre-history, it is necessary for those of us who see the future clearly, to act.

Throughout the world people intuitively sense that something is seriously wrong with the way we are treating our environment. They are demanding a more long-term and thoughtful approach to man's use of the natural resources which surround him.

Broadly-based conservation organisations have sprung up in many countries, but sometimes their policies are negative because they can see only the damage being done to the environment by our present activities, and offer no positive solution. It is the responsibility of those of us in the environmental professions to help find these solutions.

Positive work is being done at an international level through such organisations as UNESCO, the International Union for the Conservation of Nature, ICOMOS, and the International Federation of Landscape Architects, which has close affiliations with these.

On a national and local level concerned citizens and professionals are also meeting in the conservation organisations. They play a watch-dog role which is gradually becoming more influential and effective. Let us hope it will not be 'too little too late'.

292

Falling Water, Bear Run, near Mill Run, Pennsylvania by Frank Lloyd Wright. The handling of the relation of building to site is breathtakingly beautiful: '. . . the great reinforced concrete slabs which carry the living space out over the water . . . recall, in their rhythmic stratification, the jutting ledges of the stream bed.'[18]

293

Three girls contemplate the lake in Melbourne Botanic Garden. This landscape masterpiece was created by William Guilfoyle in the second half of the nineteenth century.

294

Another view of the Leder garden in Zurich.

295

Garden for Idete Monteiro, near Petropolis, Brazil by Roberto Burle Marx. Plant materials in this garden are indigenous. Its sympathetic contours form the whole surrounding landscape into the garden.

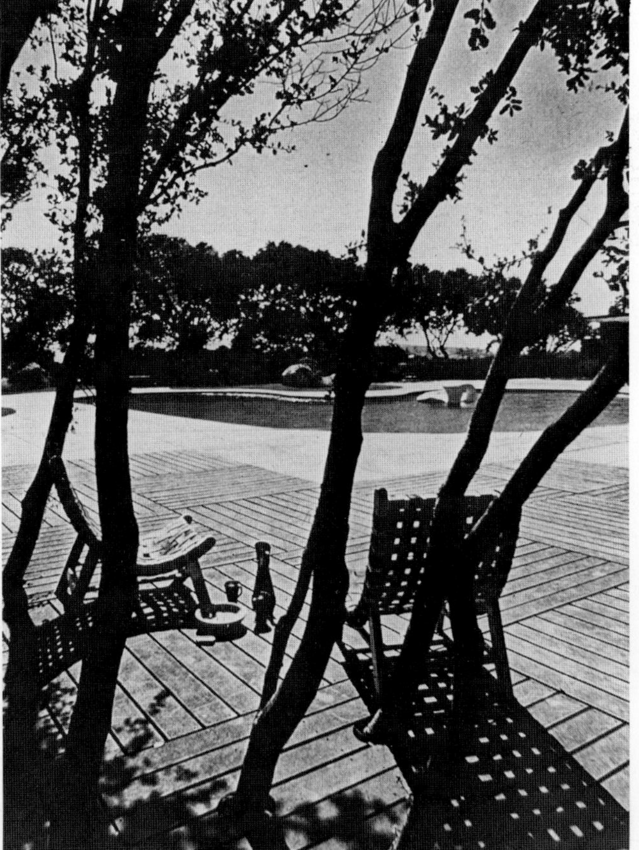

296

Garden at Sonoma, California by Thomas Church. Here informality has been extended to the shape of the pool, with great success. Church was a leader in the twentieth-century movement that stressed the fact that even small gardens were places to live in, not just to look at.

297

Tea-trees come up through a timber terrace at Sonoma, emphasising the value of keeping as many of the existing trees as possible. This device was often used by Church.

298

Another view of the pool area at Sonoma, in the garden created for Mr and Mrs Dewey Connell. Thousands of years of aesthetic experience have gone to make this garden.

299

Garden in the UNESCO complex in Paris. This is obviously inspired by the historic gardens of China and Japan.

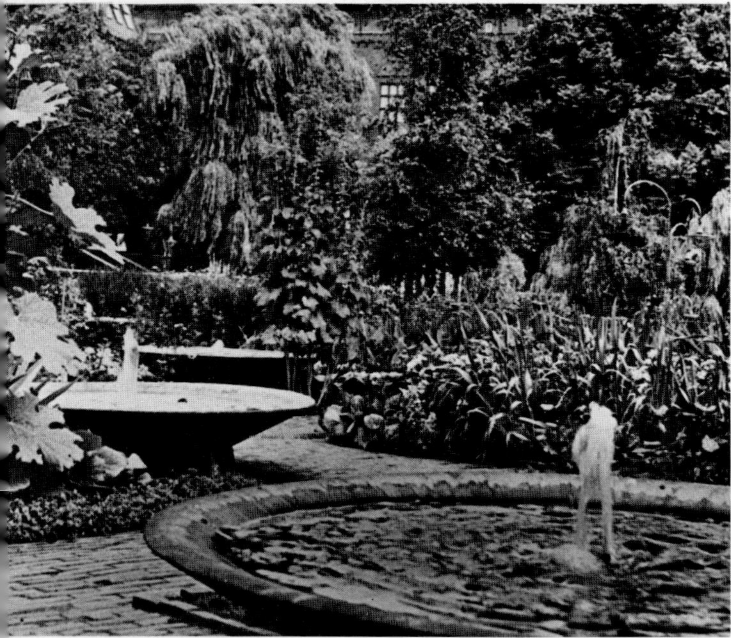

300

Private park, Saronno, Italy by Pietro Porcinai, landscape architect. The architects were Peressutti and Rogers.

301

Flower parterre, Tivoli Gardens. An informal arrangement of water basins and fountains in Copenhagen.

302

Children's wading pool in Stockholm Park designed by Holger Blom. One of the many delightful open spaces created by Blom in this beautiful city.

303

Huge weeping tree in Frankfurt Park. The early informal parks of Frankfurt provided inspiration to travellers from the New World, like Andrew Jackson Downing and Frederick Law Olmsted. They are still fine today.

LUCKY LAGER
The real lager beer
GUARANTY
SAVINGS

304

Roof garden at the Kaiser Center, San Francisco by Theodore Osmundson. Open spaces are being consumed by the motor car in most of our modern cities; so it is fine to see gardens being created several storeys above ground level.

305

One of the very latest 'Hanging Gardens' is this delightful one for Edgar Kaiser Jr. in Vancouver B.C. Eleven floors up, it was designed by Theodore Osmundson and Associates.

306

Hartford Plaza, Connecticut. A more formal roof garden, surrounded by high-rise buildings. Sasaki, Walker and Associates were the landscape architects.

307

A beautiful paved mall in Malaga. Another victory for pedestrians over the all-consuming motor car.

308

A contemporary fountain in the centre of Malaga, southern Spain. Garden traditions in Malaga go back to ancient times. The city has many delightful modern precincts to complement the ancient ruins of the Alcazaba and Gibilfaro.

309-10

Two views of Crestwood Estate, a Radburn-type residential development landscaped by the authors in Perth, Western Australia. Children move freely from home to school and play happily in the park system completely free from the threat of the motor car. 309 is a walkway and 310 an underpass.

311

Ord River Dam in North Western Australia. The author's problem was to fit the large man-made structure into the natural environment with the least possible scarring. An approach road planned to cut through the abutment hill was taken around the contour; blasting for aggregate was conducted out of vision of the dam; and all construction work took place in the dam basin and was inundated by the new Lake Argyle.

312

The Narrows Interchange in Perth, Western Australia. The landscape scheme, designed by John Oldham, provides for 40 acres of pedestrian park separated from the road traffic by underpass and overway. It is now functioning successfully.

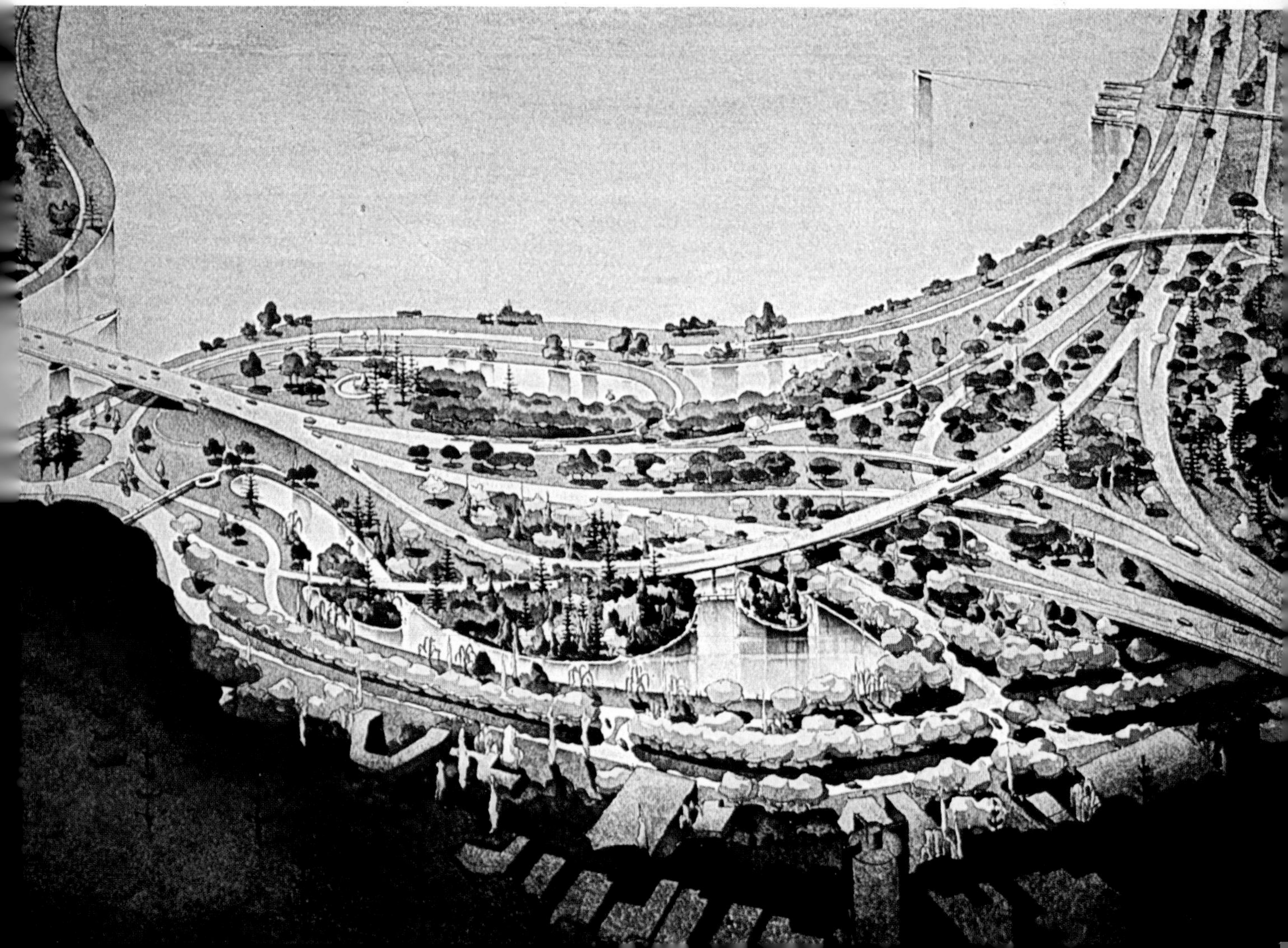

THE EVOLUTION OF LANDSCAPE DESIGN AND GARDEN ART

The chart is greatly simplified. Only major developments are shown.

Arrows indicate the direction of flow of ideas influencing Garden Art and Landscaping.

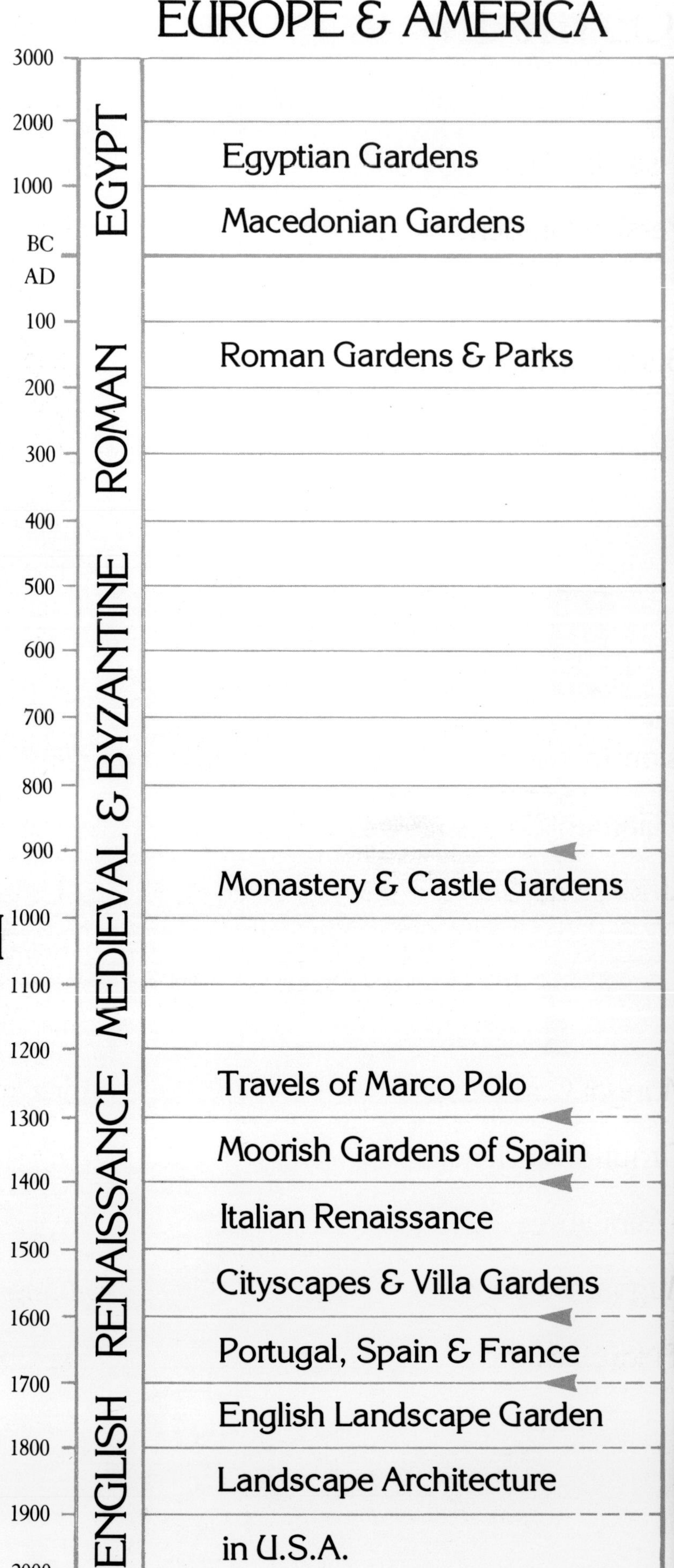

Date	CENTRAL ASIA	China	CHINA & JAPAN	Japan
3000–2000		SH'ANG		
2000–1000	Assyrian Hunting Parks		Sh'ang Hunting Parks	
1000–BC	Persian Gardens & Parks		Informal Imperial Parks	
AD–100		HAN	& Landscape Poetry	
100–200	Buddhist Temple Gardens			
200–300				
300–400			Landscape Theory Develops	
400–500			In Parks, Poetry & Gardens	
500–600				NARA
600–700		T'ANG	Large Informal Imperial	
700–800	slamic Gardens		Parks, Gardens & Poetry	
800–900	Garden Courts in Asia		1st Landscape Painting	HIEAN
900–1000	frica, Spain & N. India		Hsi. Ma. Kuang Garden &	
1000–1100		SUNG	Paintings of the Sung	
1100–1200			Sung Gardens seen during	
1200–1300	ongol Conquests		Mongol Period by Marco Polo	ASHIKAGA
1300–1400	imurid Gardens		Ming Restoration	
1400–1500	Miniatures	MING	Landscape Gardens of Japan	
1500–1600	ughal Gardens		& Ming Gardens & Themes	
1600–1700	f Northern India		Edo Garden Parks of Japan	EDO
1700–1800		CH'ING	& Ching Garden Palaces	
1800–1900				MEIJI
1900–2000				

APPENDIX II
CULTURAL BACKGROUND OF CHINA

313

This symbol for a park, used by the ancient Chinese about 1500 B.C., bears a close resemblance to that used in Western Asia from earliest times. Perhaps the very earliest Chinese parks were formal ones, as in Western Asia and the Mediterranean.

As the history of China is less well known to most readers than that of Europe and the Middle East, we have prepared the following brief summary. We owe a debt for much of the material to the brochure distributed at the China Exhibition in London in September 1973.

Chinese culture has been continuous for thousands of years. Its origins began around the fifth millennium B.C. in the basins of the Yellow River and the Yang Tse Kiang. By the late third millennium B.C., the ancestors of the Chinese were producing some of the finest neolithic pottery the world has seen, laying the basis of their supremacy in ceramics.

The first historical principality in China, the Shang state, centred on Honan, represents also the earliest phase of bronze-using culture in East Asia. Recently much earlier bronze artifacts have been discovered in Indo-China. The Shang state was long regarded by Western scholars as mythical; but recent archaeological discoveries have, like those of Troy and some other Western centres, taken historical records back to this period and have revealed the variety of Shang art, the unsurpassed skill of the bronze casters, and the extent of Shang rule and culture.

The Shang state dates from around 1600 B.C. The Shang kings, constantly warring, ruled a slave-owning theocracy, enslaving enemies who might be slaughtered in royal tombs. The palaces and public buildings of the period have not survived because, like most Chinese structures, they were built of timber; but immense tombs still being excavated throw a vivid light upon the civilisation of the time. Rulers were buried with all the things they were likely to need in the hereafter, including guards and servants, ornaments and works of art, chariots complete with war horses with harness and equipment, and even favourite pets – including an elephant. It is in these tombs that the splendid bronze ritual vessels and artifacts were found, for which the Shang period has become famous.

The Shang rulers consulted an oracle on practical and ritual affairs by inscribing and burning animal shoulder bones and tortoise carapaces. This was the origin of the Chinese written language – not, as some Western writers fancifully thought, birds' foot-prints on the sand. To appease ancestors' spirits, they used superbly decorated and intricately-shaped bronze vessels in rites of human and animal sacrifice.

We know that the Shang monarchs built parks and gardens because the archaic form of the language that they used, contained a symbol for 'park'. This was a lozenge-shaped pictograph, not unlike a medieval shield in shape, which contains a symbolic tree in each of its quarters. It bears a close resemblance to the earliest garden symbols used in ancient Western Asia.[1] Though, like most pictographs, it is greatly simplified, its appearance suggests that the earliest parks in China were formal in character. This seems highly probable as row planting is the easiest possible arrangement of trees – just as the primitive beat of a drum is the simplest form of music.

The Shang dynasty was succeeded by that of the Chou (1027-771 B.C.) and then followed a period called The Autumn Annals (771-475 B.C.). Confucius lived at the end of this period and is said to have edited the historical work after which it was named.

During the period of the Autumn Annals, the power of the Chou declined and the Empire broke up into a number of Warring States that gave the next period its name (475-221 B.C.). Though the age was turbulent, philosophy flourished under the leadership of Chuang Tsu, a Taoist poet and philosopher; and Mencius, a disciple of Confucius. A rapid advance in metallurgy took place, iron coming into widespread use.

In 221 B.C. the first Ch'in Emperor, Shih Huang Ti united China by subduing the other States. This Ch'in Emperor was a despot. He distrusted intellectuals because they tended to question authority, and it was he who ordered 'the burning of the books' whereby priceless works of history and philosophy were destroyed. He ordered, on pain of death to those who failed to comply, the burning of all books other than functional treatises useful to the State, mostly of technical value. Some outraged scholars, at the risk of their lives, did manage to conceal a few important works of philosophers, among which were some writings of Confucius, Chuang Tsu and Mencius.

There are references in the writings of Confucius and Mencius which show a love and understanding of Nature.

The Ch'in dynasty was not wholly destructive. It introduced many valuable reforms to consolidate the unification of the country, including completing the Great Wall. It is the hunting park of the Ch'in Emperor Shih Huang Ti which is the subject of the prose poem quoted in Chapter 2. The Ch'in dynasty, unpopular and short-lived, was displaced by the Han (206 B.C.-220 A.D.). The author of the above poem was a Han intellectual who composed it in 179 B.C.

The Han armies controlled Central Asia as far as Fergana in the West. Their territorial expansion was paralleled by a revival of the arts and an intellectual renaissance. Magnificent works were created in sculptoral bronze, in lacquer and jade, in painting and embroidery. A series of superb bas-reliefs were engraved on the walls of the Han tombs.

During the Han dynasty, silk became a major export to the West, carried by a relay of traders in the lands through which The Silk Road ran from North-West China, finally passing into the hands of the Parthians who in turn traded the silk with merchants of Rome. There it became so popular that it drained the Roman Empire of much of its gold. Roman art forms were probably influenced through silk embroidery and other imported Chinese artifacts.

The Han dynasty lasted for about four hundred years, after which China became disunited during the period of the Six Dynasties and Sui (220-618 A.D.). Buddhism was introduced from India and found wide acceptance. Buddhist monasteries became centres of the arts and their missionaries carried Chinese culture across the China Sea to Japan. The arts of literature, painting and landscape design thrived.

In 618 A.D. China was re-united under the dynasty of the T'ang (618-906 A.D.). Once again Chinese power and influence flowed westward along The Silk Road. Extensive trade with Western countries brought to China exotic goods and ideas. This too stimulated a new wave of creative activity. The arts flourished, with notable advances in sculpture and ceramics. Silk stuffs, silver ware and polychrome pottery produced in the capital city of Chang-an reflected the polished, luxurious and cosmopolitan life of one of the greatest cities of the civilised world of that period.

The expansion of T'ang was terminated by the rise of Islam in Western Asia, with its rapid expansion eastwards.

When peace was established after the Battle of Talas River (751 A.D.), Islamic embassies visited Chang'an and an important cultural interchange took place in the following centuries. During the T'ang dynasty, links with Japan also became stronger.

The collapse of the T'ang dynasty was followed by a period called The Five Dynasties and then arose the Sung (909-1279 A.D.). This era was the glory of Chinese art and culture, the Golden Age when the arts of landscape painting and landscape design reached a peak. The last years of the Sung saw the conquest of China by the Mongols under Genghis Kahn. His grandson was the famous Emperor Kublai Khan to whose court came Marco Polo to stay as an administrator for seventeen years. The period of the Mongol occupation is known as Yuan (1271-1368 A.D.).

The Mongols were ousted from China and a new dynasty of Ming Emperors established (1366-1644 A.D.). This and the Ching dynasty which followed (1644-1912 A.D., often called the Manchu as they had come from Manchuria) proliferated and elaborated the creative accomplishments of the Sung. It was during this period that the penetration of China by invaders from the West by sea took place; first came the Portuguese, then the Dutch, British and French; later the Germans, Americans and Japanese. The story of the domination of China by foreigners is modern history. It was terminated in 1949 by the liberation armies of the Communists under the leadership of Mao-Tse Tung, and the present People's Republic of China was established.

REFERENCES

Chapter 1. The Ancient 'Sense of Landscape'

1 *Journey Among Men,* Jock Marshall and Russell Drysdale, Hodder & Stoughton, pp. 157-8.
2 *The Roots of Civilisation,* A. Marshak, McGraw Hill.
3 Unpublished monograph by Professor S. Hallam, Dept. of Anthropology, University of Western Australia.
'Fire-Stick Farming' by Rhys Jones, Research Fellow, Dept. of Pre-history, Australian National University, Canberra, A.C.T., Australia.
4 *The Roots of Civilisation,* A. Marshak, McGraw Hill, p.10.
5 *A History of Garden Art,* M. L. Gothein, J. M. Dent & Sons, vol.1., p.8.
6 ibid., p.10.
7 ibid., p.23.
8 ibid., p.5.
9 ibid., p.29.
10 ibid., p.30.
11 ibid., p.32.
12 ibid., p.40.
13 ibid., p.41.
14 ibid., p.72.
15 ibid., pp.73, 74.
16 ibid., p.45.
17 Ad. Quint. Frat. 111. 1.5 quoted in *Love of Nature among the Romans,* Sir A. Geike, p.137.
18 ibid., Id. 1 xvi. 5-16, p.80.
19 *A History of Garden Art,* M. L. Gothein, J. M. Dent & Sons, vol.1, p.104.
20 ibid., p.103
21 ibid., p.143.
22 ibid., p.140.
23 *The Silk Road,* L. Boulnois, George Allen & Unwin, pp.8-10.
24 *China A Short Cultural History,* C. P. Fitzgerald, Cresset Press, p.244.

Chapter 2. Chinese Gardens

1 *Anthology of Chinese Literature,* Cyril Birch (ed.), Penguin, pp.164-174
2 *China, Mother of Gardens,* E.W. Wilson, Arnold Arboretum, p.278.
3 *Marco Polo. Travels,* John Masefield (ed.), Everyman.
4 *China A Short Cultural History,* C.P. Fitzgerald, Cresset Press, p.449, 450.
5 *The Murmuring Stream*, J. D. Frodsham, University of Malaya Press, vol. 1. p.15.
6 ibid., p.147.
7 *The Chinese Theory of Art*, Lin Yutang, Panther, pp.45, 46.
8 Bulletin of Research in Chinese Architecture, June 1934. A. Soper.
9 *Gardens of China,* Oswald Siren, Ronald Press, p.72.
10 *Design of Cities,* Edmund N. Bacon, Thames & Hudson, p.52.
11 ibid., p.232.
12 *China A Short Cultural History,* C. P. Fitzgerald, Cresset Press, p.449.
13 *A History of Garden Art,* M.L. Gothein, J.M. Dent & Sons, vol.2, pp.241, 242

Chapter 3. The Gardens of Japan

1 *Gardening as a Fine Art,* F.C. Cowell, Weidenfeld & Nicolson, p.125.
2 *The World of Japanese Gardens,* Loraine Kuck, Walker Weatherhill, pp.89, 91.
3 *A History of Far Eastern Art,* Sherman Lee, Thames & Hudson.
4 ibid., p.380.

Chapter 4. Islam and the Mongol Empire

1 *Early Islam,* Desmond Stewart and eds., Time Life, pp.83, 84.
2 *Science and Civilisation in China,* Dr Joseph Needham, Cambridge University Press, vol.1, p.236.
3 ibid., pp.215, 216.
4 *Persian Gardens and Garden Pavilions,* D. W. Wilbur, Tuttle, pp.41, 42.
5 ibid., p.179
6 *History of the Mongol Empire,* M. Prawdin, Allen & Unwin, p.140.
7 *Painting and Culture of the Mongols,* M.S. Ipsiroglu, Thames & Hudson, p.36.
8 ibid., p.11.
9 *History of the Mongol Empire,* M. Prawdin, p.143.
10 *Persian Gardens and Garden Pavilions,* D.W. Wilbur, Tuttle, pp.53, 55.
11 *The World of Ottoman Art,* Michael Levy, Thames & Hudson, p.7.

Chapter 5. India and the Mughal Gardens

1 *Gardens of the Great Mughals,* C. S. Villiers Stuart, A. C. Black, pp.231-5.
2 *Memoirs of Barbur,* quoted in *Persian Gardens and Garden Pavilions,* D. W. Wilbur, Tuttle, p.77.
3 ibid., p.75.
4 *Gardens of the Great Mughals,* C. S. Villiers Stuart, A. C. Black, p.172.
5 ibid., pp.255-8.
6 ibid., p.92.
7 ibid., pp.116-121.
8 *Rebuilding Shahjahanabad,* Jagmohan, Vikas, Delhi, pp.14, 15.

9 *Twilight at Delhi,* Ahmed Ali, Champak Library, p.136.
10 *Rebuilding Shahjahanabad,* Jagmahan, Vikas, New Delhi, pp.ix, x.
11 *Persian Gardens and Garden Pavilions,* D.W. Wilbur, Tuttle, p.79.

Chapter 6. Medieval Europe and the Italian Renaissance

1 *Science and Civilisation in China,* Dr Joseph Needham, Cambridge University Press, vol.1, p.5.
2 *Garden Craft in the Bible and Other Essays,* Eleanor Sinclare Rhode, Herbert Jenkins, p.66.
3 *Penguin Atlas of Mediaeval History,* Colin McEvedy, Penguin, p.68.
4 *Novum Organum,* Francis Bacon, Routledge, 1905.
5 *Marco Polo. Travels,* John Masefield (ed.), Everyman, pp.290-309.
6 Collected Poems of W.B. Yeats, p.399.
7 *A History of Garden Design,* Derek Clifford, Faber and Faber, p.38.
8 ibid., p.17.
9 *Studies in Landscape Design,* G.A. Jellicoe, Oxford University Press, p.1.
10 ibid., p.4.
11 ibid., p.6.
12 ibid.
13 ibid., p.7.
14 *Design of Cities,* Edmund N. Bacon, Thames & Hudson, p.91.
15 *Landscape of Man,* Geoffrey and Susan Jellicoe, Thames & Hudson, p.166.

Chapter 7. The Navigators

1 *A History of Garden Design,* Derek Clifford, Faber and Faber, p.58.
2 *A History of Garden Art,* M.L. Gothein, J.M. Dent & Sons, vol.1, p.375.
3 ibid., p.377.
4 *Baroque and Rococo Silks,* Peter Thornton, Faber and Faber, p.18.
5 *A History of Garden Design,* Derek Clifford, Faber and Faber, p.68.
6 *Saint-Simon at Versailles,* Lucy Norton (trans.). Our quote ibid., pp.77, 78.
7 *A History of Garden Design,* Derek Clifford, Faber and Faber, p.73.

Chapter 8. The 'Natural' Awakening in France and England

1 *Collected Works of Sir William Temple,* Bart., vol.3, p.330.
2 *Marco Polo. Travels,* John Masefield (ed.), Everyman, pp.242, 243.
3 China and the Gardens of Europe, Cavald Siren, Ronald Press.
4 *Collected Works of Sir William Temple, Bart.,* vol.3, p.225.
5 *The Moralist,* Anthony Ashley Cooper, 1709.
6 *The Spectator,* Joseph Addison, no.414.
7 'Epistle to the Earl of Burlington', Alexander Pope.
8 *Outline of English Literature,* Newnes, p.263.

Chapter 10. The English School of Landscape Gardens

1 *China and the Gardens of Europe,* Cavald Siren, Ronald Press, p.33.
2 *The Art of Landscape Gardening,* Humphrey Repton, John Nolan (ed.), Introduction p.xxiii, Houghton Mifflin.
3 *A History of Garden Art,* M.L. Gothein, J.M. Dent & Sons, vol.2, p.316.
4 *British Parliamentary Papers,* vol.15 of 1833.
5 *The Park and the Town,* G.F. Chadwick, Architectural Press, pp.90, 91.
6 *Forty Years of Landscape Architecture,* F.L. Olmsted Jr. and T. Kimbal, Putnam & Sons, vol.1, p.96.

Chapter 11. A New World of Landscape Architecture

1 *A History of Garden Art,* M.L. Gothein, J.M. Dent & Sons, vol.2, p.310.
2 *The English Garden,* Edward Hyams, Thames & Hudson, p.113.
3 *Forty Years of Landscape Architecture,* F.L. Olmsted Jr. and T. Kimball, Putnam & Sons: Downing's editorial in *The Naturalist,* Aug. 1851, vol.11, p.27.
4 *Outline of English Literature,* Newnes, p.397.
5 *Forty Years of Landscape Architecture,* F.L. Olmsted Jr. and T. Kimball, Putnam & Sons, vol.1, p.60.
6 ibid., vol.1, pp.108, 109.
7 ibid., vol.11, p.45.
8 *Olmsted Papers: Central Park,* p.46.
9 *Forty Years of Landscape Architecture,* F.L. Olmsted Jr. amd T. Kimball, Putnam & Sons, vol.1, pp.119, 120.
10 *Frederick Law Olmsted, Senior,* Fabus, Milde, Weimnayr, University of Massachusetts Press, p.3.
11 ibid., p.43.
12 ibid.
13 *Dictionary of American Biography,* p.71.
14 *Frederick Law Olmsted, Senior,* Fabus, Milde, Weimnayr, University of Massachusetts Press, p.99.
15 *Forty Years of Landscape Architecture,* F.L. Olmsted Jr and T. Kimball, Putnam & Sons, vol.1, pp.68, 69.
16 *A History of Garden Art,* M.L. Gothein, J.M. Dent & Sons, vol. 2, p.373.
17 ibid., p.375.
18 *Modern Gardens in the Landscape,* F. Kessler, Museum of Modern Art, New York, p.95.

Appendix 1

1 *The World of Japanese Gardens,* Loraine Kuck, Walker Weatherhill, p.35.

SELECT BIBLIOGRAPHY

Chapter 1. The Ancient 'Sense of Landscape'

Boulnois, L. *The Silk Road,* Cresset Press, London, 1966.

Berrall, J.S., *The Garden,* Thames & Hudson, London, 1966.

Casson, L., *Ancient Egypt,* Time Life, Nederland, 1966.

Childe, V.G., *Man Makes Himself,* Collins, London, 1965.

Clifford, D. *A History of Garden Design,* Faber and Faber, London, 1962.

Cuppy, W., *The Decline and Fall of Practically Everybody,* Dobson Books, London, 1951.

Drinkwater, J., *An Outline of Literature,* Newnes, London, 1963.

Gilgamesh, The Epic of, Penguin, London, 1960.

Gothein, M.L., *A History of Garden Art,* J.M. Dent & Sons, London, 1928.

Hallam, S., *Anthropological Monograph,* unpublished.

Homer, *The Odyssey,* Riev, E.V. (trans.), Penguin, London, 1952.

Lloyd, Seton, *The Art of the Ancient Near East,* Thames & Hudson, London, 1961.

McEvedy, C., *An Atlas of Medieval History,* Penguin, Harmondsworth, 1961.

Marshak, A., *The Roots of Civilisation,* McGraw Hill, 1972.

Marshall J. *et al., Journey Among Men,* Hodder & Stoughton, London, 1962.

Margueron, J.C., *Mesopotamia,* Frederick Muller, Geneva, 1965.

Morcombe M., *Australian National Parks,* Lansdowne, Melbourne, 1969.

Needham, J., *Science and Civilisation in China,* Cambridge University Press, Cambridge, 1965.

Plato, *The Republic* and *Statesmen,* Davis, H. *et al.* (trans.), London, 1901.

Sami, A., *Percepolis,* Musavi Printing Office, Shiraz, 1967.

Sherrard, P. (ed.), *Byzantium,* Time Life, Nederland, 1967.

Velikovsky, I., *Oedipus and Akhnaton,* Doubleday, New York, 1960.

Wheeler, M. *Roman Art and Architecture,* Thames & Hudson, London, 1964.

Chapter 2. Chinese Gardens

Bacon, E.N., *The Design of Cities,* Thames & Hudson, London, 1967.

China, a Tourist Guide, Foreign Language Press, Peking, 1974.

China, The Genius of, Exhibition catalogue, Times Newspapers Ltd, London, 1973.

Birch, C. (ed.), *Chinese Literature, an Anthology,* Penguin, New York, 1965.

Cox, E.H.M., *Plant Hunting in China,* Collins, London, 1945.

Danby, H., *The Garden of Perfect Brightness,* Williams & Norgate, London, 1950.

Fitzgerald, C.P., *China. A Short Cultural History,* Cresset Press, London, 1961.

Fitzgerald, C.P., *A Concise History of East Asia,* Heinemann, Melbourne, 1966.

Frodsham, J.D., *The Murmuring Stream,* University of Malaya Press, Kuala Lumpur, 1967.

Gothein, M.L., *A History of Garden Art,* J.M. Dent & Sons, London, 1928.

Kuck, L., *A World of the Japanese Gardens,* Walker Weatherhill, New York, 1968.

Lee, S.E., *A History of Far Eastern Art,* Thames & Hudson, London, 1964.

Lin Yutang *et al., Imperial Peking,* Elek, London, 1961.

Mirams, D.C., *A Brief History of Chinese Architecture,* Hong Kong, 1940.

Mirsky, A., (ed.), *The Great Chinese Travellers,* George Allen & Unwin, London, 1965.

Needham, J., *Science and Civilisation in China,* Cambridge University Press, Cambridge, 1965.

Masefield, J. (ed.), *The Travels of Marco Polo,* Everyman, London, 1967.

Schafer, E.H. *et al., Ancient China,* Time Life, Nederland, 1968.

Siren, O., *Gardens of China,* Ronald Press, New York, 1949.

Siren O., *China and the Gardens of Europe,* Ronald, New York, 1950.

Sullivan, M., *A History of Chinese Art,* Faber and Faber, London, 1967.

Sullivan, M., *The Birth of Landscape Painting in China,* London, 1962.

Swann, P., *The Art of China, Korea and Japan,* Thames & Hudson, London, 1963.

Waley, A., *Chinese Poems,* George Allen & Unwin, London, 1948.

Wilson, E.H., *China, Mother of Gardens,* Arnold Arboretum, 1929.

Wu Luen Tak (ed.), *China Magnificent,* Liang You Book Company, Hong Kong, 1966.

Yule, Sir H., *Cathay and the Way Thither,* Hakluyt Society Publications, 1913–15.

Chapter 3.The Gardens of Japan

Asano, K. *et al., Invitation to Japanese Gardens,* Charles E. Tuttle, Tokyo, 1970.

Engel, D.H., *Japanese Gardens for Today,* Charles E. Tuttle, Tokyo, 1959.

Gropius, W. and Tangye, K., *Katsura: Tradition and Creation in Japanese Architecture,* Yale University Press, 1960.

I.F.L.A. Congress brochure, 1964.
Keene, D. (ed.), *Japanese. Anthology of Literature,* Penguin, London, 1956.
Johnes R., *Japanese Art,* Spring Books, London, 1964.
Kuck, L., *The World of the Japanese Garden,* Walker Weatherhill, New York, 1968.
Lee, S.E., *A History of Far Eastern Art,* Thames & Hudson, London, 1964.
Leonard, J.N. *et al, Early Japan,* Time Life, Nederland, 1969.
Smith, B., *Japan, a History of Art,* Doubleday Windfall, Tokyo, 1964.
Tatui, M., *Japanese Gardens,* Board of Tourist Industry, Tokyo, 1936.

Chapter 4. Islam and the Mongol Empire

Antequera, M., *The Alhambra and Generalife,* Ediciones Miguel Sanchez, Granada, 1971.
Coats, P., *Great Gardens of the World,* Spring Books, London, 1963.
Flaudin *et al, Voyage in Perse: Perse Moderne,* Paris, 1854.
Ipsiroglu, M.S., *Painting and Culture of the Mongols,* Thames & Hudson, London, 1967.
Irving, W., *Tales of the Alhambra,* Padre Sudrez, Granada, 1965.
Levy, M., *The World of Ottoman Art,* Thames & Hudson, 1976.
McEvedy, C., *An Atlas of Medieval History,* Penguin, Harmondsworth, 1961.
Needham, J., *Science and Civilisation in China,* Cambridge University Press, Cambridge, 1965.
Pirenne, H., *Mahammed and Charlemagne,* Unwin University Books, London, 1939.
Prawdin, M., *The Mongol Empire,* Allen & Unwin, London, 1961.
Rice, D.T., *Islamic Art,* Thames & Hudson, London, 1965.
Robinson, B.W., *Persian Painting,* Victoria and Albert Museum, London, 1965.
Robinson, B.W., *Persian Miniature Painting,* Victoria and Albert Museum, London 1967.
Stewart, D. *et al, Early Islam,* Time Life, Nederland, 1968.
Wilbur, D.N., *Persian Gardens and Garden Pavilions,* Charles E. Tuttle, Tokyo, 1962.
Yan, V. *Jenghiz-Khan,* Hutchinson's International Authors, London.

Chapter 5. India and the Mughal Gardens

Beveridge, A.P., (trans.), *Memoirs of Barbur,* London, 1922.
Cameron, R., *Shadows from India,* D.B. Taraporevala & Sons, Bombay, 1958.
Crowe, Dame S. *et al, Gardens of Mughal India,* Thames & Hudson, London, 1972.
Hambley, G., *Cities of Mughal India,* UBS Publishers, Delhi, 1968.
Hurlimann, M., *India,* Thames & Hudson, London, 1967.
Hurlimann, M., *Delhi, Agra, Fatapur Sikri,* Thames & Hudson, London, 1965.
Jagmohan, *Rebuilding of Shahjahanabad,* Vikas, Delhi, 1975.
Lee, E.S., *A History of Far Eastern Art,* Thames & Hudson, London, 1964.
Pannikar, K.M., *A Survey of Indian History,* Asia Publishing House, Bombay, 1964.
Poreinae, P., *et al, Gardini d'occidente et d'oriente,* Fratelli Fabbri, Milan, 1966.
Prawdin, M., *The Builders of the Mogul Empire,* George Allen & Unwin, London, 1963.
Rhode, E.S., *Garden Craft in the Bible,* Herbert Jenkins, London, 1927.
Stuart, C.M.V., *Gardens of the Great Mughals,* A.C. Black, London. 1913.
Schulberg, L., *et al, Historic India,* Time Life, Nederland, 1968.
Wilbur, D.M., *Persian Gardens and Garden Pavilions,* Charles E. Tuttle, Tokyo, 1962.

Chapter 6. Medieval Europe and the Italian Renaissance

Bacon, E., *The Design of Cities,* Thames & Hudson, London, 1967.
Berrall, J.A., *The Garden,* Thames & Hudson, London, 1966.
Clifford. D., *A History of Garden Design,* Faber and Faber, London, 1962.
Cronin, V., *The Florentine Renaissance,* Collins, London, 1967.
Faure, G., *Gardens of Rome,* Nicholas Kaye, London, 1960.
Gothein, M.L., *A History of Garden Art,* J.M. Dent & Sons, London, 1928.
Hadfield, M., *Gardens,* Weidenfeld & Nicolson, London, 1962.
Jellicoe, G.A., *Studies in Landscape Design,* Oxford University Press, London, 1960.
Masson, G., *Italian Gardens,* Harry N. Abrams, New York, 1961.
Mumford, L., *The City in History,* Secker & Warburg, London, 1961.
McEvedy, C., *An Atlas of Medieval History,* Penguin, Harmondsworth, 1961.
Needham, J., *Science and Civilisation in China,* Cambridge University Press, Cambridge, 1965.
Pirenne, H., *A History of Europe,* George Allen & Unwin, London, 1939.
Pirenne, H., *Mahammed and Charlemagne,* Unwin University Books, London, 1968.

Plumb, J.H., *et al, The Renaissance,* Horizon Books, London, 1961.

Masefield, J., (ed.), *The Travels of Marco Polo,* London, 1967.

Olschki, L., *Asiatic Exoticism in Italian Art of the Early Renaissance, Art Bulletin,* New York, 1944.

Rhode, E.S., *Garden Craft in the Bible,* Herbert Jenkins, London, 1927.

Chapter 7. The Navigators

Berrall, J., *The Garden,* Thames & Hudson, London, 1966.

Clifford D., *A History of Garden Design,* Faber and Faber, London, 1962.

Coats, P., *Great Gardens of the World,* Spring Books, London, 1963.

France, Parks and Châteaux of, Commissariat Général du Tourisme, Paris, 1960.

Gothein, M.L., *A History of Garden Art,* J.M. Dent & Sons, London, 1928.

Parry, J.H., *The Age of the Reconnaissance,* Mentor Books, New York, 1964.

Parry, J.H., *Europe and the Wider World 1415-1715,* Hutchinson, London, 1966.

Norton, L., (trans.), *Saint Simon at Versailles.* Our reference, Clifford, D., *A History of Garden Design,* Faber and Faber, London, 1962, pp.77-8.

Thornton, P., *Baroque and Rococo Silks,* Faber and Faber, London.

Trigg, H.I., *Formal Gardens of England,* B.T. Batsford, London, 1902.

Chapter 8. The "Natural" Awakening in France and England.

Addison, J., *The Spectator,* no. 414.

Cooper, A.A., *The Moralist,* 1709.

Danby, H., *The Garden of Perfect Brightness,* Williams & Norgate, London, 1950.

Drinkwater, J., *et al, An Outline of Literature,* Newnes, London, 1962.

Frodsham, J.D., *The Murmuring Stream,* University of Malaya Press, Kuala Lumpur, 1967.

Gay. P., *et al, The Age of Enlightenment,* Time Life, Nederland, 1966.

Gothein, M.L., *A History of Garden Art,* J.M. Dent & Sons, London, 1928.

Marvell, A., *Poems,* 1681.

Needham, J., *Science and Civilisation in China,* Cambridge University Press, Cambridge, 1965.

Pope, A., *Poems.* 'Epistle to Richard Boye, Earl of Burlington', 1732.

Peattie, D.C., *Green Laurels: The Lives and Achievements of the Great Naturalists,* Garden City Publishing Co., New York, 1938.

Siren, O., *China and the Gardens of Europe of the Eighteenth Century,* Ronald, New York, 1950.

Temple, Sir W., Bart, *Miscellanea,* vol.1, 'Upon the Gardens of Epicurus', 1680.

Chapter 9 The English School of Landscape Gardens

Austen, J., *Mansfield Park,* Oxford University Press, Oxford, 1933.

Austen, J., *Pride and Prejudice,* Oxford University Press, Oxford, 1933.

Chadwick, G., *Works of Sir Joseph Paxton 1803–1865,* Architectural Press, London, 1961

Chadwick, G., *The Park and the Town,* Architectural Press, London, 1966.

Chambers, Sir W., *A Dissertation on Oriental Gardening,* London, 1772.

Clifford, E., *A History of Garden Design,* Faber and Faber, London, 1962.

Drinkwater, J., *et al, An Outline of Literature,* Newnes, London, 1948.

Gothein, M.L., *A History of Garden Art,* J.M. Dent & Sons, London, 1928.

Hyams, E., *The English Garden,* Thames & Hudson, London, 1964.

Jellicoe, G. and S., *Landscape of Man,* Thames & Hudson, London, 1975.

Jourdain, M., *The Works of William Kent,* Country Life, London, 1948.

Olmsted, F.L., *Walks and Talks of an American Farmer in England,* David Bogue, London, 1852.

Repton, H., *The Art of Landscape Gardening,* Houghton, Mifflin, Boston, 1907.

Stroud, D., *Capability Brown,* Country Life, London, 1957.

Stroud, D., *Humphrey Repton,* Country Life, London, 1962.

Woodbridge, K., *Landscape and Antiquity,* Oxford University Press, Oxford, 1970

Chapter 10. A New World of Landscape Architecture

Church, T., *Gardens are for People,* Reinhold, New York, 1955.

Colvin, B., *Land and Landscape,* John Murray, London, 1948.

Crowe, Dame S., *Tomorrow's Landscape,* Architectural Press, London, 1958.

Downing, A.J., *A Treatise on the Theory and Practice of Landscape Gardening adapted to North America,* Wiley & Putnam, New York, 1841.

Eckbo, G., *Landscape for Living,* Dodge Corporation, New York, 1950.

Eliot, C.W., *Charles, Eliot, Landscape Architect,* Houghton Mifflin, Boston, 1902.

Fabus *et al, Frederick Law Olmsted Sr.,* University of Massachusetts Press, Boston, 1968.

Fein, A., *Landscape into Cityscape,* Cornell University Press, Ithaca, N.Y., 1968.

Gothein, M.L., *A History of Garden Art,* J.M. Dent & Sons, London, 1928.

Kessler, F., *Modern Gardens in the Landscape,* Museum of Modern Art, New York, 1964.

Massingham, B., *Miss Jekyll,* Country Life, London, 1966.

Morrison, C., *Melbourne's Gardens,* Melbourne University Press, Melbourne, 1956.

Newton, N., *Design on the Land,* Harvard University Press, Cambridge, Massachusetts, 1971.

F.L. Olmsted Jr. & Kimball, T. (eds.), *Olmsted, F.L. Sr., Forty Years of Landscape Architecture,* Putnam & Sons, London, 1963.

Symonds, J.O., *Landscape Architecture,* McGraw Hill, New York, 1961.

ACKNOWLEDGEMENTS

The far-reaching scope of *Gardens in Time* has meant that many other talented writers have been in the field before us. We owe a deep debt of gratitude to many of these but our greatest is to Marie Luise Gothein whose monumental work produced early in this century has been a mine of information for those who came after her.

We also owe a special debt to Constance Villiers-Stuart for her work on the Mughal Gardens of India; Lorraine Kuck for her *World of the Japanese Garden*; Joseph Needham for *Science and Civilisation in China*; and John Simonds for *Landscape Architecture.*

The works of other writers have been exceedingly stimulating and helpful. These include Julia Berrall, Derek Clifford, Sylvia Crowe, Hope Danby, Garrett Eckbo, Sherman Lee, M.S. Ipsiroglu, Geoffrey and Susan Jellicoe, Norman Newton, Osvald Siren and Peter Swann.

We wish to thank Kenzo Ogata for first introducing us to the techniques of Japanese gardens, and the leading members of the Japanese Institute of Landscape Architects for their great assistance in this field.

We thank Hubert Owens for his constant encouragement; and Theodore Osmundson for the same reason, and forgive him for almost invariably being in the way when we wanted to take our most important photographs (taking the same picture himself).

Our publishers, Lansdowne Press, have been most helpful, especially Helen Frazer and Peita Royle as editors and Bruno Grasswill on layout.

Hal Bruce did a superb job on colour conversion of hundreds of our slides; and Bob Hart in relieving us of detailed administrative work when research and writing pressures were on.

We thank the publishers Harry N. Abrams Inc., George Allen & Unwin, Adam and Charles Black, Cambridge University Press, Cresset Press, J.M. Dent & Sons Ltd, Elec Books Limited, Faber and Faber, Hodder & Stoughton, Herbert Jenkins, McGraw-Hill, Museum of Modern Art, Newnes, Oxford University Press, Penguin, Putnam and Sons, Ronald Press, Charles Scribner & Sons, Thames & Hudson, Time-Life, Charles E. Tuttle Company, University of Massachusetts Press, Vikas, Viking Penguin Inc., Walker Weatherhill and Weidenfeld & Nicolson for permission to quote from their various publications.

Acknowledgement is also made to the following people and organisations for the pictures, plans and photographs as numbered. All other pictures are by the authors. Aero Express 198; Anthos 92; Archaeological Survey of India 94; Art Institute of Chicago 218; Bibliothèque Nationale 24, 25, 26, 27, 206; Bochkor 141, 142; J. Bowles 193; British Museum 13, 23, 28, 88, 135; Bruin 159; China Tourist Guide 36, 40; Chicago Park District 289; T. Church 296, 297, 298; City of Liverpool 255; Cleveland Museum of Art, Gift of Hanna Fund 29, Gift of Katherine Holden Thayer 33, purchase from J.H. Wade Fund 209; D. Clifford 183; Country Life 247, 284; Miss Cremers 200; Dame Sylvia Crowe 301; Department of Environment U.K. 216; Dumbarton Oaks, Trustees of Harvard University 275; Duperac 146; Flandin 133; Freer Gallery of Art 87, 208; The Frick Collection 140; Marcel Gautherot 295; M.L. Gothein 10, 19, 180, 181, 182, 236; Gropius & Tange 58; Gulistan Museum 90; Hakutsuru Art Museum 204; Collection of Alice & Nasli Heeramaneck 118; Hendrick 292; Mr George Howard 217; Shigaki Kaizuka 31; J.E. Kidder 57; J.M. Kraus 264; L. Kuck 52, 313; Lauris 152; J. Malyshev 201; J. Mayuyama 37; Musée des Arts Decoratifs 68, 86; National Gallery London 219; National Gallery of Victoria 51, 202, 213; National Palace Museum 30, 32, 203, 211; New York Public Library 8; Nezu Art Museum 203; Olmsted Trustees 269; T. Osmundson 18, 278, 304, 305; Le Pautre 191; F.M. Piper 230; Pietro Porcinni 303; Rohde 263; Schirmer 268; O.C. Simonds 281; O. Siren 34; Trustees of the Sistine Chapel 146; Staedelsches Kunstinstitut 136; Stowe Library 235; Tokyo National Museum 203; Topkapi Sarayi Muzesi 84, 89; Touring Club Italiano 171, 172; Indigo Trigg and J. Tarney 195, 196, 197, 215; Unknown 207, 232, 234, 265, 266, 267, 282; Victoria and Albert Museum 91, 206; J. White 245.

INDEX

Numbers in index that are bold refer to pictures, those that are in roman to text pages.